Ammonius
On Aristotle Categories

Ammonius
On Aristotle Categories

Translated by
S. Marc Cohen &
Gareth B. Matthews

Duckworth

First published in 1991 by
Gerald Duckworth & Co. Ltd.
The Old Piano Factory
48 Hoxton Square, London N1 6BP

Introduction © 1991 by Richard Sorabji
Translation © 1991 by S. Marc Cohen and Gareth B. Matthews

All rights reserved. No part of this publication
may be reproduced, stored in a retrieval system, or
transmitted, in any form or by any means, electronic,
mechanical, photocopying, recording or otherwise,
without the prior permission of the publisher.

A catalogue record for this book is available
from the British Library.

ISBN 0 7156 2253 6

Photoset in North Wales by
Derek Doyle & Associates, Mold, Clwyd.
Printed and bound in Great Britain by
Redwood Press Ltd, Melksham

Contents

Introduction *Richard Sorabji*	1
Translation	7
Prolegomena	9
Commentary	22
On Substance	45
On Quantity	65
On Relatives	76
On Qualified and Quality	97
On Doing and Being Affected	112
On Opposites	113
On Contraries	124
On Priority	126
On Simultaneity	127
On Change	128
Textual Emendations	130
Appendix: the commentators	132
English-Greek Glossary	142
Greek-English Index	145
Subject Index	162

Introduction

Richard Sorabji

Ammonius (AD 435/45-517/26) brought the ideas of his teacher Proclus from Athens to the chair of philosophy in Alexandria. He succeeded his father Hermeias in the chair, but he gave new life to it. His pupils included all the most important remaining Neoplatonist philosophers of the sixth century AD: Philoponus, Simplicius, Damascius, Asclepius and Olympiodorus. His father-in-law was Syrianus and his brother Heliodorus.

The *Categories* commentary, translated here, is described as being written up by pupils from the voice of, that is from the seminars of, Ammonius. Only one of the commentaries surviving in his name, that on the *de Interpretatione*, is not so described.

He is the first author to hand down to us the set of ten introductory questions about the study of Aristotle which thereafter are standardly prefixed to Neoplatonist commentaries on Aristotle's *Categories*. We know from elsewhere that the set of ten was already laid down by Proclus in his *Sunanagnôsis* (reading of a text with a master).[1] There follows a set of particular questions about the treatise to be commented on, in this case the *Categories*. Some of these questions are repeated when Ammonius comes to comment on the categories of relative and quality.[2]

Perhaps the most important question is the point of studying Aristotelian Philosophy. The aim is to ascend to the supreme

---

[1] Elias *in Cat.* 107,24-6. For this and other information, see Richard Sorabji (ed.) *Aristotle Transformed: The Ancient Commentators and Their Influence*, London and Ithaca N.Y. 1990.
[2] 66,5; 80,15.

Neoplatonist God, the One.³ This will be made possible by a reading of Aristotle and Plato, culminating in Plato's two supposedly theological works, the *Timaeus* (on the second God, the divine Intellect) and the *Parmenides* (on the One). Ammonius' belief in the One is clearly expressed in this passage and again in 36,25, where he gives the standard Neoplatonist view that one can speak only negatively of it, saying what it is not. This commitment to the One is important, because Ammonius was accused of making some disgraceful compromise with the Christian authorities in Alexandria.⁴ And one of the reasons why the pagan Neoplatonist school lasted so much longer in Alexandria than in Athens has been thought to be that the Alexandrians were closer to Christian monotheism, having abandoned the supreme One, in favour of the Creator-Intellect.⁵ It is clear, however, that Ammonius accepted the One in addition to the Intellect and was free to express his belief.

Ammonius reveals his own view on the reinterpretations of Aristotle's *Categories* which Porphyry and Iamblichus had devised, in order to protect the work from Plotinus' criticisms. Plotinus' major complaint was that Aristotle's scheme of categories took no account of Platonic Forms. Porphyry's reply was that the work was designed for beginners, and therefore was not intended to be about real things, but only about words insofar as they signify things. Iamblichus went further: Aristotle's accounts of the various categories do apply, and apply first and foremost, to the Platonic Forms and to things at that higher level.⁶

In Ammonius, we find agreement with Porphyry that the *Categories* is designed for beginners.⁷ It is therefore concerned not with Platonic Forms, but with things perceptible to the senses⁸ and familiar to the masses,⁹ *inter alia* with the kind of

---

³ 6,9.

⁴ Damascius, *Life of Isidore* 250,2; 251,12-14.

⁵ Karl Praechter, 'Richtungen und Schulen im Neuplatonismus', *Genethliakon für Carl Robert*, Berlin 1910, 105-55, with reply by Koenraad Verrycken, ch. 10 in *Aristotle Transformed*.

⁶ For the evidence, see P. Hadot, 'The harmony of Plotinus and Aristotle according to Porphyry', translated in *Aristotle Transformed* ch.6, from the French of *Plotino e il Neoplatonismo in Oriente e in Occidente*, Accademia Nazionale dei Lincei, Rome 1974, 31-47.

⁷ 36,11; 53,6; 55,12.   ⁸ 33,25; 41,10.   ⁹ 33,25.

substance that has matter as well as form.[10] But as to Porphyry's idea that Aristotle is talking about words which signify things through the medium of concepts, Ammonius claims that Aristotle is talking about all three: words, things and concepts.[11] Hence Ammonius sometimes describes him as talking about things,[12] sometimes as talking about words.[13] Where Aristotle uses two different expressions, 'said of' and 'is present in', Ammonius suggests that he employs the first expression ('said of') to show that he is talking about words which are said, while he employs 'is' to show that he is talking about things.[14] Universals are merely *said of* individuals, because they do not depend on individuals for their being.[15] Aristotle also describes himself at 2a12 as talking about what is *said* to be the most primary substance, because according to Ammonius, Aristotle's own view coincides with Plato's, that it is universals, not these perceptible individuals, that are really the primary substances.[16]

Ammonius does not at all endorse Iamblichus' interpretation, according to which Aristotle's account of substance does after all apply to higher realities such as the Platonic Forms and the divine Mind in which they are lodged. Nor yet does Aristotle's account apply to Universal Soul.[17] The entities to which Ammonius here refers, the Universal Soul and Forms inhering in a divine Mind, are all derived, of course, from the Platonist, not the Aristotelian, tradition.

Ammonius evidently sides with the view, which became standard from Porphyry onwards, that there is fairly substantial harmony between Plato and Aristotle. He does not, however, in his section on the qualities required of a commentator,[18] go as far as his pupil Simplicius, who in a corresponding passage makes it one of the commentator's duties to display the harmony of Plato and Aristotle in most things. What Ammonius does say in this section is that the commentator must be dispassionate about Aristotle and not act as if he was paid to prove him right at every point.[19]

Ammonius has a splendid explanation for Aristotle's obscurity of style. The obscurity is deliberately designed so

[10] 34,5; 45,22.   [11] 9,17ff.   [12] 18,16.   [13] 26,23; 93,9.   [14] 26,23.
[15] 40,19-21; cf. 26,12-14.   [16] 36,13-14.   [17] 37,1-22.
[18] 8,11-19; cf. Simplicius *in Cat.* 7,23-32.   [19] 8,15-18.

that 'good people for that reason may stretch their minds even more, whereas empty minds that are lost through carelessness will be put to flight by the obscurity when they encounter sentences like these'.[20] Ammonius also has to discuss the number and state of the manuscripts and the authenticity of the work.[21] He does not, like many modern scholars, suspect the authenticity of chapters 10-15, but he does think their positioning requires discussion. He also has occasion to explain how Greek grammar sometimes followed different rules nine hundred years earlier in the time of Plato and Aristotle.[22]

Ammonius imports not only Platonist, but also Pythagorean, ideas into his commentary on Aristotle. He thinks, for example, that the numbers 4 and 10 have a special significance.[23] And he is taken in by a pseudo-Pythagorean treatise on categories, probably from the first century BC, which purports to come from Archytas. Since the real Archytas preceded Aristotle, this gives Ammonius the impression that Aristotle did not invent the scheme of ten categories, but merely gave it its particular order.[24] Among the Platonist ideas of Ammonius, which would not be approved by Aristotle, we find the view that our souls pre-existed and enjoyed knowledge before our incarnation,[25] and the opinion that universals are prior to individuals and do not depend for existence on them.[26] But the second, as remarked above, is fathered onto Aristotle.[27]

Quite apart from its historical interest, Ammonius' commentary is valuable in a further way. It provides a gymnastic, probably unmatched in modern literature, requiring the student to think through the viability of Aristotle's scheme of categories. According to Aristotle, what characterises a particular accident like Socrates' whiteness (to take an example that Ammonius would accept) is that it is

[20] 7,7-14; cf. 25,14.
[21] 13,20ff.
[22] 17,8-9;18,9-11.
[23] 24,23ff.
[24] 14,1-2. For Pseudo-Archytas *Peri tôi katholou logôi*, see Thomas Alexander Szlezak, *Pseudo-Archytas über die Kategorien*, Peripatoi vol. 4, Berlin and New York 1972.
[25] 15,4ff.   [26] 26,12-14.   [27] 40,19-21.

in something (in Socrates), not as a part (of Socrates), and that it cannot exist separately from what it is in.[28] But in that case, why will not form be an accident of matter? And conversely, will not Socrates' fragrance fail to be an accident of him, since it exists separately from him when it floats off into the surrounding air?[29]

There are other problems too. If there is a category of passion to match that of action, why not one of being had to match that of having?[30] Where do points and privations fit in the scheme?[31] Are the differentiae which differentiate kinds of substance themselves substances?[32] Since place and time fall under the category of quantity, how do the separate categories of where and when relate to them?[33] In fact, it turns out that the first four categories are the basic ones, in Ammonius' view, and the other categories arise from interrelations among the first four.[34] The category of relatives is particularly tricky. Position (*thesis*) is a relative, but one type of position, posture (*keisthai*), is a separate category.[35] Knowledge is a relative, but one branch of knowledge, music, is a quality.[36] In fact, everything which counts as a relative (e.g. a father) can also be classified as a thing in its own right (e.g. a man) under a different category.[37]

A further question is why the categories have the order which they have.[38] The order is regarded by Ammonius as Aristotle's particular contribution to the subject. To show why the category of quantity comes second after that of substance, Ammonius appeals to Aristotle's other works, in this case to *Metaphysics* 7.3. There, on one interpretation, Aristotle speaks of a first subject (*hupokeimenon prôton*),[39] or prime matter. This subject has as a first layer of properties – length, breadth and depth,[40] in other words items drawn from the category of quantity. Ammonius takes it[41] that prime matter, endowed with these quantities, acts in its turn as a second subject which is endowed with further properties drawn from

---

[28] Aristotle *Cat.* 1a24-5.
[29] 27,9-29,4.   [30] 33,16-19.   [31] 33,22-4.   [32] 45,7ff.
[33] 69,10-14; 92,9.   [34] 92,6ff.   [35] 69,9-10.   [36] 91,15-21.
[37] 91,29-92,2.   [38] 54,6; 66,7.   [39] Aristotle *Metaph.* 7.3, 1029a1-2.
[40] Ibid., 1029a14.   [41] 54,4ff.

the other categories.⁴² So endowed, it constitutes familiar physical objects like Socrates, or bronze. This sort of analysis had already been given by Porphyry.⁴³ It is intended to show that quantity constitutes a fundamental level in the make up of substances, and so deserves its place as the second category. In fact, Aristotle himself was somewhat haphazard as regards the order in which he listed the categories. But it has been plausibly suggested that Aristotelians came to feel that they must provide a justified order, because this is what had been done by the Stoics for their very different set of categories.⁴⁴

It can be seen that Ammonius imports many alien elements into his study of Aristotle's categories, and yet that that makes him no less adept at provoking reflection on the categories themselves.

Readers should know that, since the preparation of our volume, I. Hadot has argued for the authenticity of certain passages that were excluded from the Busse text which we have followed.⁴⁵

Acknowledgments

The present translations have been made possible by generous and imaginative funding from the following sources: the National Endowment for the Humanities, Division of Research Programs, an independent federal agency of the USA; the Leverhulme Trust; the British Academy; the Jowett Copyright Trustees; the Royal Society (UK); Centro Internazionale A. Beltrame di Storia dello Spazio e del Tempo (Padua); Mario Mignucci; Liverpool University. I further wish to thank Eric Lewis and John Ellis for assistance on this volume. The translators wish to thank Thomas Hünefeldt for his assistance with the indexes; his work was funded by a grant from the University of Washington whose support is also gratefully acknowledged.

---

[42] For these see Aristotle *Metaph.* 7.3, 1029a12-13.
[43] Porphyry *ap.* Simplicium *in Cat.* 48,11-33.
[44] Hans Gottschalk, 'The earliest Aristotelian commentators', ch. 3 in *Aristotle Transformed.*
[45] Simplicius *Commentaire sur les Catégories, Traduction Commentée sous la direction d'Ilsetraut Hadot*, Fascicule 1, Leiden 1990, 98-9.

Ammonius

On Aristotle Categories

Translation

Prolegomena to the Ten Categories by the Philosopher Ammonius

Since we want to delve into Aristotle's philosophy, as a useful introduction to it for us, let us raise some questions, ten in number. (1) Where do the names of the philosophical schools come from? (2) What is the division of the Aristotelian writings? (3) Where should one begin the Aristotelian writings? (4) What obvious utility does the Aristotelian philosophy have for us? (5) What will guide us to it? (6) How should an auditor of philosophical lectures (*logôn*) prepare himself? (7) What is the form of the narrative? (8) Why has the Philosopher obviously made a point of being obscure? (9) How many and what sort of prerequisites are there for the study of each of the Aristotelian writings? (10) What sort <of person> should a commentator on them be?

The philosophical schools get their names in seven ways. One is after their founder, as the Pythagoreans, Epicureans, and Democriteans are named after those who founded each of these schools – Pythagoras, Democritus, and Epicurus. Another is after the country of the founders, as, for instance, the philosophy called Cyrenaic. Another is after the place where they studied, as, for instance, the Stoics, since they studied in the Painted Stoa, or the members of the Lyceum or the Academy, who also take their appellations from a place. Another is after their kind of life, as, for instance, the Cynic (*kunikoi*) philosophers, who were called dogs (*kunes*) on account of their frank speech and contentiousness. For a dog can distinguish family members from others, and that is how these philosophers behaved. They received those worthy of philosophy hospitably, but chased away those unworthy and incapable of mastering philosophical reasoning. That is why they are called Cynics, and also why Plato said, 'even a dog has something of the philosopher in him'.[1]

Philosophical schools are also named after their manner of disputation in philosophizing, as, for instance, the undecided (*ephektikoi*) philosophers. They thought themselves quite unworthy of the name of philosophers, since they sought the nature of things, but did not succeed. For they said that there is total ignorance (*akatalêpsia*) and that no one knows anything. Although Plato refutes them with other strong arguments, he also uses this sort of refutation, which is drawn from their own doctrine: 'Do you claim', he says, 'that you know there to be total ignorance, or that you do not know? If you do not know this, we will surely not believe you, since your claim is just talk.[2] But if you do know it, then there is cognition (*katalêpsis*).'

In support of their claim that there is no knowledge, they used this argument: 'If there is to be knowledge, the knower must conform to what is known; and if the knower is to conform, then either what is known must stand fast and always be the same, or if it should change, the knower would have to go along and change with it. If, therefore, things are not fixed but always change, and our soul cannot follow along and change with them, the result will necessarily be ignorance.' Now indeed they were right to say that things change and are always in flux and effluence, i.e. in flow and change. That is why when one of the ancients[3] said that one cannot step into the same river twice in the same place, another one[4] replied to him with the truly penetrating thought that one cannot do it even once. For at the same time one puts one's foot in, water flows over it, before the rest of the body goes in. Now, as I said, they were right in asserting this, but they were wrong to suppose that our soul cannot follow along. For Plato proved that good souls not only do not come upon things afterwards, but actually anticipate them and meet them first with the speed of their own movement, and in this way they apprehend them.

---

[1] *Rep.* 376A.
[2] Literally, 'your claim comes from your jaws': *humin apo gnathôn apophainomenois*. This is not a verbatim citation of any surviving passage in Plato's dialogues.
[3] Heraclitus, as reported by Plato (*Crat.* 402A).
[4] Cratylus, as reported by Aristotle (*Metaph.* 1010a13).

Prolegomena

The schools are also named after something accidental, as with the Peripatetics. For since Plato walked while he taught, wishing to exercise his body, lest its deterioration be an obstacle to his mental activities, his successors – that is to say, Xenocrates and Aristotle – were named Peripatetics (*hoi apo tou Peripatou*). Of these, Aristotle taught at the Lyceum and Xenocrates at the Academy. But later on, the place was omitted and the followers of Aristotle were called Peripatetics (*Peripatêtikoi*) after the activity of their teacher, whereas in the case of the followers of Xenocrates, it was the activity that was omitted and they were called Academics after the place.

Schools are also named for the goal (*telos*) of their philosophy, as with the Hedonists. For they said that pleasure is the goal of life; not, indeed, the pleasure which the masses seek – I mean affective pleasure – but the soul's total freedom from emotion.

Since, therefore, we have stated in how many ways and from what source the schools of philosophers have been named, let us <take up> the second <question> and produce a division of the Aristotelian writings. Now some of them are particular, some are universal, and some are in between the universal and the particular. The particular are those that he wrote to someone in particular, either letters or other such <writings>. The universal <are those> in which he inquired into the nature of things, such as *de Anima, de Generatione et Corruptione*, and *de Caelo*. In between are the historical ones that he wrote, such as the some two hundred and fifty constitutions written by him. He did not write these for anyone in particular, nor are they universal (for the Constitution of Athens or <those> of other <cities>, for example, could not be universal). He wrote them so that people after him, reading and making judgments about how to govern justly and how not, might choose some and shun others and be helped in this way. But let us put aside the particular and the in-between.

Among the universal <works> some are systematic[5] and some are notebooks.[6] The <works> called notebooks are those in which only the main points (*kephalia*) are registered.

---
[5] *Suntagmatika*, literally, 'drawn up in order'.
[6] *Hupomnêmatika*, literally, 'commentaries'.

Note that in ancient times, those who proposed to write would compile in summary fashion their own particular discoveries into an exposition of the subject; then they would take many thoughts from even older books, in order to confirm the ones that were correct and refute those that were not. Last of all, of course, they composed their writings, making them beam with the beauty of their words and the ornamentation of their narrative. In this way the notebooks differed from the systematic <works> in ordering and in beauty of expression. Some of the notebooks are uniform, e.g. when an inquiry is conducted into some one thing; others are diverse, <e.g.> when <it is conducted> into many things. Some of the systematic <works>, on the other hand, are in dialogue form, e.g. those which are set out dramatically in question and answer form among several characters; others are *in propria persona*, e.g. the ones Aristotle wrote as <coming> from himself.

The dialogues are also called popular (*exôterika*), whereas the writings in propria persona are also <called> axiomatic (*axiômatika*) or school <works> (*akroamatika*). It is worth asking why on earth they were named this way. Some say that the dialogues are also called popular because Aristotle does not openly exhibit his own aim in them but rather models his discussions after those of other people.[7] But this is false. They are called popular because Aristotle wrote <them> for those who understand superficially. The philosopher deliberately used a clearer style in these works and his proofs are not so much demonstrative as they are plausible, <deriving> from received opinions (*endoxa*). The others are called school <works>,[8] since they would have to be listened to attentively by one who is serious and in fact a genuine lover of philosophy.

Among the school <works> some are theoretical, some are practical, and some instrumental. The theoretical ones are concerned with the discrimination (*diakrisis*) of the true and the false; the practical ones are concerned with the

---

[7] The explanation is evidently etymological: the dialogues were called popular (*exôterika*) because they were modeled after other people (*ex allôn*).

[8] *Akroamatika* ('school works') means, literally, 'to be heard orally'. Ammonius proposes another etymological explanation: the school works were so called because they have to be listened to attentively (*akroasasthai*).

Prolegomena 13

<discrimination> of the good and the bad. But since in the 5,1
theoretical realm some things creep in as apparently true
without being true, and similarly in the practical realm some
things are coloured with the name of the good without being
good, we need some instrument to discriminate such things.
What is it? Demonstration. Next, among the theoretical
works, <there are> the theological, the mathematical, and 5
the natural (*phusiologikon*); and among the practical works
<there are> the ethical, the economical, <and> the political;
and among the instrumental works, some go into matters
concerning the first principles (*arkhai*) of the method, some
into matters concerning the method itself, and some into
matters concerning other ways of contributing to the method.
<By 'the method'> I mean the demonstrative one (*apodeik-
tikê*). Since a demonstration (*apodeixis*) is a scientific
(*epistêmonikos*) syllogism, before knowing it one must know 10
the syllogism in general. But since this name 'syllogism' does
not denote a simple, but rather a compound (for it signifies an
aggregation (*sullogê*) of statements (*logôn*)), before <turning
to> the syllogism, it is therefore necessary to study the
simples of which they are composed; these are propositions
(*protaseis*). But these too are compounds, out of nouns and
verbs, which will be taught in the *Categories*. Propositions
<will be taught> in *de Interpretatione* and the syllogism in 15
general in the *Prior Analytics*. These then are the principles of
the method. The *Posterior Analytics* teaches us the method
itself, that is, the demonstrative syllogism. But again, just as
physicians who pass on medical information to the young
mention teachings of noxious things along with beneficial
ones so that they might choose the former and avoid the
latter, so also here, since sophists cause trouble for those who 20
seek the truth and want to mislead them with sophistical
syllogisms, the Philosopher also writes them down so that we
may avoid them. These are said to be included in the method
in another way, just as if someone wanting to teach how
statements should be put together were to cover syllables
before nouns and verbs, and letters even before <syllables>. 25
Letters, syllables, and nouns and verbs are said to be the
principles of the method of how writing should be composed –
those concerning the composition itself concern the method

itself. But if one also wanted to count the vices of discourse, one would say that he discusses things that are included in the method in another way as well. And this is the division of Aristotle's writings.

6,1 In the third place, let us ask where one should begin. The natural sequence would be to begin with the ethical treatise, so that after first disciplining our own character, we might in that way get to the other writings. But he has used demonstrations and syllogisms in that <treatise>, too, and we are likely to be ignorant of them, being untutored in this kind of discourse. So,
5 for this reason, we must begin with logic, having first, of course, disciplined our own character without the ethical treatise. After logic we must go on to ethics, and then take up the physical <treatises>, and after those the mathematical ones, and finally the theological ones.

In the fourth place, in addition to these <questions>, one
10 must ask what purpose and what obvious utility the Aristotelian philosophy has for us. We answer that it is to ascend to the common principle (*arkhê*) of all things and to be aware that this is the one goodness itself, incorporeal, indivisible, uncircumscribed, infinite and of infinite potentiality.[9] For <goodness> is not the only thing that is good. Notice that just as what we call white is a body that has received whiteness, whereas <what we
15 call> whiteness is the quality itself, so too a body that has received goodness and participates in it is called good, whereas goodness is a kind of substance and being (*huparxis*).

In the fifth place, in addition to these <questions>, let us ask what will guide us to the aforementioned principle. And we reply: first, the ethical treatise, and then after that the one on
20 physics, and then the mathematical one, and finally after these we will grasp theology.

In the sixth place, let us ask how one should prepare oneself to listen to what is to come in Aristotle's writings. We reply that one must be educated in character and pure of soul. 'For the impure is not allowed to attain the pure', as Plato said.[10]

[9] Ammonius alludes here to the idea of an ascent to a mystical union with the One (the supreme God of the Neoplatonists), an ascent which he supposed would be facilitated by a reading of Aristotle and Plato, culminating in Plato's supposedly theological treatises, the *Timaeus* (on the divine intellect) and the *Parmenides* (on the One).
[10] *Phaedo* 67B1.

Seventh, it is our task to inquire what the form of the narrative is. We reply that the Philosopher evidently has different styles of communication. In the school <works> he is dense and terse and aporetic in his thoughts, yet not overly refined in his expression, for the sake of the discovery and clear knowledge of the truth; but he is also one who makes up words, if need be. However, in the dialogues, which he wrote for the general public, he deliberately employs a certain volume and overelaboration of speech and metaphor; moreover, he changes the form of speech depending on the personalities of the speakers, and, in a word, he knows how to embellish any type of discourse. And in his letters, finally, it is evident that he has successfully adopted an epistolary style, which must be concise and clear and free of any harsh combination or expression.

Eighth, let us ask why on earth the philosopher is contented with obscure teaching. We reply that it is just as in the temples, where curtains are used for the purpose of preventing everyone, and especially the impure, from encountering things they are not worthy of meeting. So too Aristotle uses the obscurity of his philosophy as a veil, so that good people may for that reason stretch their minds even more, whereas empty minds that are lost through carelessness will be put to flight by the obscurity when they encounter sentences like these.

Next, the ninth <question> to be asked is how many and what kind of <issues of> interpretation of any Aristotelian work should be anticipated. We reply that they are six in number. <First,> there is the aim (*skopos*) of the book (for just as an archer, for example, has a mark toward which he shoots and which he wants to hit, so also a writer has some end in view, which he is eager to attain. One must then inquire what this is). Second, in addition to this, <we must ask> what use we will derive from the work, if this is not apparent along with the aim (for it generally follows). Third, what is its order? Fourth, what is the explanation (*aitia*) of the title, if it is not clear beforehand, as in the case of *de Caelo* or of *de Generatione et Corruptione*? Fifth, is it a genuine or a spurious book of the Philosopher? (Many people have composed works signed with Aristotle's name which must be rejected on the basis of both form and matter. The form here is the intricacy of the thoughts and the truth that is evident in the language; the matter is the expression and the narration of the teaching.)[11] Sixth, one should ask what main points it is divided into. Just as it is someone who has carefully examined each of the limbs and joints of a human being who knows best the whole human being composed of them, so too it is one who has gone through in detail the main points into which a discussion (*logos*) is divided who knows the discussion best.

In the tenth place, after everything <else>, one must inquire what sort <of person> a commentator on Aristotle's writings needs to be. We reply that he must know very well that which he is about to comment on, and must also be an intelligent man, in order to present the Philosopher's thought and to examine closely the truth in what he says. For one must not, so to speak, sell oneself completely and accept what is said and in all earnestness support everything one comments upon as true, even if it is not. Rather one must examine each point closely and, if it should turn out that way, prefer the truth to Aristotle. In this way, then, should the commentator prepare his commentary.

But since we want to begin with the treatise on the *Categories*, let us now examine the questions raised a little way back; the first <concerns> the aim. Notice that commentators have differed on this, some saying that the Philosopher is discussing words (*phônai*), some <saying> things (*pragmata*), and some, concepts (*noêmata*). Those of each group support their claims with textual passages. Those who say it is about words say that when he says 'Among things that are said, some are said in combination, some without combination' (1a16) he is obviously distinguishing words. Those who say it is about things say that he is obviously distinguishing these when he says 'Among the things that there are, some are said of some subject and some are in a subject'.[12] And those who say it is about concepts <point out> that after completing the doctrine of the ten categories he says 'Concerning genera, that is

---

[11] Reading *hê tês didaskalias apangelia* with Pelletier. The MSS read *hê tês apangelias didaskalia*, 'the teaching of the narrative'.
[12] 1a20.

Prolegomena   17

sufficient'.[13] The genera he is talking about are clearly later in origin and are notional entities (*ennoêmatika*), whence also Porphyry says 'Therefore the description we have given of the concept of *genus* includes nothing excessive or deficient'.[14] So Aristotle's aim concerns only concepts (*noêmata*). Although these people appear to disagree when they say these things, in reality they all speak the truth, even though not completely, but only in part. It is as if in defining 'man' one person were to say that man is an animal, and another were to say that 'rational' by itself is enough, and yet another that <man is> mortal. The three speak the truth, but none of them states the complete definition.

The Philosopher's aim here, therefore, is to treat words that mean things through mediating concepts. So when one says that one of the things we mentioned is the aim, one necessarily implies the remaining two as well, as we will show. For in saying that it is about words one means that it is about meanings (*sêmantikai*), for there is not even one study by a philosopher dealing with meaningless <words>. These meanings clearly signify things through mediating concepts. For when talking about a certain thing one first has the concept of it, and then one expresses (*phêsin*) it. So it is altogether necessary that one will be discussing all three. But even those who say that it is about things must bring in the means <i.e. the concepts>. Accordingly, since some of these are in bare thought, such as goat-stags and the like, whereas some really exist independently (*huphestôta*), <those people> will surely say that the Philosopher is not talking about things found in bare thought, but rather about things that have a real and independent existence. Aristotle will teach us

---

[13] 11b15 (in part).
[14] *Ouden ara peritton oude elleipon periekhei hê tou genous rhêtheisa hupographê tês ennoias* (*Isag.* 3,19). The most natural interpretation of Porphyry's remark is that he is trying to elucidate the concept of *genus* by means of a description (*hupographê*) since he thought that *genus* could not, strictly speaking, be defined (cf. Boethius, *in Isag., Editio Secunda*, CSEL 48, 180,20-2). If this is so, Ammonius has surely misinterpreted him; Porphyry's remark about the concept of genus no more commits him to the idea that a genus is a concept than Frege's discussion of the concept *horse* indicates that he thinks that a horse is a concept. But another (less plausible) reading of Porphyry's remark is also grammatically possible: 'Therefore the description we have given of a genus embraces nothing more or less than a concept.' Such a claim would well serve Ammonius' purpose, since it suggests that a genus is nothing but a concept.

about these things, not by pointing at them with his finger, but rather by means of words that signify them through mediating concepts. And as for those who say that concepts are the sole purpose, we reply that concepts are concepts of
5   things and that he who is engaged in teaching about these things teaches through words that signify them. Thus whichever one of the three one were to mention, one would necessarily have to admit the other two as well. So we were right to say that the Philosopher's aim is to lecture about words that signify things through mediating concepts. And this is reasonable. For the book at hand is primary both for
10 the treatment of logic (*tês logikês pragmateias*) and for all of the Aristotelian philosophy. Thus as a primary treatment of logic it teaches about words; but also as an introduction to the rest of the Aristotelian philosophy it makes a division of beings, that is, of things. That <this is done> through mediating concepts is clear from the fact that when the extremes are taught, necessarily the means are also taught along with them.
15   We said a little while back that there are two branches of philosophy, the theoretical and the practical, and that whereas the theoretical concerns the recognition (*katalêpsis*) of the false and the true, the practical concerns the discrimination of the good and the bad. But since in each of these <branches> something that is not true masquerades as
20 true, or something that is not good <masquerades> as good, in order for people not to be deceived by them they need an instrument to discriminate such things for them, one that they can use as a rule or a standard to reject what is
11,1 unsuitable. And this <instrument> is demonstration. But a demonstration is a syllogism, and a syllogism, as we have already said, is not a simple thing but rather a collection (*sullogê*) of statements which are, to be precise, propositions (*protaseis*) and which are composed of nouns and verbs.[15] <We> also <said> that nouns serve as subjects (*hupokeitai*) whereas verbs are predicated, and these are composed of
5   syllables. But these <syllables> do not *per se* signify anything, and, for this reason, there is no study of them by the

---

[15] We have followed Pelletier's emendation here. The received text reads: '... and they are composed of nouns and verbs which are, to be precise, propositions'.

Prolegomena 19

Philosopher. We will not stop with nouns and verbs, although we will not go beyond to their syllables, either. It is therefore necessary that there be something intermediate between them. Accordingly we say that prior to <nouns and verbs> there is the first application (*thesis*) of simple words. For one should be aware that nature, recognizing that the <human> animal was going to be sociable, gave him speech so that by means of it <people> might indicate their own thoughts to one another. And after they banded together, human beings agreed with one another that this, for example, would be named 'wood', and that, 'stone'; and that the word 'Socrates' would signify a certain substance, and 'walk' (*peripatein*), a certain action (*energeia*). In this way, then, all words <came to> name what they signify. In sharpening the focus (*epibolê*) for a second time,[16] people observed that articles, but not tenses, can be attached to some words, which they called nouns, and that tenses, but not articles, are attached to others, which are <the ones they called> verbs.

Aristotle's aim, then, is to treat not simply nouns and verbs, but rather the first application of simple words signifying simple things by means of simple concepts. Then are all words discussed in the *Categories*? I think not, for they are infinite <in number>, and infinite things do not lend themselves to science (*epistêmê*). But he reduces <them all> to certain universal words, not an indefinite <number>, but limited to the number ten. And all words are reduced to these, which are: substance, quality, quantity, relative, where, when, doing, being affected, position, having. And this is the aim.

The usefulness is clear immediately. If the book, the *Categories*, is the beginning of the study of logic, and logic, as we have said, discriminates for us the true from the false and the good from the bad, the aforementioned book is therefore useful to us. Moreover the order is also immediately obvious to us, since we said that the first application of simple words precedes <that of> nouns and verbs, whereas nouns and verbs <precede> simple propositions, and they <precede>

---

[16] *Epibolê* is an Epicurean term for the focusing in thought or perception that yields an impression of the shape or other property of an external object; cf. Epicurus, *Letter to Herodotus* 46-53. For Epicurus' slightly different version of the two-stage development of language, cf. ibid. 75-6.

universal syllogisms, and they <precede> demonstrative syllogisms. It is with reference to the order of these things, accordingly, that the books have been composed as well.

We must ask why on earth he entitled the book the *Categories*. We answer accordingly that he proposes to teach about genera and species and that the species are subjects (*hupokeitai*) for their genera and the genera are predicated (*katêgoreitai*) of their species. Therefore individuals (*atoma*) are subjects only, subordinate <species and genera> are subjects for those that precede them and are predicated of those that come after them, and the ultimate genera (*genikôtata*) are only predicated. So since the ten expressions (*phônai*) <under investigation> are <names> of ultimate genera (i.e. are only predicated and are never subjects) that is why he entitled it the *Categories*.[17]

One should be aware that forty copies of the *Analytics* have been found in the ancient libraries, but <only> two of the *Categories*. One of these has the beginning, 'Among things that there are, some are called homonyms, whereas some are called synonyms'.[18] The second is the very one we now have in front of us. This is preferred, since it has the advantage in order and material and everywhere declares Aristotle <its> father. All agree that the work is a genuine composition of Aristotle. For it is evident that in all of his writings he makes mention of the theories here. Wherefore, if this is spurious, so are those; but if those are genuine, this will be genuine also. Nevertheless one should be aware that the discovery of the categories is not his, but rather existed previously;[19] however, their organization is due to him.

The book is divided into three parts: one is that of the 'pre-categories',[20] one the categories themselves,[21] and one the 'post-categories'.[22] The pre-categories will be a useful

---

[17] Literally, 'the predications', or 'the predicables'.

[18] This is apparently a running together of the opening of the *Categories* with 1a20ff.

[19] The supposed inventor of the categories to whom Ammonius refers is Aristotle's predecessor Archytas. But the treatise on categories Ammonius alludes to was wrongly attributed to Archytas and is in fact of much later composition. Cf. Introduction for details and references.

[20] *Praepraedicamenta*.

[21] *Praedicamenta*.

[22] *Postpraedicamenta*.

<introduction> for us into the doctrine of the categories. For, since he was going to mention in the doctrine of the categories certain words that are unknown to us, that is why he wishes to teach about them beforehand, so he would not appear to throw his account into confusion. He discusses the post-categories at the end. For since in teaching the categories he used certain <other> words that are not known, he goes on <later> to define them. But we must ask why on earth he did not also teach <them> before the categories. We reply that at the beginning he mentioned those <words> that he anticipated would not be known at all. But some he kept for the end, since they would be known from ordinary usage without our having a precise understanding of them. That is the reason he used them in the doctrine of the categories without defining them. For in ordinary usage everybody uses the word 'simultaneous' (*hama*) and the word 'before' (*proteron*) and the noun 'motion' (*kinêsis*). Accordingly he gives a more precise account of what is signified by them. But some have said that these have been appended spuriously by people who want to read the *Topics* right after the *Categories*. And indeed they even entitle the book before us the 'Pretopics' (*pro tôn topôn*). But these people do outright battle with the manifest facts and the order. If he really taught that the primary position of simple words immediately precedes <that> of nouns and verbs, and he teaches in the *Categories* about the position of simple words, whereas in *de Interpretatione* <he teaches> about nouns and verbs, then each of the two <books> is connected to the other like a chain, and before the latter one cannot read anything other than the *Categories*, nor after the former anything other than *de Interpretatione*. And the same argument and order <applies> all the way up to the *Posterior Analytics*, that is, the *Apodictics*.

\<Commentary\>

1a1. Things are called homonyms that have only their name in common.

If souls were on high, separate from the body, each of them would on its own know all things, without need of anything else. But they descend at birth and are bound up with the body, and, filled up with its fog, their sight becomes dim and they are not able to know things it is in their nature to know. This is why they need to communicate with one another, the voice serving their needs in conveying their thoughts to one another. Now everything is made known (*dêlountai*) both by a name and by an account (*logos*). And this is reasonable enough, since each of the beings is both one substance (*ti esti*) and is also composed of many proper parts which, in conjunction, satisfy its nature. For example, man is both one substance and is composed of a genus and its constitutive differentiae; it is signified as one being by the sound 'man', which is a simple name, and is signified as a compound of certain parts by an account which goes through each of the properties of a man, e.g. *mortal rational animal*.

It therefore follows from this that if we take two things, they will either (a) have both in common — I mean both name and account — or (b) differ with respect to both, or have one in common but differ with respect to the other, and this in two ways: either (c) they have their account in common but differ in name, or, conversely, (d) they have their name in common but differ in account. Thus, there are four different cases.

Now if they have both in common, they are called *synonyms*, since they share with one another a definition (*horismos*) together with their name,[23] as it were. This is the way that

---

[23] *Sun tôi onomati.* Ammonius is suggesting a possible etymology for the word *sunônumon*.

genera are predicated of their own species, for man is called 25
animal and is also a sensible animate substance.

But if they differ with respect to both, they are called
heteronyms, as is the case with man and horse. For you would
not call a man a horse, nor a horse a man, nor again do they
have the same definition, but different ones.

Now if they have their name in common, but differ in
account, they are called *homonyms*, as is the case with the two 16,1
Ajaxes. For they have the name 'Ajax' in common, but not the
same definition; in defining Telamon's Ajax we say 'the one
from Salamis', 'the one who fought Hector in single combat', or
some such thing, whereas we define the other one differently –
as 'the son of Oileus', or 'the Locrian'.

But if they have their account in common but differ in 5
name, they are called *polyonyms*, as is the case with *sword*,
scimitar, and *sabre*.

Of these four, Aristotle here discusses only two – I mean
homonyms and synonyms – since he takes only these to be
useful in his doctrine of predication, and because from them 10
the other two are obvious, since they are their opposites. For
polyonyms are opposed to homonyms in that the latter have
their name in common but differ in account, whereas
polyonyms, as we said, differ in name but have their account
in common. Moreover, heteronyms are opposed to synonyms.
For the latter have both in common, while the former differ 15
with respect to both. Therefore, one who knows these will
thereby know their opposites as well. The Philosopher's
brevity was deliberate, for opposites are known by the same
knowledge. Therefore the remaining two should be learned
along with the account of the first two.

He put homonyms before synonyms, not because[24] being is
predicated homonymously of the ten categories, but because 20
in a course of study simpler things should always come before
those that are not as simple. Now homonyms are simpler than
synonyms, in that they have in common only their name,
whereas synonyms have, along with that, their account in
common.

It should be said that some things are just different

---

[24] MS M reads: '... not, as some say, because ...'.

24   Commentary

25   (*heteron*), while others are heteronyms. Things that are entirely other, such as man and horse, are different (for they have neither the same name nor the same definition), while heteronyms are those that differ in both these respects but are the same in their subject, such as ascent and descent. For neither the name nor the definition of these is the same, yet their subject is the same; for they are thought of in relation to
17,1   the same staircase. Similarly, too, seed and fruit, which differ in both respects, are thought of in relation to the same grain. For that <grain> is called fruit in reference to having already grown, but seed in reference to future growth.

1a1. Things are called homonyms that have only their
5   name in common; the account of being (*logos tês ousias*) corresponding to the name is different.

The thought behind this passage is completely clear; those things are homonyms, he says, that have their name in common but differ in definition (*horismos*). The statement raises the following questions: Why does he say 'homonyms' and not 'homonym'? And why does he say *legetai* and not *legô*
10   or *legontai*?[25] And why does he say 'name in common' and not say further 'verb' as well? Next, why does he say 'account of being' and not say 'definition' or 'description'? And why does he not make mention of accidents as well?[26] (The Philosopher has thus <been> interpreted according to the order <of presentation>, ignoring the things said here. In fact, he first teaches about accent and inflection, and then mentions those
15   things, bringing them in as subordinate.)[27]

---

[25] *Legetai* is the third person singular, *legô* the first person singular, and *legontai* the third person plural of the verb 'to call'.

[26] A definition (*horismos*), for Aristotle, is an account of being (*logos tês ousias*) or an account of what something is (*logos tou ti esti* – cf. *An. Post.* 2.10, 93b29-94a19). *Ousia* here has the generic sense of 'being' or 'essence'. But Aristotle also uses *ousia* in the more specific sense of 'substance' as the name of the first category. So Ammonius wonders whether Aristotle's claim that homonyms have different *logoi tês ousias* commits him to denying that accidents, which are not *ousiai* (substances), can be homonyms. He answers this question below (20,23-21,2), correctly distinguishing between the specific and generic senses of *ousia*.

[27] This parenthetical remark is obscure and difficult to translate. Busse proposes that it be rejected. Pelletier suggests that it may be an interpolation by a student of Ammonius, and that 'the Philosopher' here refers to Ammonius rather than (as it normally does) to Aristotle.

See how precisely he says not 'homonym' but 'homonyms', using the plural form of the word, since homonyms are thought of as many things, or at least two, but one never speaks this way in the case of one thing. One should know that homonyms always require these three things: accent, inflection, and breathing. For if we find names that differ in one of these respects, they are not homonyms, as, for example, with *argós* (idle) and *Árgos* (the city). The accent here is changed; the paroxytone means a city in the Peloponnesus, the oxytone means a sluggish person. Because of the change in accent, then, these are not called homonyms. It is the same with inflection. For we say *ho elatês* and mean a charioteer, and we say *tês elatês* and mean the wood of the silver fir tree. Thus, because of the change in inflection,[28] these are not homonyms. We say the same about breathing, also. For we say *oion* and the word with rough breathing (*hoion*) means 'of what sort', but the unaspirated word (*oion*) means 'the only' and it is not a homonym. With the word 'Ajax', however, the accent is the same and the inflection is the same, and even the breathing is the same for both. It will follow, therefore, that they <sc. the two heroes named 'Ajax'> are homonyms.

The Philosopher sees that, even though homonyms are multiple, they are, at any rate, signified by a single expression. For this reason he himself makes his statement with *legetai* (singular) and does not say *legontai* (plural). For it was always the custom among Attic speakers to use that form of expression. Thus Plato said, 'These things, Gorgias, are said (*legetai*) about Themistocles'.[29] Moreover, it is clear that this word (sc. 'homonyms') was in use among the ancients and is not a coinage of his. For when it is his own he says, 'I call' (*kalô*), as he says in the *Analytics*, 'I call a term that into which a proposition is resolved'.[30]

1a1. They are called homonyms ...

One must understand *things*.[31]

---

[28] *Ho elatês* is in the nominative case, *tês elatês* in the genitive.
[29] *Gorg.* 455E.
[30] *An. Post.* 24b16.
[31] As opposed to expressions. Ammonius is clear on the point that for Aristotle it is things, not expressions, that are homonyms.

1a1. ... that have only their name in common.

Do we not then find homonymy among verbs? We do, indeed, say *erô* and it means both 'I will say' and 'I am erotically affected'. How is it, then, that he says those things are homonyms that have only their name in common? We say to this that he understands 'name' (*onoma*) here, not in opposition to 'verb' (*rhêma*), but in a more common way, according to which each semantic expression is called a name. As Aristotle says in *de Interpretatione*: 'In and of themselves, then, verbs are names' (16b19). Thus *erô* is a homonym and has a common name, but a different definition, and there is homonymy among verbs.

1a1. Only.

'Only' is said in two ways, either as opposed to *yoked together*, as when we say there is only one person in the bath, as opposed to another person besides, or as when we say there is only one left behind in battle (to be sure, having with him, perhaps, a spear and clothing, or something else, he is not alone, but is called 'alone' for lack of his companions); or else to mean *unique*, as when we speak of the only sun. In this passage 'only' is used in the first way.

1a1. Common.

'Common' is said in two[32] ways; either <it means> what is partaken of indivisibly, for example, animal (for we all partake of it indivisibly; it is not as if some partake only of *substance*, some only of *animate*, some only of *sensation*), or <it means> what is partaken of divisibly, like a field (for not everyone touches the whole, but each <touches> a part). Surely it is what is partaken of indivisibly that he means here.[33]

---

[32] The text reads 'four ways', but Ammonius mentions only two. There may be a lacuna here.

[33] MS M adds: For the 'Aj' of the word 'Ajax' is not predicated of one thing and the 'ax' of another, but the whole is predicated indivisibly of both Telamon's <son> and Oileus' <son>.

1a1. ... the account of being (*logos tês ousias*) 15
corresponding to the name is different; for example, both
a human and a drawing are animals.[34]

The Philosopher has confidently cited all these examples,
since someone might object that there are no homonyms at all,
but rather synonyms. For the Ajaxes have in common a name
and a definition – *mortal rational animal*. So he was right to
say 'the account of being corresponding to the name is 20
different', lest we select just any definition rather than the
one corresponding to the name they have in common. For one
of the Ajaxes is Telamon's son, from Salamis, who fought
Hector in single combat; the other is Oileus' son, the
fleet-footed Locrian. Therefore the definition corresponding to
the name is different for each of them. 20,1

But someone might say that it is possible to call homonyms
synonyms as well, as in the case of the two Ajaxes. For they
are homonyms, in that they have a name in common but a
different definition corresponding to the name; one is
Telamon's <son>, the other Oileus'. But on the other hand
someone might say, 'Even with respect to the account 5
corresponding to the name they are synonyms;[35] for both
Oileus' and Telamon's <sons> are men[36] and so they will be
synonyms'. How, then, do they differ from one another? In this
way: homonyms, such as the Ajaxes, have a commonality
between them with respect to a name, e.g. to 'Ajax', and the
two of them also have a commonality with homonymy itself, in 10
that they participate in that homonymy. Of course, that does

---

[34] *Zôion* may mean either 'animal' or 'image' (not necessarily the image of an animal). A better example of homonymy in English might be 'ball', meaning either a sphere or a dance.

[35] At this point, MS M adds: for in so far as they are Ajaxes, they have <something> in common with one another with respect to the name 'Ajax', but also with respect to the definition corresponding to the name.

[36] There may be a lacuna here. The text as we have it appears to conflate two arguments, one of which (a) takes *man* and the other of which (b) takes *homonym* to be a shared predicate ('name') whose definition is also shared by the two Ajaxes. Pelletier, noting that Ammonius discusses only the second of these (cf. 20,7-20,12 below), proposes reading 'homonyms' in place of 'men'. Busse wants to reject the entire passage (20,1-20,12). For further details on argument (b), cf. Philoponus (*in Cat.* 20,22): 'Some say that perhaps even homonyms are synonyms, since they share both the name *homonym* and also its definition. For *homonym* itself is predicated of the Ajaxes, and so is its definition; for each of them has only his name in common with the other, but a different definition.'

not make them synonyms; for here we are considering only their relation to each other.[37]

1a2. Account (*logos*).

For what sort of reason does he say account (*logos*) instead of definition (*horismos*)?[38] We answer: it is because we cannot give definitions to all things; for the supreme genera do not receive definitions. Rather, there are times when we use descriptions (*hupographai*). Still, there is homonymy even among things for which we use descriptions. This is why he does not say 'definition', since that would leave out things signified by description. On the other hand, if he had said 'description', he would have omitted things signified by definitions. So this is why he has used 'account', since it is predicated in common of definition and description.

1a2. [The account] of being [corresponding to the name]...

Why is there not homonymy among accidents? We actually observe it: sharp is predicated of *taste* and *tone* and *voice* and *knife*. For we say 'sharp taste', and similarly with all of the others. So why <does he say> 'the account of being (*logos tês ousias*) corresponding to the name'? We reply that he says 'being' (*ousia*, 'substance') here, not in contradistinction to accidents, but in the more general sense of the being (*huparxis*) of each thing. In this respect even accidents are said to be (*huparkhein*) among the things that there are (*en*

---

[37] Ammonius seems to have in mind the following argument. Consider any two homonyms, such as the two Ajaxes. Since they are homonyms, the name 'homonym' can be predicated of each of them. But the definition of 'homonym' can also be predicated of each. So the two Ajaxes have both a name and the definition corresponding to it in common, and that makes them synonyms. Therefore, all homonyms are synonyms.

His reply appears to be that this argument considers not just the relation between the two homonyms, but between each of them and something else (viz. homonymy itself), whereas to qualify as synonyms they would have to be considered (with regard to sameness of name and definition) just in comparison with one another. (This seems a not quite satisfactory way of saying that synonyms must have the same definition corresponding to their common proper name – the definition Aristotle would call the *logos tês ousias*.)

[38] cf. n. 26.

tois ousi). So he says 'of *ousia*' as much as to say (*anti*) 'of the nature of each thing in accordance with which it exists' (*kath' hên huphesteken*).

1a4. For if one were to set out what it is [for each of them to be an animal].

If one wanted, he says, to give a definition of each of these as being an animal, one would give two different definitions. Of the genuine human being: *mortal rational animal*. Of the drawing: perhaps, *image (zôion) drawn with such and such colours*.[39]

1a5. What it is to be *zôiôi* [animal, image] is distinct for each one.

And this is why he doesn't say 'to be an animal' (*zôion einai*) but 'what it is to be an animal (*zôiôi einai*)'.[40] We say that things are characterized either by their matter or by their form or by both together, that is, by their matter and their form. If, then, he had said *zôion einai* ('to be an animal'), he would have signified their matter and their form, whereas in saying *zôiôi einai* ('what it is to be an animal') he signifies that with respect to which it is characterized, that is, its form. For the being of a thing is its form, and proper definitions are derived from it, since definitions should be made up of genera and constitutive differentiae.

This, then, is the division of homonyms: among homonyms (1) some are so by chance (and these are called accidental), for example, if someone were perchance to discover here and in Byzantium someone called Socrates. These are not further divisible. And (2) some are homonyms by intention, of which

---

[39] Ammonius seems to have forgotten what his point is. He is supposed to be giving two different definitions of *zôion*, and not a definition of *anthrôpos*. Perhaps he offers *mortal rational animal* (the stock definition of *anthrôpos*) not as a definition of *zôion*, but only as a way of making clear that its definition will be different from that of *zôion* in the other sense. The *zôion* that is a human being is a mortal rational *zôion*, and that is clearly a *zôion* in the sense of *living thing*; the *zôion* that is a drawing is a *zôion* drawn with such and such colours, and that is clearly a *zôion* in the sense of *image*.

[40] The dative + infinitive construction, *zôiôi einai*, literally 'being for an animal', is a phrase Aristotle standardly uses to refer to an essence. *zôiôi einai* is often translated 'essence of animal'.

20 (A) some are homonyms of one another and paronyms of what they are called after. Among these (i) some are called after the efficient cause, as when both a scalpel and a book are called medical, and (ii) some are called after the final cause, for example, a healthy drug. (These are both after one (*aph' henos*) <cause> and towards one (*pros hen*) <cause>. Those that are after one are after the efficient cause, and those that are towards one are towards the final cause.) (B) Some are both homonyms of one another and also homonyms of what they are
25 called after. Among these (i) some differ temporally from what they are called after. (And among these (a) some are called in memory of another; for example, someone remembering his own father, or teacher, or some such person, might call his own son by that person's name; (b) some by chance, as when someone calls a child Felicity; (c) some by hope, as when one
22,1 names <someone> hoping <he will> become <as one has named him>.[41]) But (ii) some are not temporally different from what they are called after. Among these, in turn, (a) some are called according to the similarity among the things <as when we call a prudent person Prudence>. (b) Some are called according to participation: for example, a female musician and musical knowledge are both called *mousikê*, a philological
5 woman and philological knowledge are both called *grammatikê*.[42] Some are called according to analogy, that is to say, as this is to this, so is that to that, for example, foot of a bed and foot of a mountain. And among those called according to a similarity among things, (a1) some are because of the similarity of their behaviour (*energeia*), for example, calling a certain person Swift (*Gorgias*) from his hurrying (*gorgeuesthai*); (a2) some because of the similarity of the form, for example, between the
10 image and the original, and (a3) some according to metaphor, as head and foot (*literally*, feet) of <Mt.> Ida.

---

[41] This passage is apparently mutilated, but the sense of the original is evident from the remarks of other commentators. Philoponus comments: 'As when someone calls his own son Plato thinking he will be a philosopher.' Olympiodorus comments: 'As when someone names his own son Socrates or Plato hoping that he will be such as they have been.'

[42] Ammonius appeals to the Platonic notion of participation (*methexis*) to make the point that a female musician (*mousikê*) is so called by virtue of her participation in musical knowledge (*mousikê*).

1a6. They are called synonyms.

After completing the discussion of homonyms he treats synonyms. His teaching concerning synonyms is clear from <that concerning> homonyms. He even uses the same example here, since he wants to show that one can often call the same thing both a synonym and a homonym, first in one respect and then in another. For example, Ajax is both a homonym of the other Ajax and a synonym. He is a homonym because, though he shares a name <with the other>, he differs <from him> with respect to the definition of Ajax. But he can also share the definition of *human being* and is therefore a synonym.

1a12. Things are said to be paronymous in case one gets its name from another.

One must recognize that there are four things to consider concerning paronyms; more specifically, the first two are commonality and difference with respect to the name, and the second two are commonality and difference with respect to the thing. Take, for example, grammar (*grammatikê*) and grammarian (*grammatikos*). With these there is obviously commonality with respect to the name, but also a difference concerning the last syllable: with one it is *kos* and with the other, *kê*. It is the same with respect to the thing. <For there is commonality in the thing, in that the grammarian is so called because he partakes of grammar, and there is also a difference in the thing.>[43] For the grammarian is a substance, whereas grammar is a science, which is to say, a quality, i.e. an accident. If one of these <four things> should be missing, you will not have paronyms. Thus suppose there is commonality and difference with respect to the name, and suppose there is also commonality but no difference with respect to the thing; then you will not have paronyms – for example, *platanos* (plane) and *platanistos* (plane).[44] Here we would not call them paronyms; for they are the same.

Again, suppose that all the other features <are present>,

---

[43] Insertion by Olympiodorus.
[44] The first term is a later, simplified, form of the second.

but there is no commonality with respect to the thing; then, similarly, they will not be paronyms, as is the case with *Helenê* (the woman) and *Helenos* (the man). Again, suppose that all the other features <are present>, but there is no difference in the last syllable; then they will not be paronyms, as with the science of music, *mousikê*, and the woman musician, *mousikê*. These are homonyms and not paronyms.

Again, suppose the other <features are present>, but there is no commonality with respect to the name. Then, similarly, you will not have paronyms, as with virtue (*aretê*) and good (*spoudaios*). It is therefore necessary that paronyms have all the aforementioned features, as is the case with the art of grammar and the grammarian. For they are so called paronymously.

The Philosopher, then, has embraced all the aforementioned features in a very concise way. Saying 'from another' reveals both commonality and difference with respect to the thing. If something <merely differs> from another, it is clear that it has commonality with the other, but if it <differs> completely from another, it is clear that it also has a difference. Now in saying 'gets its name with some difference in grammatical form (*ptôsis*)'[45] Aristotle presents the commonality and the difference in the name. *Grammatikê* (grammar) differs from *grammatikos* (grammarian) in the form of the ending of the name. What the Philosopher calls *ptôsis* is the variation (*analogia*) of the last syllable and not, as the grammarians <use the term>, the difference between the nominative and the genitive and dative.

One must recognize that some people say that paronyms are exactly in the middle between homonyms and synonyms. They have in common with them that both they and the other <two> will have commonality in the name, but they differ from homonyms in that the latter, that is the homonyms, involve completely different things, whereas the paronyms have a commonality <with respect to the thing>. Paronyms differ from synonyms in that the synonyms impose a complete commonality in the things, whereas the paronyms require a difference as well.

---

[45] *Ptôsis* can mean, generically, any grammatical modification, or, specifically, the case endings of nouns and adjectives.

One should be aware, however, that paronyms are not exactly in the middle, but come closer to synonyms. For they share with them commonality in the name and in the thing. They differ from them only in that paronyms do not have complete commonality in the thing and in the name, but have only a diminished commonality along with a difference in these respects. But paronyms are separated from homonyms by no small amount. They approach them only insofar as there is commonality in the name, but even in this commonality one sees a difference. Whereas homonyms will have complete commonality – the same name – with paronyms there will be some difference. Thus paronyms come closer to synonyms.

1a16. Among things that are said, some are said in combination…

Why did Aristotle put things <said> in combination ahead of those <said> without combination? For good reason. Since he is about to divide those without combination, he mentions them last so that he can proceed directly to his teaching concerning them. And indeed he does divide them when he says 'examples of things said without combination are *man, ox, runs, wins*' (1a18-19). He puts the two nouns together on purpose, and the two verbs together, so that one doesn't connect the noun with the verb and take him to be saying <them> in combination.

1a20. Among the things that there are, some [are said] of a subject.

The natural sequence would be to produce an account of the categories themselves, but since he wants to produce a more general fourfold division before his teaching concerning the categories, he puts that in front. He does so because we first obtain the number ten by adding up the numbers from the monad to the tetrad; that is, one, two, three, four added up in this way make ten. The tetrad is the substance and a kind of origin (*genesis*) of the decad, just as the tetrad, in turn, is derived from the dyad. After having divided expressions

34   *Commentary*

25,1 (*legomena*) into two he next divides beings into four and then <divides> both together into ten, going through the most appropriate numbers for division up to their totality and arriving at their most perfect limit. One should also be aware that Aristotle produces his fourfold division of beings by means of compounds (*kata to sumplekomenon*), but later he produces the inventory of ten genera without combination.[46]

5   This is the division. Some beings are universal, some are particular; and again, some beings are substances, some are accidents. Thus six pairings are generated, as we learned in the *Isagoge*.[47] Two of these are nonexistent, but the remaining four, I mean the subalterns and the diagonals, do exist. They
10 are these: some beings are (i) universal substances, some (ii) particular accidents, some are (iii) universal accidents, and some (iv) particular substances; for example, (i) man and (ii) this white (or this knowledge) and (iii) white and (iv) this man. This is our diagram:

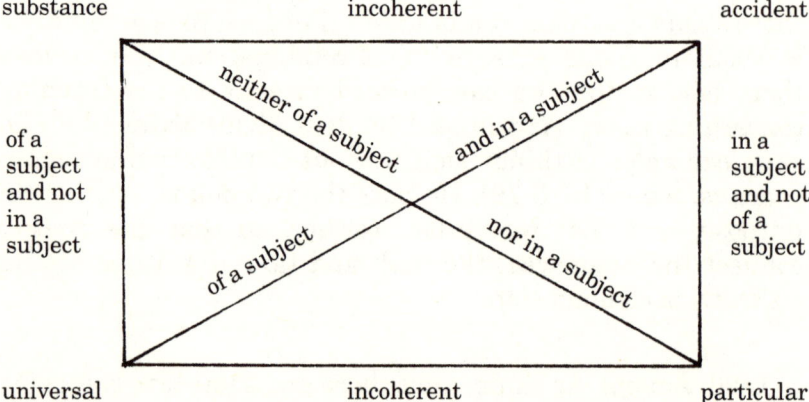

    If Aristotle had used these words, what he said would have
15 been clear; but he used other names in pursuit of obscurity, as we have said, and also because he wants to use the more appropriate names. The universal he calls 'of a subject', because it is certainly said of some subject, and the particular <he calls> 'not of a subject', because it is not said of any

---

[46] Ammonius apparently has in mind the fact that the fourfold division is made by means of compound expressions (e.g. 'said of a subject but not in any subject') whereas each of the ten categories is introduced by a single term (e.g. 'substance').

[47] See Ammonius in *Isag.* 95,19.

Commentary

subject. (He calls the one by the negation of the other.) The accident he calls 'in a subject', because it needs some other subject in order to exist (*hupostênai*); and substance he calls 'not in a subject'.

For this reason it is worth asking what Aristotle's purpose was in not calling substance 'subject' but <describing it instead> by means of the negation of the expression signifying *accident*. We reply that (1) not every substance is a subject (for surely primary and divine substances are not subjects). Therefore, it was reasonable that he did not call substance 'subject'. But then, too, having made a division of things, he wanted to make it by means of negation and affirmation, so it would be exhaustive,[48] i.e. would in fact include everything. It is as if he said, 'Among colours some are black and some are not black'. Indeed one who speaks this way has included everything, whereas one who says that among colours some are black and some are white has not included everything; for he has not <included> yellow, grey, and other colours. Therefore, it is right that Aristotle made the division by means of negation and affirmation. (2) Another reason is that 'subject' is said in two ways: on the one hand, with respect to belonging (*huparxis*), as a substance <is a subject> for accidents; on the other, with respect to predication, as particular substances <are subjects> for universal <substances>. For particular substances are subjects for universal ones not in order for the <latter> to exist (*hupostôsi*) (for the universals pre-exist) but so that <the universals> can be said of them. If therefore he had simply called substance 'subject', someone might have objected, saying that he calls the particular substance a subject for universals only with respect to predication.[49]

Using these names he sets out four pairings: first, universal substance, since it is most honourable; next, its opposite, I

---

[48] *Aphuktos*, literally, 'from which escape is impossible'.

[49] One would expect Ammonius' point to be that since a particular substance is a subject in the second sense of 'subject', but not in the first, it would be inappropriate to characterize a substance as a subject *simpliciter*, and we have translated accordingly. But the text reads, literally: '... it is only the particular substance that he calls a subject for universals with respect to predication.' This merely recapitulates his first reason for objecting to the characterization of substance as 'subject', viz. that not every substance is a subject. We surmise that in the MSS the word *monên* ('only') was misplaced.

mean the particular accident. Then he gives precedence to the universal accident over the particular substance because discourse among philosophers concerns universals.

One should consider what the Philosopher means when he says 'among the things that there are, some are said of some subject but are not in any subject' (1a20-1). It must also be noted that here, where he is reasoning about words, he uses 'said', but whenever he is talking about *things* (*ousiôn*) he uses 'is'.

1a24. But I call in a subject [what is in something, not belonging as a part, and cannot exist apart from what it is in].

Out of the six <possible> pairs, Aristotle now proposes to clarify the four that we have highlighted, that is to say, (i) the particular accident, (ii) the particular substance, (iii) the universal accident, and (iv) the universal substance. He begins with (i) the particular accident because it is clearer and simpler. Since, then, we understand things from their definitions, he gives, not a definition of it, but rather something analogous to a definition. *In something* is analogous to a genus and the rest to differentiae. *In something* is said in eleven ways: in a time, in a place, in a container, as a part in the whole, as a whole in its parts, as a species in a genus, as a genus in a species, as the <affairs> of the ruled in <the power or control of> the ruler,[50] as form in matter, as in an end, as in a subject, for example, an accident in a substance. He then takes this *in something* in his definition as a genus said of many things. He has added *not belonging as a part* so as to distinguish it from things in something as parts, for example, this hand. For it is in the man, too, as being part of him. So to separate it from them he has added *not belonging as a part*. But he has added *cannot exist apart from what it is in* to separate it from the rest.

One must recognize that some people fault this definition for both the defects of definitions, that is to say for overshooting and exceeding the definition of the thing and yet

---

[50] cf. Philoponus 32,23-4; *Anonymous Paraphrase* 6,16.

also for leaving out and not including all. They say that it does not convert with the thing defined, as must be the case with definitions and things defined, as we have said. For example, man is mortal rational animal capable of understanding and knowledge. This converts. For if something is a mortal rational animal capable of understanding and knowledge, it is a man. Some then say that the definition given does not fit all accidents, and others say it fits other things also besides accidents. For they say that Socrates being in a place is in something and not as a part in a whole (for he is not part of the place) and he cannot exist apart from what he is in (for he cannot exist apart from a place), so that according to the definition Socrates is an accident, which is absurd. We reply then that Socrates can exist apart from what he is in. For if we suppose him to have left behind the place where he was earlier and gone to another place, he is no less Socrates, whereas the accident separated from its subject has been destroyed. Moreover, one must recognize that place goes along with Socrates not as completing his essence but rather as attending in the way that a shadow goes along with someone walking in the light and not at all as completing his proper essence. It is especially necessary to add 'in' (*en*) to 'belongs' (*huparkhon*), so that it will be *that which inheres* (*enuparkhon*) *in something*; for we do not say that a substance inheres in a place but just that it is *in* it. We say this – I mean that they inhere – only of accidents.

Again it is said, 'Form is in matter and is not part of matter and cannot exist apart from matter. Therefore according to the aforesaid definition form, too, is an accident'. We reply that, in the first place, the form, even if it is not part of the matter, is yet part of the composite (for in this way we also say that the hand is not part of the rest of the body but rather of the whole body), and, in the second place, the form is constitutive of the substance of each thing and when it is destroyed the subject is destroyed. But the accident does not constitute the substance of the subject and when it is destroyed the subject is not damaged. These comments are directed towards those who say that the definition fits other things as well.

Those, however, who say that it does not fit all accidents say that he has defined only the inseparable ones. Thus the fragrance in the apple is separable and comes to us at a distance from the apple, but it is still an accident. If, then, it is separable from its subject, it would not be comprehended by the definition given. We reply to them that we solve this in two ways. First, Aristotle does not say *in which it was* but *in which it is* (therefore it is impossible for the fragrance to exist apart from the place[51] in which it is; for it is either in the apple or in the air). Further, not only does the fragrance of the apple come to us, but it comes with some substance of the apple. A sure sign of this is that after some time the apple will shrink and shrivel up, which shows that some substance of the apple in which the fragrance belongs is dissipated.

But if someone says, 'And yet when the apple was still on the tree the fragrance came to us no less from the nonshrivelling, sometimes even growing, apple', we reply to him: 'You do not understand nature's faculty of nourishment and growth. Do we not see growth taking place among all animals? And doubtless we do not for that reason say that they are not reduced each day by dissipation because, nevertheless, there is a greater amount brought in by reason of nourishment than the quantities of waste. Nature is so arranged that not only is evaporation imperceptible but growth, to the contrary, is comparatively perceptible.' We then say the same for the apple. For it is not that the effluence from the tree is imperceptible to us and thanks to this no substance is dissipated from it. It is rather that the substance that goes into it by reason of nutrition is greater than what goes out.

But it is possible to be persuaded of this in another way. Passing by a stinking place we block our nostrils with a garment and breathe air without the stench. For that reason it is clear that the stench cannot pass through the garment because of its thickness. But the air, having subtle parts, travels through. Thus it is clear that this scent comes to us with some substance of the subject. This is also shown by the smoke given off from incense, which immediately comes to

---

[51] Deleting *mêlou* (apple) and reading *topou* (place, genitive) for *topôi* (place, dative). Unamended, the text reads: 'it is impossible for the fragrance to exist apart from the apple in which place it is.'

view because of the incessant effluence and the thickness of the substance that is its subject.

In something is said in eleven ways, as has already been stated: (1) in a time (for the Trojan War or the Peloponnesian War occurred in a certain time); (2) in a place (for we say that Socrates is in a place, for example, in the Lyceum); (3) in a container (for we say that wine is in the pitcher – *in a place* differs from *in a container* in that the container is a movable place, whereas a place is an immovable container); (4) as a part in the whole, for example a finger in a hand or a hand in the whole of the body; (5) as a whole in its parts (for we say that the whole man is seen in his *parts* and not in a *part*); (6) as a species in a genus, for example man in animal; (7) as a genus in a species, for example animal in man; (8) as the <affairs> of the ruled in <the power or control of> the ruler (for we say that this particular thing is 'in' this particular ruler); (9) as form in matter, for example the human form in matter or the triangular or square figure in bronze; (10) as in an end, as for example <we say> that medicine is 'in' health; (11) as in a subject, for example an accident in substance. Someone might say that a genus is found in a species or a species in a genus as a whole in its parts or as the parts in the whole. We reply to this that a whole is not preserved without all of its proper parts, whereas a genus is preserved when even one species or one individual is preserved; for Socrates is Socrates and a man and an animal. So it is clear that whereas one part does not make up a complete whole, one species does make up a complete genus.

Having then clarified the particular accident for us, the Philosopher gives us an example of a universal accident and says: 'some things are both said of a subject and in a subject' (1a29-b1). Having then given examples of both universal and particular accidents he now goes on to the example of a particular substance and says 'but some things are neither in a subject nor said of a subject' (1b3-4). But he introduces this additional principle: 'absolutely without exception, things that are individual and one in number are not said of any subject' (1b6-7). He wants to show by means of this that no individuals, whether accidents or substances, are predicated of anything. Moreover, he divides and separates individual accidents from self-subsistent individuals. *Absolutely* (*haplôs*) is said in three ways: either strictly (*kuriôs*) or solely or universally. Here he has used it with the meaning universally. For he means 'universally, things that are individual and one in number'. We have written at length in commenting on the *Isagoge* of Porphyry about how many ways individual is said.⁵² We shall now say in how many ways *one* is said, for it is also said in many ways: either one in species, as we say Socrates and Plato are one in species in that they are men; or one in genus, as when we say man, cow, and horse are one in genus in that they are animals; or in number, as when we say Plato is one – but *one* here means *individual*, and this is what Aristotle says, for the sake of clarity, when he means *one* <in this sense>. Individuals, then, beings that are one in number, are never said of any subject but are often found in a subject, as this white is in body. For this reason, therefore, he has added *nothing prevents*, since they are not all in a subject. For Socrates is not in a subject, but this grammar, as Aristotle says, is in a subject, the soul. And to speak universally, things that are one in number and not substances are not said of any subject, but are in a subject.

1b10. When one thing is predicated of another [as of a subject, whatever is said of what is predicated will also be said of the subject].

The exemplar <for this> is that of universal substance. When one thing is predicated essentially (*ousiôdôs*) of another, he says, and in turn another thing is predicated of it, the last will also be predicated of the first. One might raise this objection: 'If it is true that whatever is said of what is predicated will also be predicated of the subject, and *genus* is predicated of *animal* and *animal* of *man*, then *genus* will also be predicated of *man*.' But this is not what Aristotle meant. For the Philosopher said 'whatever is said of what is predicated', i.e. as attributes of it (*hôs pragmata autou*) and as characterizing its essence (*ousia*), 'will also be said of the subject'. And he was right to add 'as of a subject', in the sense of 'essentially'

---

⁵² There is no such discussion in the surviving text of Ammonius' commentary on Porphyry's *Isagoge*.

Commentary 41

(*ousiôdôs*) and 'really' (*pragmatikôs*). For if something is predicated accidentally of what is predicated, it need not also be said of the subject. For *genus* is predicated accidentally and relatively (*kata skhesin*) of *animal*.

1b16. Of heterogeneous things not subordinate one to another [the differentiae, too, are different in kind].

Aristotle adds[53] some small assumptions which will be useful to him in setting out his lesson. He says that the specific differentiae of heterogeneous things are always different; for example, <those> of substance and quantity. For *animate* and *inanimate* are differentiae of substance, but *continuous* and *discrete* <are differentiae> of quantity. So the differentiae are different when the genera are different. But 'different genera'[54] is said in many ways. For <genera> called different include: (1) those entirely distinct from one another, such as *knowledge* and *animal*; (2) those not entirely separate, for example *winged* and *aquatic* (for they have a common genus, animal); even (3) subordinate genera, such as *substance* and *body*. Aristotle therefore says 'and not subordinate one to another'. For those <sc. genera one of which is subordinate to the other> can have the same differentiae; for example, both *living thing* (*empsukhon*) and *animal* (*zôion*) have <the differentiae> *mortal* and *immortal*, *rational* and *irrational*.

He was right to add 'in kind'. For here, take note, we have the same differentiae of different genera: we call some utensils 'footless', for example, a censer or a pestle or the like, and some 'footed', such as a chair or a bed and things like that. Likewise we say of animals that some are footless and some are footed. However, the same differentiae are not specific and not predicated strictly, but by a kind of analogy.

1b18. For the differentiae of animal [are footed, winged, aquatic, and two-footed].

---

[53] Reading *proslambanei* with MSS MF, rather than *prolambanei* ('anticipates'), with Busse (following Philoponus).
[54] Reading *hetera genê* with MS M.

Differentiae of genera can divide them in many ways. For example, the differentiae of animal are *rational* and *irrational*, but <animal can be differentiated> also, based on permanence of life, as *mortal* or *immortal*; and, based on place, as *winged*, *aquatic*, or *terrestrial*; and, based on the feet, as *footed* or *footless*. These different things are also differentiae. Although Aristotle uses the example of a differentia based on place, he inserts in its midst other differentiae as well. He does so deliberately, wishing to show that taking other differentiae makes no difference.

1b20. [Yet nothing prevents] differentiae of genera that are subordinate one to another [from being the same].

Aristotle was right to say 'nothing prevents'. For subordinate genera will not necessarily have the same differentiae. Rather, the essential differentiae of subordinate genera are always entirely the same, but not always the accidental [differentiae]. For this reason he has added 'nothing prevents'. It often happens, however, that they are the same, on account of the aforementioned general rule: 'whatever is said of what is predicated will also be said of the subject.'

1b25. [Each] of the things [said] without any combination [signifies either substance or ...].

Earlier, Aristotle handed down to us the four-fold division of universal substance, particular substance, universal accident, and particular accident. Now he presents a ten-fold division, by means of examples, in order to give us some notion of them, and later to teach [us] about each in detail. This is connected to his remark above (1a16): *among things that are said, some are said in combination, some without combination*. Now in accordance with this[55] he says *of the things without any combination*; in saying *without any* he makes clear that there are many combinations. For (1) we can use a simple expression with a compound meaning, as when I say 'I run'[56]

---

[55] Reading *dê akolouthôs toutô to*, following Busse's conjecture.

[56] In Greek, person and number of verbs are indicated by their inflection, and pronouns are not needed. Ammonius' sentence contains just one Greek word: *trekhô*.

Commentary

(for I refer to myself and to my action); (2) the expression may be compound but its meaning simple, like *mortal rational animal* (for the expression is compound, but its meaning is *man*); (3) both <expression and meaning> may be compound, as when I say 'Socrates runs'; or (4) both may be simple, like the categories themselves. So Aristotle is here distinguishing those things said without any combination, i.e. the ten categories.

1b27. To give a general indication of what these things are – examples of substance are man and horse.

At the start Aristotle kindly furnishes us with an explanation of the categories, first to give us a notion of his teaching about them, and so we may later accurately examine each category in particular. He says that substances are *man* and *horse*, but you must understand that the rest of the things that are self-subsistent (*authupostata*) and need nothing else to exist are also substances. So much for substance; we will understand the rest of the categories clearly from the text.[57]

2a3. Examples of *having* are *wearing shoes* and *being armed*.

Since *having* is opposed to *being had*, some people wonder why Aristotle says that there is a category only of *having*, but not one of being had, just as <there is> in the case of *being affected*, which is opposed to *doing* and of which he has made a category – I mean <the category of> *being affected*. Our response is that being had can be subsumed under the <category> of *being arranged*, but *having* cannot <be subsumed> under any of the others. This is why he had to define a category for it.

Now some people say that not every entity can be subsumed

---

[57] At this point MS M adds: Here it should be indicated that although every quality is in a subject, they are not all assigned the same kind of subject. Rather, some, such as heat and cold, exist in body, while others, such as geometry, have their being in the soul. Since he wanted to indicate the two types of quality by means of examples, the Philosopher mentioned some, saying 'examples of quality are white and grammatical', taking white as an example of a quality in a corporeal subject and grammatical <as an example> of one assigned to be in the soul.

under the ten categories. Under what category should we subsume a *point* or a *privation*? With respect to *point*s, our response is that Aristotle is here discussing things known by perception, and to 'the many'. But a point is not an independently existing thing; it is a principle (*arkhê*) of things in general. One would be similarly puzzled about matter and form, but as we shall explain,[58] the present discussion concerns neither the simple substance that is superior to the composite, nor the simple substance that is inferior to the composite, but composite substance. With respect to *privation*, some have said that it belongs in the same category under which *possession* is subsumed, since opposites are subsumed under the same category. But we say it is not to be subsumed under any one of the categories. For they are categories of *beings*, whereas privation is not a being, but a privation of being.

2a4. Each of the things mentioned above [said just by itself is no assertion].

Since he wants to inform us that he is not here proposing to distinguish affirmations from negations, Aristotle says that each of the categories by itself does not signify anything true or false. For if I say 'Socrates walks', then if he in fact walks, I have spoken truly, and if not, I have spoken falsely; and likewise for negations. But if I say 'man' ten thousand times I am speaking neither truly nor falsely; and the same goes for 'walks'.

However, someone might object that one who says '(I) walk'[59] is speaking either truly or falsely. For if he is in fact walking he speaks truly, and if not he speaks falsely. We reply that one who says '(I) walk' (*peripatô*) has virtually included the 'I' (*egô*), as if he had said 'I walk' (*peripatô egô*). Thus once again the pronoun has been included in the verb to produce a truth or falsehood, since a single category all by itself cannot do this. For it is obvious that none of the categories[60] is by

---

[58] Reading, with Busse, *phêsomen* ('we will say') for *ephamen* ('we said'). The explanation referred to occurs below at 35,27ff.

[59] *Peripatô*, first-person singular, means 'I walk'. Cf. n. 56.

[60] Ammonius clearly means that a single predicate from any category does not by itself constitute an assertion.

On Substance

itself either an affirmation or a negation, but that they combine with one another to do this. For example, in 'man walks' an affirmation is generated from a substance and an action. And by inserting a negative particle in the middle we get a negation, such as 'man does not walk'.

2a5. [Each of the things mentioned above said just by itself] is no assertion.

Most of the manuscripts (*biblîon*) that appear to have it right do not have 'or negation'. For if no single category signifies an affirmation, then certainly none signifies a negation. For it would need a negative particle;[61] and one would suppose *action* to signify affirmation rather than negation.

2a7. For it seems that every affirmation or negation [is either true or false].

Aristotle says 'seems', since in not all cases is an affirmation or negation obviously true or false.[62] An example <would be> if someone says '(I) run' or '(I) do not run'.[63] The reason why Aristotle says 'seems' is that in these cases one virtually supplies the unexpressed 'I'. Either that <is the reason>, or <it is> because the 'seems' is redundant, or because it is a copyist's error, or because he means it is thus apparent to everyone.

<On Substance>

2a11. Substance in the most proper sense of the word, that which is primarily and most of all called substance ...

Substance is first in order among the categories and for this reason he naturally puts it in front of the others. It is

---

[61] Omitting *heterou* with MS F.
[62] The text says, literally: 'in not all cases is an affirmation true, nor in all cases is a denial false.' We follow Pelletier in amending the text to read as we have translated: *ou pantôs hê kataphasis kai hê apophasis phanerôs alêtheuei ê pseudetai*.
[63] cf. n. 56.

entailed⁶⁴ by the other categories, but it does not entail them; it<s destruction> destroys them but it is not destroyed by theirs, because it is self-subsistent whereas the other categories have their being in it. From the fact that there is substance it is not necessary that there are the other categories, but if there were not substance the others could not exist.

Some substance is simple, some composite. Some simple substance is better than composite, some is inferior. Man and things of that sort are composite substances. The substance of the gods is simple substance that is better than the composite. Simple substance that is inferior to the composite is prime matter and form. These latter <two> gain recognition on account of the composites, and things recognized because of something else are always inferior to that on account of which they are recognized. Thus, among crafts we call bridle-making inferior to horsemanship, for horsemanship uses the finished product of bridle-making as an instrument. The bridle is a means, horsemanship is an end. And with other things it is similar. But Aristotle will not discuss here what is simple and superior to the composite (for that is theology), nor what is simple and inferior to the composite (for that is the inquiry into natural causes and phenomena [*phusiologia*]), but rather the composite and relational, insofar as it is signified in such a way.

He says of this substance that some is primary and some secondary, calling the particular primary and the universal secondary. For this reason it is worthwhile to ask why he says this, since universals are more worthy than particulars. Our response is that things prior by nature are secondary to us and things prior to us are secondary by nature. For example, matter and form, then the common elements, are prior by nature. From them come the sperm and the blood and then, in this way, the man. But for us the man is prior, for we discover the man first and then the things previously mentioned, which are recognized on account of it. Since, then, the explanation is aimed at beginners and to beginners

---

⁶⁴ *Suneispherein* literally means 'join in payments', and LSJ do not attest its use in the sense of 'entails'. Still, that is what it assuredly means in this context. Cf. Plato's similar use of the related verb *epipherein* at *Phaedo* 104E10ff.

immediate things are more manifest, it is fitting that in the present circumstance he calls particulars primary. For it is from particulars that we are led to universals.

It is because he does not approve of this manner of speaking that he does not say 'that which primarily and most of all *is* <substance>', but '<that which primarily and most of all> is *called* <substance>'. One must notice how Aristotle expresses himself here. Because, as we have said, he disapproves of calling the particular substance primary; he says it is that which is *said* not of any subject. For the really primary substance, that is, the universal, *is* of some subject. So he says 'is said' to indicate his disapproval. But since he knows that neither primary substance nor secondary is in a subject, he says 'is': '*is* not in any subject' (1a21). He agrees to 'is' here because <the claim> is acceptable to him.

2a12. That which is neither said of any subject ...

Some people question why Aristotle defines the most worthy thing by means of negations, since they are less worthy than affirmations. We reply that this is not inappropriate. We, too, when we want to refer to the divine, do not affirm something of it, but rather, as Plato says, we resort to negation.

Others are puzzled, saying that perhaps the definition given of substance fits both the truly primary and divine substance and also the individual soul.[65] For God is neither said of any subject nor is he in a subject, and the soul is, of course, the same. We reply that in neither case does the definition fit.

It is absolutely unthinkable to have this definition in mind for divine substance. 'Not being in[66] a subject' means *as opposed to things in a subject*, and <the definition> fits things that have some relation to those in a subject. But the divine is completely unrelated and transcendent (*exêirêmenon*) both from everything in a subject and from everything not in a

---

[65] Ammonius apparently has in mind Iamblichus' type of theory. Cf. Introduction for details.

[66] The MSS have 'of a subject'; we follow Pelletier in reading 'in a subject'. The MS reading may be the result of haplography: 'not being of a subject' means <*as opposed to things said of a subject*, and 'not being in a subject' means> *as opposed to things in a subject*. Cf. Philoponus *in Cat.* 52,14.

48   *Commentary*

10   subject that is nevertheless a subject for accidents. As for the soul, if one understands the transcendent one, again the definition, for the same reason, does not fit (for although it has the thoughts and the knowledge of all things before it, it is itself unrelated and transcendent). If one understands the individual soul, perhaps the definition applies to it. For after it has fallen into a relation and is seized by forgetfulness, it is then driven to the memory of previous things and becomes a
15   subject for grammar at one time, for medicine at another time, and in the same way for other skills. It is not surprising that the definition fits the soul at one time but not at another, for it has an intermediate order between the things which completely transcend matter and those completely involved in matter. When the soul is separated (*exêirêtai*) from bodies, the definition does not apply to it; but when fallen into matter it is
20   caused to forget. The definition then applies and there is no paradox.

   2a14. What are called secondary substances.

   It is worth considering what manner of division Aristotle is
38,1   using in the case of substance. For some of his divisions are of (1) genera into species, some are of (2) a whole into parts, and some are of (3) an ambiguous expression into its different senses. We reply first that it is not of a genus into species, because it never happens that one of the divided species includes another. For example, some animals are rational and
5   some irrational, but we cannot say 'Some animals are irrational and some are horses'. For the second is included under the first. And it is in just this way that primary substance is included under secondary. Nor is he dividing as a whole into parts. For one cannot say 'One <part> of the whole is the hand and another is the finger'. For in the same way the finger, too, is included under the hand. Rather, one <part> of
10   the whole is the hand and another is the foot. Nor, for the same reason, is he here dividing an ambiguous expression into different senses. For among things divided as an ambiguous expression into different senses we do not find one included under another. For example, the expression 'dog' is predicated of the constellation and of the philosopher and of

On Substance

the terrestrial dog, but none of these is included under any of the others. And, above all, one finds only homonymy, not commonality of definition, among ambiguous expressions divided into different senses. But with primary and secondary substance there is commonality not only of name but also of definition. For Socrates, who is a primary substance, is called by the name of the secondary, that is, by the name 'man'; moreover, Socrates and the universal *man* also have the same definition. Likewise, an animal is called both *sensible animate substance* and *animal*. Thus we say that he gives an ordering (*taxis*) of substance, but not a division.

2a14. The species in which the things primarily called substances fall [are called secondary substances].

Why does he not say 'genera and species are called secondary substances', rather than 'the species in which ...'? Our answer is that this is quite unassailable. For if he were to say 'genera and species', then since there are genera and species in the other categories (e.g. in <the category of> quality colour is a genus and white and black are species), we could assume there to be secondary substances even in the accidental <categories>. That is why he does not speak of just any species, but of the species in which primary substances are found.

2a15. These, as well as the genera of these species.

Here the Philosopher draws together what he said above. By saying 'these' he means primary substance, and by saying 'as well as the genera of <these> species' he means secondary substance.[67]

2a16. For example, the individual man.

Aristotle takes <this> as an example of a primary substance. And from the example it is obvious that primary substance is

---

[67] Ammonius seems confused. His idea apparently is that Aristotle understands the species to be the genuine primary substance, so that among universals it is only the genus, not the species, that is a secondary substance. Perhaps he is drawing on *Metaph.* Z, which has seemed to many interpreters to link primary substance to

included under secondary. For the individual man is in the species *man*, and *animal* is the genus of this species. Since *animal* includes the universal *man*, and the universal *man* [includes] the individual man, and the individual man is a primary substance, therefore the universal man and <the universal> *animal* are called secondary substances.

2a17. So they [man and animal] are called secondary substances.

Aristotle is right in saying 'are called', since by nature they are primary substances.

2a20. Both the name and the definition of a thing *said of a subject* must be predicable of the subject.

Aristotle here deduces the following corollary: whatever is *said of* something as of a subject, he says, shares both its name and its definition with the subject (for Socrates is called a man and a mortal rational animal), but what is *in* a subject never shares its definition, although it sometimes shares its name. For whiteness is in body and does not share its definition <with body>; we would not call the body a colour penetrative of sight. But it does share its name, for we call the body white. Notice, however, that this is not always the case. Consider: virtue (*aretê*) shares neither its name nor its definition with a subject. Someone who partakes of virtue is not called 'virtued' (*aretaios*) but 'good' (*spoudaios*).[68]

2a34. Everything else [is either said of primary substances as subjects or is in them as subjects].

Again, Aristotle does well to say 'is said'. For universals do not

---

species as opposed to both individuals and genera. But Aristotle's text in the *Categories* is unambiguous: individuals are called primary substances, their species and genera are called secondary substances.

[68] In English, of course, a person with virtue is called 'virtuous'. But in Greek, the adjective corresponding to the noun *aretê* (virtue) is the non-cognate form *spoudaios*, usually translated as 'virtuous'. Here the usual translation would obscure Ammonius' point; we therefore render *spoudaios* as 'good'. We have translated his neologism, *aretaios*, as 'virtued', to preserve the odd sound Ammonius intended this expression to have.

On Substance

need primary substances, i.e. particulars, in order to exist, but in order to be *said of* them.

2a35. ... or is in them as subjects.

Again, the 'is' is good here. For accidents have their being in particular substances. Aristotle wants, then, to heap praise on primary substance. Since things are divided into three – into universal substances, particular substances, and accidents – each of them, he says, will need primary substances, some in order to exist (for accidents have their being in substances) and some in order to be predicated (for what are the universals to be predicated of other than the particulars?). And if primary substances were to be destroyed, accidents, too, unable to exist (*hupostênai*) in anything, would be destroyed. In the same way universals, unable to be said of any subject, would be destroyed, too.

It is not what is prior to the many but what is in the many that is called universal. This <remark> has been added on account of what is said in Porphyry's *Isagoge*, <viz.> that it would be possible for the genus to exist even on the hypothesis that all the species had been destroyed.[69] There, of course, <Porphyry> was discussing intelligible genera and species, which are prior to the many, whereas here <Aristotle> is discussing perceptible genera and species, that is, those in the many.

2b5. ... or is in them as subjects.

That is, universal substances are said of particulars, whereas accidents have their being in particular substances. If there were, then, no primary substances, there would be neither universals nor accidents. It is reasonable, then, that particular substances are said to be primary. And he was right to fix on 'are said' for universals and 'are' for accidents.

2b7. Among secondary substances, [species is] more [substance than genus.]

[69] *Isag.* 15,18ff.

Now he compares secondary substances (species and genus) to each other, and proves by means of two arguments that a species is more a substance than is a genus. One <argument> is based on its relation to primary substance, that is, on its proximity; for a species is closer to the primary, that is to say particular, substance than is a genus. The other is from analogy; as a primary substance is to its species, so is a species to its genus.

2b8. For if one were to give an account of what some primary substance is [it would be more informative and more appropriate to give the species than to give the genus].

Now if one were to give an account of what Socrates is, both 'man' and 'animal' would be appropriate answers, but 'man' would be more appropriate than 'animal'. For saying 'animal' we introduce more (for it signifies both rational and irrational) and we did not indicate whether <we meant> rational or irrational. On the other hand, by answering 'man' we give a more immediate account of the nature of Socrates.

2b12. For the former is more distinctive of an individual [man].

To be a man is indeed more distinctive of Socrates than to be an animal. For the latter is more general and <is predicated> of many species. The same relation holds in the case of trees and <the genus> *plant*.

2b15. Further, primary substances [are subjects for everything else].

This comes from the second argument, the one from analogy. The reason that primary substances are called primary, he says, is that they are subjects both for accidents with respect to belonging (*huparxis*) and for universals with respect to predication. For as primary substances stand to accidents and universals, so species stand to genera. Species are subjects for genera with respect to predication, but genera are not

On Substance

<subjects> for species. For genera are predicated of species (thus we say, 'Every man is an animal', and man, i.e. the species, is the subject, and animal, that is to say, the genus, is predicated), but species are not reciprocally predicated of genera. Thus we cannot say, 'Every animal is a man', as we say 'Every man is an animal'. So for these reasons a species is more a substance than is a genus.

2b22. Among species that are not themselves genera [none is more a substance than another].

Aristotle was right to have added 'that are not genera', lest you consider *animal* <as an example>; for animal is not only a species but also a genus. Accordingly, one should not consider these,[70] but rather those that are only species, i.e. the *infimae species*, for example man and horse.

2b24. For it is no more appropriate [to give man in defining the individual man than it is to give horse in defining the individual horse].

Having gone through a review of substance vertically, that is from individuals to species and from species to genus, he wants now to make the comparison horizontally in a similar way, from species to species and from individual to individual. Accordingly, he says that there will be no difference between one species and another with respect to being a secondary substance or between one individual and another with respect to being a primary substance.

2b25. [For it is no more appropriate to give an account of an individual man as a man] than of an individual horse as a horse.

Indeed, the relation (*logos*) that *man* has to the individual man, *horse* also has to Xanthus. For just as you can assert nothing more distinctive of Socrates than *man*, so too you can

---

[70] Omitting *tout' esti ta hupallēla* ('i.e. subordinates') with MS M. Ammonius' point is not that we should ignore subordinate species, but that we should ignore those species which, being genera as well, *have* subordinate species.

54 Commentary

assert nothing more distinctive of Xanthus than *horse*.

15 **2b29. It is reasonable that, after primary substances [species and genera alone among everything else should be called secondary substances].**

Now he states the reason why he has called genera and species secondary substances, but has not said that accidents are tertiary substances. He gives two arguments, the first derived from the setting out (*apodosis*) of a definition. For he says: if to the question 'What is Socrates?' we respond 'man' or 20 'animal', we will be setting out the definition properly and intelligibly. But if we respond 'pale' or 'he runs' or some such thing, we will be setting it out improperly and unintelligibly. Thus it is reasonable that we should call species and genera secondary substances, but we absolutely do not call accidents substances.

2b37. Moreover, [it is because they are subjects for everything else that] primary substances [are most properly called substances].

The second argument is by analogy. He says that just as 25 primary substances are called primary on account of their 44,1 being subjects for the rest, so too are species and genera called secondary substances on account of their also being subjects for others. But species and genera are subjects for accidents. So they are, reasonably, called secondary substances. And it is the same, too, for the others.

5 **3a7. Not [being] in [a subject] is something common to all substances.**

Having divided substance into primary and secondary, and having compared these to one another, he proceeds in good order and now wants to give a definition of substance. But since substance is an ultimate (*genikôtaton*) genus, and we cannot give a definition of an ultimate <genus> because 10 definitions, as we know, are composed of genus and constitutive (*sustatikôn*) differentiae, he looks for a *proprium* (*idion*) of substance.[71] Indeed, this is somewhat like a definition. For just as a definition belongs to all and only that of which it is the definition and is convertible with what it defines, so too a *proprium* belongs to all and only that of which it is the *proprium*, and they are convertible with one another. This, then, is the reason he wants to give a *proprium* of substance. But he does not immediately produce an answer acceptable to him; rather, he first says that *not being in a subject* is a *proprium* of substance. This fits every substance, but not only substance – it fits differentiae, too, whereas a *proprium* must belong *to all and only*.

By saying 'common' he seems to be contradicting himself. For if he wants to give a *proprium* of substance, how can he say 'common'? Our response is that two features absolutely must belong to a *proprium*, viz. *to all* and *to only*. So by saying 'common' he meant '<belonging> to all'.

It is obvious that the *proprium* given belongs to primary substances, but it is clear from this that it belongs to secondary substances also. For *animal* and *man* are somehow in the particular man not as *in a subject*, but as *of a subject*.

3a15. Moreover, although [nothing prevents the name] of a thing that is in a subject [from sometimes being predicated of the subject ...].

Aristotle wants to show that for this reason, too, secondary substances are not in a subject, <e.g.> the particular man. For he says that what is in a subject can sometimes give its name to the subject, but never its definition. For we call a body *white*, and whiteness, which is in a subject, the body, gives its name to the subject, but not its definition. For we do not call the body *colour penetrative of sight*. But secondary substances give both their names and their definitions. For Socrates is called both a man and a mortal rational animal.

---

[71] *Idion* means 'peculiar' or 'distinctive'. Aristotle uses it in a semi-technical way to indicate a non-accidental characteristic that is distinctive, but not part of the essence, of its subject (cf. *Top.* 102a18-30). We follow the common practice of having the Latin translation *proprium* represent this semi-technical usage.

> 3a21. **This, however, is not peculiar (*idion*) to substance. Rather, their differentiae are not in a subject, either.**

Aristotle rejects the *proprium* of substance that he has given, as it belongs not only to substance but also to differentiae. And this makes it clear that he is separating differentiae from substances. Does he therefore conclude that they are accidents?[72] That would be absurd. For it seems even to Aristotle himself that they are substances, so that species are made up of them and they are predicated essentially of the species. For if they were not substances, substance would turn out to be generated out of accidents, which is absurd. So if differentiae are substances (for the parts of a substance are substances and a definition consists of the parts of a substance), how can Aristotle say 'this is not distinctive of substance but <belongs> also to differentiae', which obviously implies that differentiae are other than substance?

Now our response is that some substances are intelligible and some are perceptible. Of the perceptible, some are eternal, such as the heavenly bodies, and some are subject to coming into being and destruction. Of these, some are simple, such as *rational* and *mortal* — which are precisely the essential differentiae that nature has combined to bring man into being — and some are composite, such as genera, species, and individuals. Now Aristotle's teaching here concerns only composite substance that is subject to coming into being and destruction, I mean individuals, species, and genera. And so having compared substances with one another, he compared species alone and genera and then individuals, too, since he set himself to teach about them as well. But he made no mention of differentiae, since they are simple and he is constructing a definition of composites, as has <already> been said. It is for this reason, therefore, that Aristotle says that this <sc. not being in a subject> is 'not a *proprium* of substance'. He did not mean every substance, absolutely, but composite substance. And that was reasonable. For <not being in a subject> belongs not only to the composite, but also to the simple, i.e. to differentiae, to *rational* and *irrational*.

---

[72] Busse does not punctuate this as a question, but the context makes clear that it must be so intended.

And that is why he seemed to be distinguishing differentiae from substances.

Others say that differentiae are not substances without qualification, but that some of them are related to substance, such as *rational* and *mortal*, some are related to accidents and border more closely on them, such as the black in the raven or white in the swan, and some are exactly in the middle between substances and accidents, such as the heat in fire. (For on the one hand it partakes of accident in that it is a quality, and on the other it partakes of substance in that it completes its subject.) These people have made a clever effort, although it is not entirely correct. For under what category shall we rank these <differentiae>? Or might we need an eleventh? That is absurd.

3a29. We should not be afraid [that we might have to say] that the parts of a substance [are not themselves substances since they are in a subject, viz. the whole <substance>].

The very point one was likely to have raised as an objection to Aristotle, he himself has anticipated and solved. One might have objected as follows: 'Since the parts of substances are in something (for hands and legs are observed in a man) and similarly accidents are also in something, as whiteness or heat may perhaps be observed in a man, the parts of substances are therefore accidents – which is absurd.'

Aristotle solves this by saying that he has explained in what sense an accident may be said to be in something, <viz.> not as a part of the subject.[73] Differentiae, on the other hand, provide what is needed by the whole; that is, they constitute the subject. Thus, even if they have in common <with accidents> that they are in something, there is this difference between them: the differentiae make up <the subject> and belong <to it> as parts, whereas accidents do nothing of the sort. One must realize that Aristotle's discussion concerns not

---

[73] Busse reads '<For an accident is in something> not as a part of the subject', deriving from MS L the bracketed words, which were arguably omitted in MSS MF by haplography. Since this emendation is superfluous, we have chosen to follow MSS MF.

perceptible parts of substance, for example, hands and feet or other such things, but intelligible (i.e. real) parts, for example, *rational* and *mortal*. For some parts are perceptible and some are intelligible, and his discussion concerns intelligible parts. So the location (*taxis*) of this observation is appropriate. For after saying, 'It is not a peculiarity of substance not to be in a subject, for differentiae also are not in a subject' (3a21-22), lest one think he meant by this that differentiae are not substances (for they are indeed substances in the strict sense) he then says, 'We should not be afraid [that we might have to say] that the parts of a substance [are not themselves substances] since they are in a subject, viz. the whole <substance>' (3a29-31). The inclusion of this observation will seem inappropriate unless we recognize that Aristotle is talking about intelligible parts, such as *rational* and *mortal*. These are indeed properly <counted as> parts of man, for man is <constituted> of them.

3a31. For 'things in a subject' was not being used to mean [things belonging to something as parts].

This is what he has said: Accidents, even if they are in something, are not so as parts of substances. But he has said in what sense they are in something, namely, not as a part in the whole.

3a33. It is a characteristic of substances and differentiae [that they are said synonymously of everything they are said of].

Aristotle has turned to a second concomitant (*parakolouthêma*) of substance and immediately gives an unfavourable judgment of it. This is clear from the fact that he has included differentiae; for again it is evident that this *proprium* fits them. Anyhow, it is not only for this reason that this *proprium* does not fit substances, but also because it is not a characteristic of every substance. For a primary substance is not predicated of anything.

3a35. [For every such predicate] is predicated either of individuals [or of species].

First Aristotle teaches that some things are recipients of predication; then he connects them in the following way with synonymous predication. Individuals are not said of any subject, species <are said> of individuals, and, again, genera <are said> of both. And these things are said synonymously of the things of which they are predicated. *For whatever is said of the predicate will also be said of the subject* (3b4-5). For Socrates is called a sensible animate substance and a mortal rational animal. And man is called a sensible animate substance, and this is with good reason. For since the genus is predicated of the species and of the individual, and the species <is predicated> of the individual, and whatever is said of the predicate is also said of the subject, it is with good reason that the genus is predicated synonymously of the individuals and of the species, and the species of the individuals.

3b10. Each substance seems to signify a particular this.[74]

Having rejected the first two concomitants of substance – not being in a subject and being said synonymously of everything <it is said of> – he turns to the third: signifying a particular

---

[74] Following this lemma, and preceding the subsequent commentary, MS F adds: After rejecting the first two *propria* of substance, Aristotle goes on to the third. Let us <first> investigate their order, then why he used the <expression> 'particular this' (*tode ti*), and third why he used 'signifies' and not 'is signified'. For 'signifies' applies to words, and 'is signified' to things.
  Now since he used the <expression> 'in a subject' in many ways and has already demonstrated the way in which predication arises, it was necessary for him to put *not being in a subject* first as a proprium of substance. He put *being said synonymously of <everything> they are said of* second, since other things in addition to secondary substances are predicated synonymously of an individual substance, e.g. differentiae. He assigned the third position to *particular this*, since the remaining *propria*, such as *more and less*, and *not having a contrary*, are used for things.
  Here he used the <expression> 'particular this' only for words. Aristotle understood 'particular this' determinately (*hôrismenôs*), as applying to determinate existing things, but <he understood> 'such' (*toionde*) to apply to the indefinite and to the universal. (Indeed he was correct to withhold the term 'universal' from all things, *simpliciter*.) Plato, on the other hand, had to understand 'particular this' to apply to the universal as a determinate thing, i.e. to the Forms (for he said that they were substances in reality), and 'such' to apply to the particular (*tou kathekasta*), (for he said particulars are indeterminate because they are not at rest but have their being in flow and effluence). Both are right in what they say, since they understand <the expression> in two different ways.
  The reason that Aristotle said 'signifies' is that he sometimes transfers a property (*pathos*) of a thing to a word or a property of a word to a thing. For example, in the case of <saying> 'Socrates walks', one transfers the activity to the word 'Socrates'; or, again, <in saying> 'A man thinks', <one transfers> thinking, which is strictly a

60   *Commentary*

this (*tode ti*). 'This' (*tode*) signifies a pointing out (*deixis*), and 'particular' (*ti*) signifies a substance in the sense of a subject (*tês kata to hupokeimenon ousias*), because it is permanent and does not need anything and is not in a subject but is a subject for all <the rest> and is the cause of their unity, that is, of their
49,1   signifying one thing, such as this log or this man. For 'particular this' is said of a substance in the sense of a subject, that is, of the observable individual substance. For that is what is capable of being pointed out. But he discovers that even if this distinguishing mark is a concomitant of substance alone, it
5   is not a concomitant of every substance. For a species or a genus, he says, such as man or animal, although it seems to signify a particular this because it appears in the singular form, signifies rather a plurality and a certain quality (*poiotêta tina*). For <a species or a genus> makes apparent the commonality and uniting of particulars. On that account he says, '<A species or a genus> is not a sort (*poion*) in the sense of accident, but rather it marks off a sort with respect to
10   substance',[75] i.e. a uniting and gathering together of particular men. Indeed a sort in the sense of accident comes after the substance is generated and needs the substance in order to exist, whereas the latter <sort> certainly does not.

3b24. It is also characteristic of substances not to have a contrary.

Aristotle proceeds to a fourth concomitant of substance, although he recognizes that it belongs to other things as well.
15   For nothing is the contrary of a quantity, such as two-footed, and likewise nothing is the contrary of a number. What would be contrary to ten? If you say that three is contrary to ten, then you are taking them as large and small, and these are not contraries,[76] but relatives, which do not have contraries.

---

property of the soul, <to the man>; or, again, <in saying> 'A man builds', <one transfers to the man something> that is strictly only <a property> of the body.
   [75] This is not a precise citation of any extant Aristotelian text. Cf. 3b15-23.
   [76] Ammonius must have meant to say 'quantities' here rather than 'contraries'. Still, his argument is puzzling. It is, apparently, this: Ten and three are contraries only if they are thought of as *large* and *small*, respectively, and only if *large* and *small* are contraries. But large and small are relatives, not quantities. And relatives don't have contraries. So ten and three are not contraries. However, Aristotle says (6b15) that some relatives do have contraries, as Ammonius is well aware (cf. 69,22-70,8).

3b26. Nor is anything [the contrary] of man or animal.

There is nothing contrary to Socrates, or to man, or to animal, in the way that cold is contrary to hot or black to white.

3b30. Although someone might say that many [is contrary] to few.

In truth, these are not strictly contraries, as Aristotle himself proves a little later. But he says, by way of concession, that even if these things are contraries, nothing absurd will follow from the purported fact. For it takes only one case to overturn a universal. Therefore if nothing is the contrary of two-footed, it is clear that *not having a contrary* does not belong to substance alone.

3b33. It appears that substance does not admit [of more and less].

This is the fifth concomitant <of substance>. It is reasonable that substance does not admit of more and less, since it does not have contrariety. For there is more and less in things in which there is contrariety, and there is contrariety in things in which there is more and less. For a contradictory (*makhomenon*) comes into being by a decrease in its contrary. Aristotle does not add, in conclusion, that 'this is not distinctive (*idion*) of substance; for quantity also does not admit of more and less'. For since these concomitants are interconnected, he has left it to you to understand and supply this implied but unexpressed conclusion, which he had already stated above.

3b34. I do not mean that [one] substance [is not more] substance [than another].

For since earlier he said that the individual substance is more a substance than the species, and the species more than the genus, now he says that he does not mean by this that one substance is not more or less a substance than another, but that the same substance does not admit of more and less. For example, Socrates is not said to be sometimes more Socrates and sometimes less, nor is a man said to be more or less a man.

3b39. For one [man] is not more [a man] than another.

25 Socrates is not sometimes more a man and sometimes less, nor again is Socrates more a man, in respect of being a mortal rational animal, than Plato, in the way that one white thing is
51,1 more white than another, and similarly for the rest. A thing can even be said to be more white than itself. For what is now white can later, its whiteness having increased, become whiter than itself.

4a10. Most distinctive of substance [seems to be the fact that something the same and one in number is receptive of contraries].

5 This sixth concomitant Aristotle has rendered a *proprium* (*idion*) of substance. He says 'one in number' <to indicate> that one subject is preserved; he says 'the same' <to indicate> that it does not change with respect to its real being (*hupostasis*). For a colour goes from white to black and changes with respect to its real being; but Socrates <remaining one and the same is at one time hot and at one
10 time cold, and it is the same with the rest>.[77] He says 'receptive of contraries' meaning *having the capability of receiving contraries in turn*. <For he does not say 'receives contraries'>,[78] since <on that showing> opposites would be in the same thing in the same respect. But by 'receptive' he meant only that there is a capacity.

But how would this appear to be a *proprium* of substance? For it does not fit secondary substances. We will say that even
15 if it is not a concomitant of all <substance>, still it is a concomitant of <substance> alone. What belongs to something alone is more distinctive of it, even if it does not belong to all of it, than what belongs to all of it but not to it

---

[77] The bracketed passage does not occur in any of the MSS. We follow Busse, who derives it from Philoponus.
[78] cf. n. 77.

alone. And this is reasonable. For how could what belongs to other things also be a *proprium* of this particular thing? Of the six characteristics of substance that have been presented, the first, fourth, and fifth belong to all of it, but not to it alone, whereas the second, third, and last belong to it alone, but not to all of it. That is why the three which belong to all of it but not to it alone have been defined negatively as being far from the nature of *propria*, while the second, third, and sixth have been defined positively as being more proper (*idia*) than the others, on the grounds that, as we have said, a *proprium* must belong to that alone of which it is a *proprium*.

The final one is given precedence over the second and third, even if it seems to apply (*sêmainein*) in the same way they do (for all three belong to substance alone but not to all of it). The reason is that *signifying a particular this* and *being said synonymously of everything it is said of* are taken in connection with an expression (*phônê*), whereas the last <derives> from the very being (*huparxis*) <of substance>. The last <characteristic> would belong to all and only substance if we were to make a slight addition and say, after the *proprium* given, 'or contains what is one and the same and is receptive of contraries'. For in putting it this way we include species and genera.

4a21. [This sort of thing] is to be seen in no other case.

He anticipates just what one would likely find puzzling, and resolves it. That is, we say that spoken statements and opinions can receive contraries. For the statement which says, 'Socrates is sitting', is true if Socrates happens to be seated, but false if he happens to be walking about. And similarly concerning the opinion. For one who judges about Plato that he is sitting judges correctly if Plato happens to be seated, but falsely if he is not. Thus the same statement, and the same opinion, can receive both truth and falsity.

He resolves this in two ways, namely, by objection and by counter-objection. The objection is not to accept the puzzle at all, but to refute it as stated. The counter-objection is to admit the puzzle and to grant its premises, but to show that even if they obtain, they will do no damage to what he has said. Here

64 *Commentary*

5   he has put the counter-objection before the objection to make things clearer for beginners.

4a34. Statements and opinions, however, [remain themselves entirely unchanged ...]

Note that among substances, contraries change into each other (for what is hot becomes cold and conversely what is cold
10 <becomes> hot, and similarly what is dark <becomes> light and what is light <becomes> dark). But with statements and opinions this is not so. For a falsehood does not change into truth, nor truth into a falsehood.[79] Rather, it is by a thing (*pragma*) being changed and altered that truth and falsehood come into being. Truth and falsehood do not derive from statements or opinions.

15 **4b2. It would still be characteristic of substance that it happens in this way ...**

That is, a substance is capable of receiving contraries in a different way from an opinion or a statement.

4b4. Even if one were to allow that statements and opinions can receive contraries ...

20 With the counter-objection one proceeds by concession; in truth, they are not capable of receiving contraries. For statements and opinions are not said to be capable of

---

[79] Literally, 'the false does not change into truth nor truth into false'. *To pseudos* ('the false') can mean either a *falsehood* (i.e. a false statement) or *falsity* (i.e. the property of being false). On neither reading, however, is Ammonius' argument very plausible. If he means 'a false statement', his claim is incompatible with Aristotle's example: the true statement that a person is sitting will become false after that person has got up (4a24-26). If he means 'falsity', the claim is correct (for the property of being false does not turn into the property of being true) but the contrast with substances is lost. For when what is hot becomes cold the property of being hot does not become the property of being cold.
   Aristotle's point is that when a statement changes in truth-value, the statement itself does not undergo alteration; rather, the *facts* change. But even this point, one might argue, is none too secure. For according to Aristotle the sense in which the statement itself does not undergo alteration is that it remains *the same statement*. But neither does a body that becomes cold undergo alteration in that sense: it remains the same body. To maintain, as he wishes to, that statements do not undergo change at all, Aristotle ought to have denied that one and the same statement can be

receiving contraries in virtue of receiving anything themselves. For how will they ever be capable of receiving contraries when they do not have any independent existence (*hupostasis*) at all?[80] This is precisely what is required for there to be a future reception of contraries; but statements and opinions perish as soon as they are uttered.

Let what has been said thus far concerning substance suffice. Next we must discuss quantity.

On Quantity

4b20. Some quantities are discrete.

Having completed his discussion of substance, Aristotle now takes up quantity, for quantity is second in order among the categories. Prime matter, which is formless and incorporeal, first receives the three dimensions and becomes a three-dimensional object called the second subject, and next <receives> its qualities and becomes a quantified[81] composite. For example, when the three-dimensional <subject> receives heat and dryness, it becomes fire; when it receives coldness and wetness, it becomes water, and similarly for the others. So quantity quite rightly is second in order among the categories, quality third, <and relatives fourth>.[82] For relatives are a kind of relation (*skhesis*) to other categories, while place and time and the rest are derived (*sesulêtai*) from

---

now true and later false. The utterance may be the same on both occasions (e.g. 'He is sitting'), but the statements made are different.

[80] Ammonius certainly believes that statements have being (cf. 60,10: the existence [*einai*] of a statement consists in its being said). What he denies is that they have *hupostasis* ('real being', or 'independent existence'). His reason for denying this is, presumably, that statements exist only while being said. A statement cannot receive a contrary in the future since it will not still be in existence in the future.

[81] It is not clear why Ammonius says 'quantified' here (as all MSS agree that he does). One would have expected to be told that, upon receiving its qualities, the second subject becomes a *qualified* composite. It will, according to Ammonius' account, already have become quantified when it became three-dimensional. Perhaps his idea is that prime matter first receives the three dimensions and becomes quantified, and then receives its qualities and becomes a quantified *composite*.

[82] As Pelletier points out, the bracketed phrase must be understood if the next sentence is to be relevant.

66   *Commentary*

these.⁸³ Moreover, we divide substance into primary and secondary, and 'primary and secondary' itself involves number. Hence, *number* is used for the three-dimensional, and number is a quantity. So Aristotle is quite right to take up quantity in the second place.

Aristotle divides quantity into continuous and discrete. He further divides the discrete into two — number and statement (*logos*) — and the continuous into five — line, surface, body, time, and place. Then he cross-divides quantity into those composed of parts having position <in relation to one another> and those not so composed. Quantities composed of parts having position <he divides> into line, surface, body, and place; those not so composed into time, statement, and number.

Some people say that, properly speaking, there are three species of quantity — number, volume, and power, i.e. weight. They argue that (1) statement and time are the same as number; (2) line, surface, and body can be reduced to something common — magnitude; (3) place is the same as surface, and therefore (4) one kind of quantity is number, another magnitude, another power. (For under this last heading they place heavy and light, which are weights of quantity, for they fall under it.)

Why didn't Aristotle mention *change* (*kinêsis*)? Our response is that change is not an actuality (*energeia*), but an indefinite thing. Therefore he did not mention it, since he was addressing his discussion to beginners. For change itself is nothing other than the transition (*hodos*) from something in potentiality to something in actuality.

   4b21. Some [quantities are composed of parts] which have position in relation to one another.

In other words, those whose permanent and co-existent parts have a certain order and continuity in which they are

---

⁸³ Ammonius probably meant to say that the categories of *where* and *when* (along with the four other secondary categories) are derived from the four primary categories (substance, quantity, quality, and relatives). For, as 58,12ff. makes clear, Ammonius is aware that Aristotle considers time and place to be continuous quantities. Time and place, therefore, are not merely derived from quantities. At 69,10ff. Ammonius explains that place and time are species of quantity that give rise to the categories of *where* and *when*.

On Quantity

arranged in relation to one another in a subject.

4b22. While others are not so composed.

That is, the ones which have their existence in coming into being. He means *position* not in its primary sense of position *in place*, but in the sense of position with respect to a relation (*kata skhesin*).

4b22. Some are discrete.

Discrete quantities are, just as he himself says, those whose parts do not meet one another at any common boundary. Continuous quantities are those whose parts meet at one common boundary.

4b25. For there is no common boundary of the parts of a number at which the parts meet.

He does not prove that number is a quantity, since that is self-evident. But he does demonstrate that it is discrete, from the fact that there is no common boundary joining any of its parts.

4b28. Nor do three and seven meet at any common boundary.

That is, a number is discrete by nature. Indeed, five and five are always discrete and do not meet at any common boundary.

4b32. That [a statement] is a quantity [is obvious].

Aristotle shows that a statement is a quantity, and that it is a discrete quantity. But first he shows that it is a quantity, since a statement's being a quantity cannot simply be taken for granted if it is not supported by some kind of proof. For this reason he says that a spoken statement is a quantity because it is measured by syllables. For it is not <a quantity> in respect of its signifying something or in respect of its being compound. For if something is measured by something, what is measured is either the double or a multiple of what measures it. These are *propria* of quantity. So if a *proprium* of quantity is evidently a concomitant of a statement, then a statement would be a quantity.

But how can a statement (*logos*), which is one of those things considered <to be said> in combination (if indeed it is composed of a noun and a verb), fall under one of the categories, if the categories are of things without combination? We reply to this that *logos* here must be understood as having the more common meaning of 'word'. Moreover, since *logos* is said in many ways (it means spoken language, and it also means inner language) here he is talking about spoken language.

5a1. A line, on the other hand, is continuous.

This is reasonable, for each part of it meets another at a common boundary, a point. But one should take the division <as> in the mind and not in actuality, since <actually> dividing it would not allow it to be continuous.

5a3. For the parts of a plane [meet at a common boundary].

The geometer calls a surface (*epiphaneia*) that is exposed by slicing, a *superficies* (*epipedon*), but the ancients applied the term 'superficies' to every surface. The common boundary of a surface, at which its parts are joined to each other, is a line. A body is also called a quantity, but only with respect to the three dimensions, since it is counted under substance in virtue of being a subject for accidents and being capable of receiving contraries while <remaining> one and the same in number. But quantity is connected with corporeal substance, on which account it is reasonable to discuss it after substance.

5a6. Time and place are also like this.

That is to say, <they are> continuous, for past time and future join at a common boundary, the present (*nun*).

On Quantity

5a8. Place, too, is one of the continuous quantities.

Place, as is said in the *Physics* lectures,[84] is the limit of a container (*peras tou periekhontos*) in so far as it contains what it contains (*to periekhomenon*). For example, the place of wine is the concave surface of a jug. It is not the whole jug; for that has both convexity and concavity, and it contains the body of the wine in its concavity. Even if we were to scrape a part of the outside surface while preserving the inside, the wine would be no less contained. What Aristotle means, then, is this: if an entire body is in a place, and the body is continuous and its parts are joined at a common boundary, then the place of the body is also continuous and its parts are joined at a common boundary. For if the parts of the place were not joined at a common boundary, but rather were separated from each other, there would be some parts of the body not in a place – which is absurd.

5a15. Moreover, some [quantities are composed of parts] which have position [in relation to one another].

After having divided quantity into the discrete and the continuous and having divided it again into those quantities whose parts have a position and those whose parts do not, and having first discussed discrete and continuous quantities, he now considers the second division. Quantities whose parts have position must display these three characteristics: (1) they endure,[85] (2) their parts are arranged somewhere and do not disappear, that is, they are in something, and (3) they have an order with respect to one another.

5a23. But the parts of number ...

The parts of place are arranged in something, the body whose place it is.[86]

---

[84] cf. *Phys.* 4.4, 212a20. As Aristotle defines it, the place that a thing occupies is two-dimensional: the inner surface of the thing's surroundings. Aristotle denies that there is a three-dimensional space which a thing occupies.
[85] Reading *hupomenein* with MS M.
[86] There is evidently a lacuna in the text here, as Busse notes.

5a25. *Or [see] which of its parts adjoin one another. Nor can the parts of time ...*

For the whole of time does not exist simultaneously, but only at a moment, and it has its existence only in coming into being and passing away. How could that which does not last take a position?

5a28. *Rather, [you might say they have] a certain order.*

He means a natural order. The present comes before the future, not the future before the present. There is a natural order, as in this case, whenever <the order> cannot be reversed. But an order is *with respect to us* whenever it can be reversed without making a difference. For example, we say 'This is the first of them', beginning first with the one on the right; but, on the other hand, we might have begun, if we had wanted to, with the one on the left.

5a30. *And it is the same with number.*

Number is twofold: on the one hand, it is in the soul that does the counting, and on the other, in the things counted (just as, too, a pint is twofold, the pint as measure, for example, the copper pint, and the pint as measured, for example, a pint of wine or honey). Since, then, number is twofold, as Aristotle says[87] – that in the soul and that in the perceptible thing – it is clear that number in the soul would not be composed of parts with position (for its parts do not have any position; rather it is intelligible, in the soul alone). But number in the things counted, for example, in ten human beings or horses, is composed of parts that have position. For its parts are arranged somewhere and they have some position with respect to each other. This is why he says 'You would not *exactly* (*ou panu*) find position', and does not say, 'You would find none at all'.

5a33. *And it is the same with a statement.*

[87] *Phys.* 4.11 (219b5-9).

That is, a statement is also made up of things not having position. For it is in being said that a statement has existence, and none of its parts endure to have any position.

5b1. For example, [there is said to be] a large amount of white.

The scientist's task is not only to investigate things he himself proposes, but also to go through in detail and refute those that seem to be so but in truth are not. Now white may seem to be a quantity. For we speak of white as more and less, which is characteristic of quantity; but then we also call an action long. So Aristotle says that these are not quantities in the strict sense, but only *per accidens*. For since white is in a surface, and that can be more or less, we say that the white is more or less. It is the same with an action; for example, a war is called long *per accidens*. Thus, since a war goes on for a certain period of time – e.g. for ten years – and we say that its time is long, for this reason we say that the action, as well, is long, *per accidens*. A change, too, is called large if its time is large. For time is the measure of change. Thus, we call a revolution of the moon a month, of the sun a year, and of the entire heaven a day. So if someone were to ask how long an action is, the answer is its time, e.g. ten years. It is the same with a surface; one may say that the white is as large as the surface is. For if we are asked how much white there is, we say two cubits if that is how large the surface containing the white is. Therefore, we mean that the surface, not the white itself, is more or less. Indeed, the white in a one-cubit surface can be whiter than that in a two-cubit surface, and then we do not say that there is more white (*leukon pleon*) but that one white is whiter than another (*leukon leukou mallon*).

5b11. Moreover, there is no contrary of a quantity.

Having presented to us his division of quantity and having said which are quantities in the strict sense and which are called quantities *per accidens*, he now wishes to set out, as he did with substance, what is distinctive of quantity.

62,1 **5b14. But [could someone say that] many [is contrary] to few ...**

Here, Aristotle appropriately examines whether large and small are contraries. In his discussion of substance[88] he touches on it only lightly, conceding in his counter-objection[89] that they are contraries. Now there are definite quantities, and also indefinite ones. The definite ones are, e.g., two cubits and three cubits, and they are quantities in the strict sense; the indefinite ones are, e.g., large and small, many and few. Moreover, *large* and *small* apply to the continuous (for we call a body large or small, and it is the same with the rest of the continuous <quantities> that have position), whereas *many* (*polu*) and *few* (*oligon*) apply to that which is discrete and does not have a position. Thus, time is spoken of as more (*polus*) or less (*oligos*), and so is number. That is why, in illustrating *large* and *small* with examples, Aristotle chose *mountain* and *millet seed*. These are cases of the continuous, for each of them is a body.

5b16. For a thing is not said to be large or small just in itself.

Here Aristotle once again makes a concession. Even if large and small are contraries, they are not quantities, but relatives. For the large is called large in relation to the small, and the small is called small in relation to the large. And later he shows that they are not contraries, but rather that they make reference to one another.

5b18. For example, a mountain [is said to be] small.

If a thing were said to be large or small just in itself, a mountain would never be said to be small or a millet seed large. But we call a mountain small obviously comparing it to another mountain, or a millet seed large obviously because it is larger than another. Therefore, a thing is not said to be large or small just in itself, but in relation to something else.

---

[88] cf. 3b31.
[89] cf. Ammonius' gloss on 'counter-objection' at 53,3.

It is the same, Aristotle shows, with many and few, which do not belong to number, i.e. to the discrete; rather, they are relatives.

> 5b26. Further, two cubits or three cubits [and each thing of that sort signifies a quantity].

Aristotle constructs another dialectical proof that large and small do not belong to <the category of> quantity, but rather to that of relatives. Indeed, he says that quantity in the strict sense is also definite. For example, this line is both a quantity and definite in its own nature, being two cubits, let us say, or ten cubits. And the rest of the quantities are likewise determinate (*hôrismena*). But large and small, and many and few, are determinate neither with respect to us nor with respect to themselves; rather, they are indeterminate (*aorista*). Therefore, large and small and many and few do not belong to quantity.

> 5b30. Further, whether one reckons them [quantities or not, there is nothing contrary to them].

Having shown that they are relatives, not quantities, he now makes the concession, by way of counter-objection, that even if they should be quantities, large is still not contrary to small, nor is many to few.

> 5b30. There is nothing contrary to them.

What he means is this. Contraries must first exist in their own right and have real and independent being. Only so do they then meet in battle and declare war, that is, oppose each other. This is not possible for relatives, for they do not fight each other, but rather they bring each other in together. For relatives differ from contraries in that contraries exist first in their own right and thereafter join battle and fight, whereas relatives produce each other reciprocally. In this way, then, even if white didn't exist at all, black would remain, but if the father were taken away, the son would be gone. Since large and small <exist> not in their own right but with respect to something else, and similarly for many and few, and <since> neither large nor small exists independently in and of itself, it is clear that they are not contraries.

5b33. Besides, if large and small are [contraries].

Here is a different proof, through reduction to impossibility. Aristotle says that if we were to say that large and small are contraries, it will follow that the same thing is both large and small, that is, when compared with two different things. Therefore, it can receive contraries at the same time and will be contrary to itself, which is impossible. Therefore, large and small are not contraries.

6a1. Although a substance, for example, [is thought] able to receive contraries ...

Although a substance is able to receive contraries, it does not, however, admit contraries together at the same time and in the same part. For the same thing will never be cold and hot, or white and black, at the same time.

6a4. And it follows that these things are their own contraries.

Heightening the absurdity, Aristotle says that if large is contrary to small, it will follow that the same thing is able not only to receive contraries at the same time, but also to be opposed to itself, which is absurd. For no being is opposed to itself.

6a8. Therefore large is not [contrary to small].

Supposing first that these are contraries, Aristotle has shown that they are not quantities; then supposing that they are quantities he has shown that they are not contraries. But the truth is that they are neither quantities nor contraries, but among the relatives. But since, then, they are among the relatives, they must be in a different category, so as to take on the relation <appropriate to> relatives. And where would they be, if they are not included in the <category> of quantity and are not contraries?

6a11. But [it seems] most of all [with respect to place] that there is contrariety [of quantity].

If someone wants to contemplate contrariety in quantity, Aristotle says, he should consider *up* and *down*. For these are set at the greatest distance from one another, that is, they admit the <popular> definition of contraries. For this is how people define contraries: 'those things in the same genus that are at the greatest distance from one another' (6a17-18). But this is not acceptable to Aristotle; for there is no absolute *up* or *down*, but only *surrounding* and *centre*,[90] which are not contraries, but relatives. For surrounding is called the surrounding of something in the centre.

6a17. For those things [in the same genus] that are at the greatest distance from one another ...

Notice how nature, wanting to unite contraries, has put them under the same genus. The genus of the contraries white and black is colour, and that of hot and cold is quality. And they do battle in a single subject.

6a19. It seems that a quantity does not admit [of more and less].

He says that not having a contrary is a *proprium* (*idion*) of quantity, and he shows that it belongs to every <quantity>, but he does not mention that it does not belong to <quantity> alone. (Indeed, this <last point> should be clear from what has been said about substance.) Rather, he passed over to another *proprium* of quantity: not admitting more or less. And this is reasonable. For where there is contrariety there is more and less, but where there is not, more and less are not found. For more and less arise from a mixture of contraries. One must realize that Aristotle again rejects this, since it also

---

[90] Ammonius is assuming a spherical cosmos, with the earth at the centre, which is viewed as down, and the stars at the periphery, which is viewed as up.

fits substance, and passes over to another *proprium*, something which is indeed called a *proprium* in the strict sense.

6a26. Most characteristic (*idion*) of a quantity is [that it will be said to be] both equal [and unequal].

20 Aristotle does not mention that the *proprium* he has just given an account of is not <in the strict sense> a *proprium* of quantity; for that should be clear from what was said in the account of substance. But this one – to be called both equal and unequal – is in the strict sense a *proprium* of quantity. And if we predicate (*legomen*) both *equal* and *unequal* of something in connection with something else, <this is> not *per se*, but *per accidens*. For example, we say that this white 25 body is equal to that white body; but, in a similar way, also unequal, not in so far as it is white but in so far as it is a body. But a careful auditor might say: 'How is it that Aristotle has put body under substance and again under quantity, although we said in the introduction that no being is placed under two categories?'

We answer that he understands body in two different ways. 66,1 There is enmattered (*enulon*) body, for example, say, a stone or a log, and there is also body contemplated by thought, <for example,> a geometrical solid (*mathêmatikon*). So in the category of substance Aristotle understood enmattered body, but in quantity he understood body contemplated by thought.

On Relatives

5 Before going into Aristotle's teaching on relatives, these five things must be examined: (1) their location; (2) the explanation of the title; (3) their independent existence (*hupostasis*); (4) the manner of teaching; (5) their division into species.

(1) First, their location. For what reason have relatives been discussed before quality, given that (a) the latter[91] involves

---

[91] Reading *hautê haplê* for *haplê*, with Busse.

simple predication whereas the predication of relatives is compound, and (b) we understand simples more easily than complexes (*poluskhedôn*)? We reply that the reason why Aristotle moves directly to his study of relatives is that he mentioned them in his teaching on quantity and did not wish to leave the hearer ignorant about them for too long. This is just what he did after he mentioned quantity in his study of substance; immediately after substance he discussed quantity.

(2) Why did he use the title 'On relatives', and not 'On relative', in the singular? We answer that it is because a single thing cannot be a relative just by itself (*auto kath' hauto*); rather, relatives are always considered in pairs. For *right* is to the right of left – you would not say that something is just by itself *right*. And this is why he used the title 'On relatives', in the plural, but 'About substance', in the singular. For it is possible for a single thing, for example a man or[92] a log, to be a substance. It is the same, too, with quantity – it is possible to call *two-feet long* on its own (*monon*) a quantity.[93] But it is not the same with relatives.

(3) Concerning the independent existence of relatives, (a) some people have said that nothing is a relative by nature (*phusei*), but only by \<its\> position (*thesei*), for example, right and left and things like that. But what those people say is not right. For cases have been observed that are this way by nature; thus, the parts of the body are observed to stand in a certain relation to one another. For example, the liver is on the right and the spleen on the left, and it never comes about that the liver is on the left or the spleen on the right. (b) Some

---

[92] Reading *ê xulon* with MS M.

[93] The point is tricky, and Ammonius' grasp of it seems none too secure. The appropriate contrast between quantities and relatives would be this: whereas a thing cannot have *to the right* predicated of it except with reference (perhaps only implicit) to something that is to its left, the predicate *two-feet long* can be applied without such additional reference; a thing can be two-feet long on its own. In his gloss ('two-feet long can, by itself, be called a quantity'), Ammonius seems to miss this point. For *right* can also, by itself, be called a relative; so no contrast between relatives and quantity has been provided.

Pelletier tries to help Ammonius by translating: ' ... ce qui est long de deux coudées peut déjà, tout seul, être dit quantifié' ('what is two-feet long can already, all alone, be called quantified'). But what is at issue is whether *right* (or *two-feet long*) is a complete predicate, not whether it is a complete specification of a subject to which the predicate *relative* (or *quantity*) can be applied.

78   *Commentary*

say that everything is relative – Protagoras the Sophist is one of these. For he says that whatever anybody says is true. One
67,1 who says that honey is sweet is speaking truly (for it is sweet relative to some), and one who says it is bitter is also speaking truly. For it is bitter to those who have jaundice. But Plato refuted him by saying,[94] 'Protagoras, either you speak truly when you say that whatever anybody says is true, or you speak falsely. But if you speak falsely, it would be reasonable for us
5 not to believe you; and if you speak truly when you say that whatever anybody says is true, and we say, about you, that you are speaking falsely, then what we say is true. Therefore, once again you are speaking falsely, and not everything is relative.' Some have said, correctly, that some things are relative and others absolute (*auto kath' hauto*). *Right* and *left*, for example, are relatives; *body* and *man* are absolutes. For a man, just as a
10 man, is not a relative. And that bears on the independent existence of relatives.

(4) The manner of teaching Aristotle has employed is this. First he gives the definition the ancients proposed for relatives; then he shows that a number of absurd consequences follow from this definition. So he himself proposes a different *proprium* for them, one that belongs to all of them and only to
15 them. In order not to seem to be attacking the ancients, he presents first their definition as a *proprium* of relatives.

(5) The division of relatives is this. Some relatives involve homonymy, as *like* is like *like*; others involve heteronymy, as *right* is right of *left*. Of the latter, some relate superior and inferior, as *double* is double of *half*; some relate ruler and ruled,
20 as a master is master of a *slave*; some relate judger and judged, as what is perceived is perceived by perception; some relate participant and what is participated in, as a knower is said to be a knower by participation in knowledge; some relate cause and effect (*aitiaton*), as a *father* is a father of a *child*; some relate agent and patient, as a *striker* strikes what is *struck*;
25 some are related by a difference in place, as *left* is left of *right* and *right* is right of *left*.

6a36. Those things that are called relatives are …

[94] *Theaetetus* 170C.

On Relatives

He uses the term 'called' to indicate his dissatisfaction with the <proposed> definition. Indeed, he goes even further and shows that a number of absurd consequences follow from this definition; and so he proposes another definition.

6a36. ... those which are [said to be] just what they are ...

For example, it is not as a man that the man on the right is said to be to the right of another, but as the one on the right.

6a37. ... or in some other way [in relation to another].

Aristotle said, '[Relatives are those which are said to be just what they are] of other things'; so lest you assume that the relation is expressed only in the genitive, he says 'or in some other way [in relation to another]', i.e. in the dative or the accusative.

6b2. The following are also to be included among relatives.

Since the preceding <examples> are of quantity, and the next ones are of quality, Aristotle rightly treats them separately, saying 'The following are also to be included [among relatives]'. Alternatively, <he does so> because the former have their correlative in the genitive, while the latter have theirs in the dative or accusative.

6b2. [State], condition, perception, knowledge, and position.

Having set forth examples, Aristotle gives us a method for taking the converse (*anakampsis*) of relatives. Thus, the state is introduced <as being> what it is in relation to the genitive case (for it is said to be the state of its possessor) and, conversely, the possessor *in* the state is introduced <as being> the possessor that it is in relation to the dative case. Similarly a condition is a condition of the thing conditioned and the thing conditioned is a conditioned thing *in* the condition, and knowledge is knowledge *of* the known and the known is known *by* knowledge.

80 Commentary

20   **6b11. Lying, [standing, and sitting are positions.]**

And lying, standing, and sitting, Aristotle says, are positions. Since they are kinds of positions and position is one of the relatives, they are therefore relatives. Either the whole body is upright and is called standing, or the whole body is arranged horizontally and is called lying, or part of it is
25   upright and part is reclining and it is called sitting.

69,1   **6b12. To be lying, to be standing, and to be sitting, [however, are not positions].**

These, Aristotle says, are not positions, at least if position is a relative they are not positions. However, they are derived paronymously from the kinds of position mentioned: to be
5   standing from standing, to be lying from lying, to be sitting from sitting. And just as they are derived from the kinds of position, so, too, from their genus, i.e. *position* (*thesis*), is derived *being arranged* (*keisthai*), which is one of the categories. <Position> is, in fact, the genus of to be standing and to be reclining and to be lying and to be seated. So one
10   species of relatives, that is, position, has given rise to one of the categories, that of being arranged. And that is not surprising, since two species of quantity gave rise to two categories: place to the where (*pou*), and time to the when (*pote*). It is not that place is said <to be> somewhere (*pou*), but rather things in a place are. Similarly time itself is not <said to be> at a time (*pote*), but rather things that occur in time are.

One might raise a difficulty for the Philosopher about why
15   he subsumes position and standing under relatives when he ought to have subsumed them under the category of being arranged. We reply that he does not always assign things to the same category when one is called paronymously after the other. You know we call a grammarian after grammar; but grammatical knowledge is subsumed under quality, and the grammarian under substance. And likewise in this case we
20   subsume the activity under relatives, but the thing that is arranged under the category of being arranged.

6b15. There is also contrariety [among relatives].

Another concomitant of relatives, Aristotle says, is that they admit contrariety. And that is reasonable. For since relatives seem to be offshoots (*paraphuasin*) and not distinct things, but rather are found in other categories, they imitate the things they are attached to. For example, since nothing is the contrary of a substance or a quantity, it follows that no contrary is found in the relatives that concern them – for example, in *triple*. Triple is a relative (for it is called the triple of something) and nevertheless it has no contrary, since it is combined with a category that does not contain (*ekhousêi*) this <sc. any contrary>. It is also the same <with a relative that is attached> to a substance – with master, son, right, left. For there isn't anything contrary to these, since the things they are combined with are subsumed under a category that does not contain any contrary. However, since quality admits contrariety, relatives of quality do likewise. For example, vice (*kakia*) is contrary to virtue (*aretê*) and ignorance to knowledge. One must realize, however, that although these are contraries of one another, they do not answer (*apokrinetai*) <to this> *as relatives*. For example, virtue <is the virtue of a good person> and a good person <is good by virtue>;[95] likewise, too, vice is vice of a vicious person and a vicious person is vicious through vice. But the contrary of virtue is vice, and that of a good person is a vicious person. It is reasonable, then, to find contrariety in relatives, and <to find> that it is not a concomitant of every relative.[96]

6b16. Each of which is a relative.

One must realize that those who say that Plato defines relatives in this way and thinks that the real being (*hupostasis*) of relatives is in their being spoken of, defame the philosopher. For one can tell from what is said in the *Gorgias*[97] that he characterizes them as *being* (*einai*). For he

---

[95] Suppletions added following Philoponus.
[96] Ammonius' point here emerges more clearly in his examples than in his general characterization. It is that although a relative may have a contrary, what it is a relative *of* will not be the same as what it is the contrary *of*.
[97] 476B.

says, 'If there is an agent, it is necessary for there to be a patient also'. He says 'to be' and not 'to be spoken of'.

6b19. [Relatives] seem [to admit of] more and [less].

Another concomitant of relatives, he says, is admitting more and less. And this one is like the preceding <concomitant>, for it belongs to relatives, but not to all of them. For it was said that where contrariety is manifested, there is more and less; and, on the contrary, where there is no contrariety there is no more or less. So if there is contrariety in relatives, there is also more and less in them. However, it is not a concomitant of all of them, since contrariety is not found in them all.

6b28. Every relative [is spoken of in relation to its converse].

This is another concomitant <of relatives>. To understand what it is to be 'spoken of in relation to its converse', let us first understand what *conversion* (*antistrophê*) is. *Strophê* is a return (*apokatastasis*) to the same point one started from. This is why we say that the universe (*to pan*) revolves (*strephesthai*), since it moves in a circle and returns to the same point it started from.

Conversion is really 'equiversion' (*isostrophê*);[98] in fact, among the ancients, *anti* means 'equal' (*ison*). For example, *antitheon* means 'godlike' (*isotheon*), *antianeira* ('a match for men') <means> a woman who has strength equal to a man's, and we call our largest digit the thumb (*antikheiron*)[99] because it has strength equal to that of the other four digits in the hand.[100]

Therefore, relatives are spoken of in relation to their converses (*antistrephonta*). For example, a slave is the slave of a master, and a master is the master of a slave. One begins

---

[98] LSJ cite only Ammonius and Philoponus in their entry on this uncommon term. Their translation, 'correspondence', conceals the etymological connection to conversion, which we have tried to bring out in our neologism 'equiversion'.

[99] Although *anti* sometimes means *equal*, as Ammonius says, the whimsical etymology he proposes for *antikheiron* is scarcely credible. The thumb is, as its Greek name suggests, the *opposable* digit.

[100] There is evidently a lacuna at this point.

with the slave and returns to him once again. And not only is *slave* convertible, but so is *master*.

6b36. Sometimes, if [... what <something> is spoken of in relation to is] not properly [specified], it will not seem to be convertible.

Aristotle means that relatives ought to observe an equality with respect to one another, and so be convertible, as, for example, *human* and *capable of laughter* are convertible. When, however, they are unequal, the greater follows from the lesser as *animal* <follows> from *human*, but the lesser does not follow from the greater; for *human* certainly does not follow from *animal*. So let this be the rule with relatives: there is equality, such as <father and> father of a child, <or double and> double of a half, in precisely those <cases> that are convertible. But when they are unequal, they are no longer <convertible>. Thus, it would be a mistake to call <a bird> a *bird of a wing* on the grounds that there is <such a thing as> a *wing of a bird*. For we would not call a bird a bird by virtue of <its having> wings, since not every wing is the wing of a bird – there are winged creatures that are not birds. For among winged creatures, some are feathered, and these alone are commonly called birds (as he himself said in the *Historia Animalium*,[101] 'Creatures with feathered wings are called birds'); others, such as bats, have membranous wings; still others are sheath-winged, such as beetles, and these are not birds. Therefore, since *wing* and *bird* are not coextensive, but *wing* <applies> to more <things> than *bird* does, if we were to increase the lesser <term>, i.e. *bird*, by saying *winged creature (pterôton)*, we would produce <the statement that> *a wing is the wing of a winged creature*, and this is convertible. For we do say that a winged creature is winged by <virtue of its> wings. So in this example, it was *bird*, which is smaller than *wing*, that we increased; but in the next example, it is the greater <term whose extension will be decreased>. If we were to say that a rudder is the rudder of a boat, it would not be convertible, for we would not call a boat the boat of a

---

[101] 490a12.

rudder. Indeed, many boats – such as rowboats – do not have rudders. So, since <the terms> are unequal, we have to equalize them. Now unequals can be equalized either by decreasing the greater or by increasing the lesser. Now if *boat*
5 has the greater <extension> and rudder the lesser, we would make them equal if we were to decrease the greater by saying 'ruddered';[102] made equal in this way, they would be convertible. Let us therefore say that a rudder is the rudder of a ruddered, and conversely that a ruddered is ruddered with a rudder. Thus in the first example, *bird* was smaller in extension than *wing*, and we increased it, while in the second,
10 *boat* was larger in extension than *rudder*, and we decreased it.[103]

[102] As Ammonius indicates below (72,13), Aristotle coined the term *pedaliôton* for the converse of *rudder* (i.e. for the thing a rudder is the rudder *of*). We have translated it as 'ruddered' to help convey the neologism. Aristotle contrasts this case with that of *wing*, for whose converse a substantive term (*pterôton*) did exist in ordinary Greek. Unfortunately, the contrast is less clear in English, since 'winged' as a substantive sounds as odd, perhaps, as does 'ruddered'.

[103] Ammonius' account of the proper specification of the *converse* of a relative is less clear than one would like. The converse of a relative is what the relative is (properly) said to be related to. Thus, the converse of *master* is *slave*, and the converse of *parent* is *child*. Another ingredient in Ammonius' discussion is what we will call the *product* of a relative and its converse. Examples are such terms as 'master of a slave' and 'parent of a child'. As we will see, Ammonius is not always sufficiently attentive to the distinction between converse and product.

According to Ammonius, if *F* is a relative, its converse is properly specified as *G* if, and only if, these two conditions obtain:
 (i) every *F* is *F* of a *G* (i.e. of some *G* or other), and
 (ii) every *G* is *G* of an *F* (again, of some *F* or other).
Thus a wing is not properly specified as *wing of a bird* because the first condition is violated. That is, some wings (those, as Ammonius mentions, of bats and beetles, for example) are not wings of birds. A wing is properly specified as *wing of a winged <thing>*, however, since every wing is a wing of a winged thing (and every winged thing is winged thing of a wing).

By contrast, a rudder is not specified properly as *rudder of a boat* because, even though the first condition is satisfied (every rudder, we are to suppose, is a rudder of some boat), the second condition is not. That is, some boats, for example rowboats, are not boats of rudders, that is, not ruddered boats.

When either of conditions (i) or (ii) obtains, the subject and predicate terms (e.g. 'master' and 'master of a slave') will, of course, be *coextensive*. (Terms are coextensive if they apply to precisely the same things.) The two conditions are therefore equivalent to the following:
 (i*) '*F*' is coextensive with '*F* of a *G*'
 (ii*) '*G*' is coextensive with '*G* of an *F*'.
Ammonius frames much of the remainder of his discussion of relatives and their converses in terms of the notion of equality (*isotês*) or being coextensive (*exisazein*). At 71,16 he gives this rule (*kanôn*) relating convertibility and equality: 'There is equality, such as <father and> father of a child, <or double and> double of a half, in just those <cases> that are convertible.'

But Ammonius is often careless (if not actually confused) when he chooses

7a5. Sometimes [it may be necessary] to make up a name.

We have to invent a name, he says, when there is not an established name for what convertibility requires. For example, he made up the term for 'ruddered'. Again, a head is a relative (for it is the head of something),[104] but if it were specified in relation to *animal* and we were to say 'head of an animal', it would not be convertible. For we would not call an animal an animal by virtue of <its> head. Indeed, some animals, such as the crab, do not have a head. Therefore it is necessary to invent a name and to innovate a usage in order to produce the conversion properly. Thus, it would be specifying properly if we were to say 'a head is the head of a "headed" (*kephalôton*)'. For we are able to convert this by saying that a 'headed' is 'headed' by virtue of <its> head. And in general, when we want to make up a name, we will make the name of the converse a paronym derived from the original <term>, e.g. 'ruddered' from 'rudder' and 'headed' from 'head'. And it is the same with the others. And so every relative is spoken of in relation to its converse.

7a19. If [one were to derive] from the original [relatives the names of their converses].

He gives us a rule we can use to make up a name properly in case no name should be found in common parlance.

---

candidates for the coextensiveness requirement. For example, at 71,24 he points out that 'wing' and its putative converse 'bird' are not coextensive. This is true, but irrelevant. What he ought to have said is that 'wing' is not coextensive with 'wing of a bird'. (Ammonius' confusion was perhaps abetted by the fact that the Greek word for wing, *pteron*, can also mean 'flying creature'. But in Aristotle's ontology, a flying creature is not a relative but a kind of substance; it is clearly *pteron* in the sense of 'wing' that denotes a relative.) Again, at 72,5 he claims that the reason *boat* is not the converse of *rudder* is that 'boat' has a greater extension than 'rudder'. But what he ought to have said is that 'boat' has a greater extension than 'boat with a rudder'.

In these passages, Ammonius makes it appear, misleadingly, as if he requires that a relative term be coextensive with its converse. But, of course, this is not what he requires. ('Master' and 'slave' are converses of one another, but they are obviously not coextensive.) Rather, what is required is that a relative term be coextensive with the product of itself and its converse.

[104] Reading *hê kephalê tôn pros ti· tinos gar kephalê. ean oun apodothê* with MS M.

86 Commentary

73,1 **7a22. Thus every relative [provided that it is specified properly, is spoken of in relation to its converse].**

Every relative that has been specified properly is convertible. But if <relatives> are not specified properly, their acknowledged converses can no longer be converted. For example, we specify properly when we say, 'A slave is the
5 slave of a master', and this is convertible: 'A master is the master of a slave.' But if the slave were not specified properly, that is to say, <as> of a master, but instead <as> of a man, it would no longer be convertible. For it is not possible to say, 'A man is the man of a slave'. Therefore, if it were not specified properly, it would no longer be convertible. For conversion obtains in all and only <cases of> proper specification.

10 **7a31. Moreover, if [what a thing is said to be related to] is properly specified, [then, if everything accidental is taken away and all that is left is that which it is properly specified in relation to, it will always be said to be related to that].**

If one specified relatives properly, Aristotle says, then when everything else has been stripped away and only that with reference to which they have been properly specified remains, the conversion and, in short, the relatives, will be preserved. For example, if the slave were specified as of a master, but being two-footed or capable of knowledge were taken away,
15 the slave would continue to be called a relative; whereas if the master were taken away he would no longer be called a slave.

7a32. ... if everything [accidental] is taken away ...

Moreover, it is not surprising that he says these[105] are accidents. For he does not mean accidents in an absolute sense (*haplôs*), but rather things which would be accidents

---

[105] A few lines below, Aristotle writes: 'if everything accidental to the master is taken away (such as his being a biped, capable of knowledge, human) and all that is left is that he is a master, the slave will always be said to be a slave in relation to that' (7a35-9). Ammonius is clearly, and rightly, puzzled when Aristotle calls such predicates as *human* and *biped* 'accidental to the master', for he knows that in Aristotle's view these are *essential* characteristics of the man, who only happens ('by accident') to be a master. His solution is to say that Aristotle does not mean that

with respect to the relation of *slave* and which would be predicated <of the master> secondarily, whereas by nature it is the master <who is predicated> primarily and with respect to himself.

7b15. It seems that relatives are simultaneous [by nature].

Another concomitant of relatives, he says, is that they are simultaneous by nature and it is never possible for one to exist when the other does not. For in saying slave it is necessary at the same time to think of the master, and if there is a double there must also be a half and *vice versa*. But it is evident that he says 'for the most part' because he is going to raise a puzzle about some other cases.

7b19. They are also destroyed together.

Not only do they exist simultaneously by nature, but they are also destroyed together. Thus if there were to be no slave, there would be no master, and without there being a master there is no slave. It is the same in other cases as well.

7b23. For what is known would seem to be prior to knowledge.

Aristotle then raises a puzzle, concerning what he has just

---

being human is in any absolute sense (*haplôs*) an accidental characteristic, but that it is accidental with respect to someone specified as a *master*, and is a *secondary* predicate of the master so specified. Presumably he thinks that being human is an essential characteristic of those things of which it is a *primary* predicate. Thus, the fact that being human is an accidental characteristic of a master (so specified) can be handled as a special case, in which it is considered in relation to a subject of which it is a secondary predicate. 'By nature', Ammonius concludes, it is *master* that is predicated 'primarily' of the master so specified.

Ammonius has, in effect, raised (but failed to grasp firmly) an issue of great philosophical importance. For if *human*, like *master*, can be essential to something under one description but accidental to it under another description, the entire distinction between essential and accidental predicates is threatened with relativization. Whether a predicate is essential or accidental, it might be argued, will always depend on the way its subject is specified, and there will thus be no such thing as what is essential or primary 'by nature' in any absolute sense. (Ammonius' confidence that Aristotle's doctrine of essences is not threatened by the concession in the text seems excessive.)

said, as to whether relatives are simultaneous by nature even though what is known is evidently prior to knowledge. So *prior* <must be taken> in two ways, on the one hand <prior> in time, and on the other <prior> by nature. The prior in time is that from whose past the distance to the present is greater. Thus we say the war with the Medes is prior to the Peloponnesian war since its distance from the present is greater than that of the Peloponnesian. With the future, on the contrary, it is the prior whose distance from the present is smaller. Thus tomorrow is prior to the day after tomorrow. And that is how it is with priority in time. The prior by nature is the one <whose destruction> destroys[106] (*sunanairoun*) <the other> along with it but which is not destroyed along with <the other>, that is, the one which is entailed[107] (*suneispheromenon*) <by the other> but does not entail it, as is the case with *animal* and *human*. What is known would seem to be prior to knowledge, for if there is nothing to be known there is no knowledge, but there can be something to be known even though there is no knowledge. Similarly, if there is nothing to be perceived there is no perception, but nothing prevents there being things to be perceived, such as fire, earth, and the like, even though there is no perception.

7b24. Since for the most part it is of already existing [matters of fact that we gain knowledge].

Aristotle explains <why he says> 'for the most part' by adding 'in few cases, or none at all, could one find knowledge coming into being at the same time as what is known'. He adds this to take account of discoveries by some art or through reflection. Suppose, for example, someone invents written characters other than the common ones. In that case what is known does not already exist, but as soon as it is produced through reflection, there is knowledge <of it>.

---

[106] cf. also *Top.* 141b28 and *Metaph.* 1059b30 for definitions of natural priority in terms of the notion of destruction. The idea, to use Ammonius' example, is that the destruction of the genus *animal* (that is to say, the annihilation of all animals) would involve the destruction of the human species, whereas the species could be destroyed without destroying the genus. Hence, it is the superordinate (more generic) of two entities in the same category that is prior by nature.

[107] cf. n. 64.

7b27. Moreover, although when what is known has been destroyed, [knowledge is destroyed along with it ...]

Having set out the temporal priority of what is known and having said that 'for the most part it is of already existing matters of fact that we gain knowledge', Aristotle now returns to explain the priority in nature of what is known in terms of *destroying* and *not being destroyed*.

7b31. For example, squaring the circle ...

Having erected a square equal to a given rectilinear figure, geometers also sought, if possible, to find a square equal to a given circle. Many geometers – including the greatest ones – looked for it, but they did not find it. Only the divine Archimedes discovered anything at all close, but so far the exact solution has not been discovered. Indeed, it may be impossible. And this is, in fact, why Aristotle says, 'if indeed it is something to be known'. [It is perhaps because he produced a straight line not dissimilar to the circumference <that he was in doubt> whether it is or is not something to be known.] He therefore says that if indeed the squaring of the circle is something to be known although the knowledge of it does not yet exist, it follows from this that what is known is prior to knowledge.

7b33. Moreover with the destruction of animal [there will be no knowledge, although there may be many things to be known].

After first having shown that this concomitant[108] is defective in one example of relatives, he then shows this universally in every case.[109] If *animal* is destroyed, the sciences (*hai*

---

[108] The concomitant feature in question is *simultaneity*. Ammonius' point is that Aristotle first illustrates the non-simultaneity of knowledge and what is known in the putative case of knowing how to square the circle, and then goes on to argue for the non-simultaneity of knowledge and its objects in general.

[109] 'Universally in every case': Ammonius cannot mean *for every pair of relatives*, for most relatives are still simultaneous in Aristotle's sense. Rather, he must mean *for every case of knowledge and what is known*. Even this last claim is problematic, however, since one can know things about one's own states of knowledge. Thus, if I know that I know that *p*, the object of this second-order knowledge (viz. that I know

90   *Commentary*

epistêmai) are destroyed, too, for the soul is the subject that the sciences are in; but the things that are known by the sciences are not destroyed. For they exist in themselves, not as things
25   that are known, but rather as actual things (*pragmata*).

     7b35. It is similar [with perception].

     After working out his argument for the case of knowledge,
76,1 Aristotle next turns to that of perception and shows that what can be perceived[110] – such as a hot, sweet, <or> bitter body – is prior to perception. For even if there were no animal, a body could still be, e.g., bitter or sweet or black or white. And it is precisely these that can be perceived.

     8a6. Further, perception comes into existence at the same time as what is capable of perceiving.

5   Indeed, one cannot conceive of perception without body – a body that is capable of perceiving[111] comes into existence simultaneously with perception – but the converse does not hold. For what can be perceived – such as fire, earth, water, and the like – can exist even though there is no perception.

     8a11. Therefore, [what can be perceived] would seem to be prior to perception.

---

that *p*) does not 'exist in itself'; it will be destroyed if I and all my knowledge are destroyed. One might try to argue on Ammonius' behalf (and contrary to much traditional epistemology) that the object of this second-order knowledge, while not independent of all my knowledge, is still independent of my particular knowledge of *it*. But this will not help Ammonius, who, like Aristotle, states the independence condition in terms of all knowledge, or at least, all of a particular person's knowledge.

[110] Aristotle's word *aisthêton* covers both (what we might call) actual objects of perception (things we perceive) and potential objects of perception (things that are capable of being perceived).

[111] Reading *aisthêtikon* for *aisthêton*. The *aisthêtikon* is what is capable of perceiving, i.e. the perceiver; the *aisthêton* is the object (capable of being) perceived, i.e. the perceptible. Aristotle holds that the perceiver is 'simultaneous' with perception, in the sense that neither can exist independently of the other: there cannot be perception unless there is a perceiver, nor can there be a perceiver unless there is perception. But he adopts a firmly realist stance about the objects of perception, which are capable of existing even though there is no perception of them.

The perceptible, therefore, is *not* simultaneous with perception, and Ammonius is mistaken if (as the MSS have it) he claims otherwise. For his point about simultaneity to be correct, he would have to be taken (as our emendation proposes) to be talking about the body that is capable of perceiving, i.e. the perceiver.

One must realize that Aristotle has not provided the solution to the aforementioned puzzles. For that, one must note that relatives can be thought of in two ways: either as independent things (*pragmata*) in themselves, or as bound in a relation. Take the example of father and child. Now if we think of the father as Sophroniscus and the child as Socrates, Sophroniscus has got to be prior to Socrates. For the father as a cause is prior to what is caused. This is the way it will be if we think of each of them as <independent> things, for Sophroniscus will be prior to Socrates. But if <we think of them> as father and child bound in a relation, they will be simultaneous.

Now knowledge and what can be known[112] are also like this. If we conceive of what can be known as a thing, e.g. the stars, what can be known conceived of as a thing will be prior, for the stars are prior to knowledge about them. But if we conceive of them as relatives, what is known will be simultaneous with knowledge. For there would be nothing known if there were not knowledge about it. For I say[113] that what is known and the knowledge about it are simultaneous. But if someone should say that what is known exists potentially even before the knowledge about it, I say that the knowledge about it will also exist potentially at that time. And for relatives universally, as it is with one <member of the pair>, so too will it be with the other. For if one of them actually exists, so will the other, and if one <exists> potentially, so too will the other exist potentially. For example, when what is known actually exists, of necessity the knowledge about it will also actually exist; and when what is known exists potentially, the knowledge will also exist potentially. But when we think of what is known <as existing> before the knowledge, or of what is perceived before the perception, we are thinking of it not as what is known or as what is perceived but as a thing by itself.

---

[112] Aristotle's word *epistêton* covers both what is actually known and what is capable of being known.

[113] The MSS have 'he says' rather than 'I say'. But it is unclear who 'he' can be, for Aristotle denies that knowledge and what is known are simultaneous. Since the view expressed here seems to be that of Ammonius, we have read 'I say' in place of 'he says'.

Commentary

8a13. There is a difficulty about whether no [substance is said to be a relative].

Aristotle has completed <his examination of> the definition of the ancients and its characteristic concomitants. Since he now wants to introduce his own definition, he first establishes some absurd consequences of their definition. Thus, it is absurd for the parts of secondary substances to be found to be relatives, i.e. for substances to be accidents. Now a division like this is traditional: substance is either universal or particular, and either whole or part. That plainly yields four pairs: (1) universal part, e.g. *head* <or> *hand*; (2) particular whole, e.g. Socrates and the like; (3) universal whole, e.g. man; (4) particular part, such as this hand or this head. Three of these are not relatives, but one – universal part, such as head <or> hand – would seem <according to the definition of the ancients> to be a relative. For it is called head of someone <or something and> hand of someone <or something>. Therefore, Aristotle says that according to the definition of relatives given previously[114] it will be impossible or <at any rate> difficult to arrive at the solution (*lusai*) <that no substance is a relative>.

8a17. For the individual man is not called this man of someone <or something>.

When a man or an ox is said to be of someone, it is not in respect of <being a> man or in respect of <being an> ox, but as property.

8a28. Thus if the [definition] of relatives [given earlier] is satisfactory ...

He says that according to the definition of relatives that was given earlier, it will be impossible or at any rate very difficult to solve the problem. He says 'very difficult' because of the

---

[114] At 6a36.

On Relatives

possibility of there being some defence[115] (*apologia*). He stated the <earlier> definition <of relatives> as 'those things which are said to be just what they are of other things' (6a36). Thus a head is a relative not in respect of <being a> head, but in respect of <being a> part. For a part is called part of a whole.

8a31. But rather relatives are [those things for which *to be is the same as to stand in a certain relation to something*].

What the Philosopher means is this: that relatives are things whose being and essence is nothing other than their relation to another. For even the fact that they are spoken of <as> themselves only with reference to another does not mean that they are relatives; rather, it is the fact that they themselves also have a relation to the things with reference to which they are spoken of. If something is a relative, not only is it spoken of with reference to another thing, but it stands in a relation to that thing. But things that are not relatives may still be spoken of with reference to another, although they do not stand in a relation to it. Now if <the definition of> a relative is like this, the parts of secondary substances will no longer be relatives. For a head is spoken of with reference to various other things, just as every part is (for every part is a part of another thing) but its being in itself a head does not derive from the relation it has to that of which it is the head. Thus, it is possible to give an account of a head as a head just by itself. For a head is a substance and a particular subject. But no relative is a relative by itself. Thus, *similar* and *equal* are acknowledged to be relatives, but neither signifies a thing (*pragma ti*) that has a proprietary application.[116] Rather, the

---

[115] Ammonius presumably has in mind the possibility of defending the earlier definition against Aristotle's objection that it implies that some substances are also relatives.

[116] In discussing semantic matters, Ammonius (like Aristotle before him and ancient Greek philosophers generally) frequently fails to make clear whether he means to be talking about *words* or *things*. The present passage is especially garbled. He says that *equal* is a relative (i.e. a thing, not a word) but also that it signifies (which is what linguistic expressions do). Further, the thing it signifies has an application (*epibolê*), which is a relation that words have to the things they apply to.

It is plausible therefore to suppose that Ammonius twice makes an unnoted

94   *Commentary*

being of each of them <consists> in a relation <to something>.

Aristotle then sets out the proper definition of relatives. In
15 fact, the first definition is really only a concomitant <of relatives>; for if something is a relative, it will also be said <to be what it is of another thing>, but it is not the case that if something is said <to be what it is of another thing> it is also a relative, for the reasons stated above.

8a35. From these considerations it is clear that [if one knows definitely that something is a relative ...]

Having set out the proper definition, he draws a corollary that follows from what has already been said. A corollary is a useful result that becomes evident along with the proof of
20 something else. For example, if one claimed and proposed to show that the soul is immortal, one might reason that if it were not truly immortal but dispersed after its withdrawal from the body, good persons would not differ from bad. But in truth we all know that there is a divine providence that assigns compensation to each soul for its deeds. Because of
25 this, some of those who have conducted their lives well hasten to acquire virtues and thereby make their souls more at home with providence. (For none of us is so foolish in our thinking as to ignore this completely.) If, then, one were to consider the consequences for the soul and show that it is brought to trial, surely in the proof of this it would also become evident that providence exists.

Accordingly, Aristotle says that if one knows one of the
30 relatives definitely, one will also know the other definitely, and if <one knows one> indeterminately, then similarly one will know the other indeterminately, and if <one of them>

'semantic ascent' (i.e. a shift from talking about a thing to talking about its name). Making this ascent explicit, we can reformulate his claim as follows:

> *equal* is a relative *whose name* signifies something *whose name* does not have a proprietary application.

A bit of reflection on this formulation should reveal that the expression 'signifies something whose name' is redundant. Deleting it, we obtain:

> *equal* is a relative *whose name* does not have a proprietary application.

Clumsy verbiage thus swept aside, the point seems simple enough: the term 'equal' does not apply to anything in a proprietary way, i.e. to that thing alone, without comparison to anything else.

absolutely, then <one will know the other> absolutely, and in general, as one knows one of them, <so> also will one know the other. Thus if one does not know at all what a thing is related to in a certain way, one will not even know whether it is related to anything in that way. For if someone knows that Sophroniscus is a father, one surely knows Socrates as well; but if one does not know this,[117] one will not know whether Sophroniscus is a father.

8b7. Similarly, if one knows of this such-and-such [that it is more beautiful ...]

If one knows that a certain magnitude is a double, one will also know, he says, what it is the double of. If not, one will not know it is a double. And if one knows that something is more beautiful, one will also have to know what it is more beautiful than. If one doesn't, but only knows that it is more beautiful than the less beautiful, one will often make the mistake of calling the worst matter of all more beautiful.[118]

8b10. That sort of thing is conjecture, not knowledge.

Whereas conjecture is a vague and unreliable awareness, knowledge is an infallible awareness.

8b13. [It may turn out that] nothing is inferior to it.

It is not unlikely that what by chance we call more beautiful is the worst of all, as with the matter <discussed above>.

8b15. But now [it is possible to know definitely] of a head and a hand ...

---

[117] By 'this' (*touto*) Ammonius must mean the fact that Sophroniscus is the father of Socrates. So, too, in the previous sentence 'one surely knows Socrates' must be taken as elliptical for 'one surely knows that Sophroniscus is the father of Socrates'.

[118] Ammonius' argument seems to be this: suppose you are talking about something that is (unbeknown to you) the foulest thing in the world. There is nothing it is more beautiful than, and hence there is nothing you can know it to be more beautiful than. But you can still know that it is more beautiful than anything that is less beautiful than it is. Hence you might infer (wrongly) that there is something (viz. 'the less beautiful') that it is more beautiful than. Aristotle's requirement of 'knowing the correlative' rules out the possibility of making this mistake.

From these considerations he then shows that a head and a foot and a hand are not relatives. Assume that Socrates has all the rest of his body covered, only a hand being exposed. In that case I know definitely that it is a hand even though I do not know whose it is. Now with <a pair of> relatives, someone who knows one of them definitely will also know the other definitely. But although I know the hand definitely, I do not know definitely whose hand it is. It is clear then that a hand is not a relative. Similarly, the same reasoning applies also to the other parts.

8b21. It is perhaps difficult [to give a strong opinion] on such matters.

Aristotle speaks in a very philosophical way. For, especially in connection with investigations requiring much research, he wants us to give an opinion neither at random nor by happenstance [80,1], but after much testing and examination. Since he teaches[119] that raising a puzzle is the route to the resolution of puzzlement, Aristotle says that raising a puzzle in each of these cases is not useless. For not raising a puzzle indicates <one of> two things: either, that one has an awareness of everything, like providence (for whom nothing is a puzzle), or that one is totally deprived of awareness; for what one is not aware of does not puzzle <one>. But since we are in the middle between those above us and those beneath us, we know in a kind of middle fashion <by> systematically inquiring into the puzzle. For just as firesticks rubbed against each other send forth fire, so also do puzzled souls through their inquiry send forth the light of truth. Therefore, since Aristotle earlier thought that the definition of relatives as things said of other things runs the risk of making some substances into relatives, he now says that perhaps we should not assert so confidently that things said of other things are not relatives. For people often defend <the first definition> against the puzzle we mentioned.

---

[119] Reading *mathêsetai* with MS F.

On Qualified and Quality

In the case of quality we have used the same manner of teaching as we did with relatives. Thus here, too, we must preface that teaching with an examination of (1) the location of the category, (2) its definition, (3) the title, *On Qualified and Quality*, and, in addition to those, (4) the subdivisions of the category.

The location of the category should already be clear to us from what was said in the case of relatives. Concerning its definition, we want to know why in giving the definition of quality he says[120] *that by virtue of which those sharing in it are said to be qualified*,[121] thereby taking just what was in question as obvious and agreed upon. Our reply will be that this definition leads us to our conception of *quality* in terms of the *qualified*. For the qualified, inasmuch as it is grasped in perception, is more obvious, and in general we proceed from that to our conception of a quality. Thus, from looking at the white in milk and the white in snow and the white in carbonate of lead we arrive at our conception of whiteness; likewise, from tasting honey and dates and figs we arrive at our conception of sweetness. Therefore Aristotle bases his explanation on the qualified thing that has received the aforementioned qualities – I mean whiteness and sweetness – since it is more obvious. But the qualified itself is what partakes of the quality, and the quality is what is partaken of. So that is why he also put the qualified first in the title,[122]

---

[120] Ammonius slightly amplifies the text of the *Categories*. What Aristotle says (8b25) is this: 'that by virtue of which people are said to be qualified.'

[121] Aristotle's term *poion* (cf. Latin *quale*) means, literally, 'of what sort'. The translation 'qualified' is meant to bring out the connection Aristotle sees between being *of a sort* (*poion*) and having a *quality* (*poiotês*, cf. Latin *qualitas*). The latter term – an abstract noun derived from the interrogative adjective *poion* – was, as Ammonius points out (81,25), a coinage of Plato's that Aristotle borrowed. *Poiotês* means, literally, 'of-what-sort-ness'; small wonder it sounded odd to Plato's listeners. Curiously, the abstract noun ('quality') survives in English, but the interrogative adjective does not.

[122] The text of the *Categories* that has come down to us contains no such title. Pelletier wonders whether we should take 'he' to refer here to Ammonius, rather than to Aristotle (the sentence presumably having been added by a disciple of Ammonius). This seems implausible, in view of the reference to the title at 80,18. We wonder, instead, whether Ammonius was working with a text that had already been amplified with section sub-headings.

98   *Commentary*

since this is what the quality is observed in.

In addition to these things, we must also discuss the subdivisions of the category. Bear in mind that Aristotle
5 provides us with four species of quality: (1) state (*hexis*) and condition (*diathesis*); (2) capacity (*dunamis*) and incapacity (*adunamia*); (3) affective quality (*pathetikê poiotês*) and affection[123] (*pathos*); (4) figure (*skhêma*) and shape (*morphê*).

A state is, for example, what we say a geometer has with regard to the theorems of geometry; a condition is, for example, what we say a person with some mistaken notions
10 has of the theorems of geometry. This is the first species of quality. The second is capacity and incapacity, which is a fitness or unfitness for natural things. We call capacity *fitness* and incapacity *unfitness*.[124] The third species is affective quality and affection. An affective quality is one such as the coldness in snow or the heat in fire. This <kind of quality>,
15 however, is twofold; <a quality is affective> either because it produces an affection or because it is generated by an affection. The coldness of snow and the heat of fire are called affective qualities not because they are generated by an affection but because they produce an affection. For it is not that some change occurs in the subject so that fire and snow may receive those qualities, but rather they instill affections –
20 <the sensations of> heat and cold – in other things.[125] But the heat in a heated piece of iron is called an affective quality because it is generated by an affection. We also call it an affection when someone who is at first pale turns red with shame – we say that this redness is an affection. The fourth species <of quality> is figure and shape. One should note

---

[123] 'Affection' (our translation of *pathos*) is used in the philosophical sense of a kind of accidental and alterable quality, and not in the more common sense of an emotional state of love or good will.

[124] The point of this curious remark is presumably that 'fitness' (*epitêdeiotês*) is the common expression that corresponds to Aristotle's technical term 'capacity' (*dunamis*).

[125] Ammonius is not as careful here as he should be. He gives heat (*thermotês*) and cold (*psukhrotês*) as examples of both affective qualities and affections. But it is more properly the *sensations* of heat and cold that are affections. When the fire warms your skin it produces in you the *pathos* of (perceived) heat; when it warms your coffee, it produces in the coffee no *pathos*, but only the affective quality of heat. Aristotle puts the point more clearly (9b3-7): 'heat and cold are said to be affective qualities not because the things which have taken them on are somehow affected, but because each of the qualities mentioned produces an affection of the senses ... .'

that 'figure' is applied to inanimate objects, and 'shape' to animate. One should note, too, that Plato used the word 'quality' in the dialogue *Theaetetus*, and he was the original inventor of the word. He says, 'You seem to me not to know what the word "quality" means, on account of its being used in a general way.'[126] But Aristotle extended the word 'quality', <applying it> not only to bodies but also to the soul. He said that knowledge and virtue are qualities in the soul.

It is possible to raise a difficulty for Aristotle and argue that he has not made the division suitably. For we apply 'state' not only to the soul but also to the body. Indeed, we say that health is a state of the body and so is consumptive fever. But under which of the four species of quality Aristotle mentions do we include these qualities? So that the division may be complete let us then say this: one kind of quality has to do with fitness and another has to do with actuality. The kind having to do with fitness makes up the second species, the one described by Aristotle as having to do with capacity and incapacity. The kind having to do with actuality is either perfective (*teleiôtikê*) or hurtful (*kakôtikê*) or neither perfective nor hurtful.[127] Of the perfective, one kind produces an affection of our senses and another kind does not produce an affection. The kind that does not produce an affection is either hard to lose (*dusapoblêtos*) or easy to lose (*euapoblêtos*). If it is hard to lose, it is a state, either of the soul or of the body; if it is easy to lose, it is a condition. A state of the soul is <e.g.> knowledge <or> virtue, while one of the body is like health.

Now if someone should say that health produces an affection, since we perceive it, our reply will be that we do not perceive health but rather the principal affective qualities of

---

[126] *Theaetetus* 182A.

[127] Ammonius' wording here is ambiguous. Has he divided the kind of quality having to do with actuality into three sub-species – (a) perfective (b) hurtful and (c) neither – or into two – (d) perfective or hurtful and (c) neither? The first (tripartite) division may seem to be the one intended, since Ammonius appears to take up species (a) explicitly in the next sentence (82,6). But it is more likely that he had the second (dichotomous) division in mind, for all his other divisions are dichotomies. Further, he seems to want to make at least some explicit comment about each of the sub-species he distinguishes; yet he nowhere discusses (b). It is likely, therefore, that his remarks at 82,6, which appear to be about (a), are intended to be about (d): he says 'perfective' but he means 'perfective or hurtful'.

health. For those who have a fever perceive the unnatural heat that is present; when it is gone, they do not perceive the health itself. This is also why the incurable do not perceive the faint <signs> of an illness that are present. For the illness in that case is not manifest except to doctors, and even the doctors themselves have certain diagnostic signs through which they track down illness and health.

One kind of affection-producing <quality> is hard to lose, and another is easy to lose. If it is easy to lose, it makes up one section (*tmêma*) of the third species mentioned by Aristotle, which I call affection, for example, the blushing of someone who turns red with shame. For a human nature, conscious of a blunder it made and not wanting to be dishonoured or shunned, sends something very valuable to its surface as a curtain for the affection. And among the more valuable of all things in nature are breath and blood. So nature dispatches blood to the surface, and the colour of that humour produces the blushing. But if it is hard to lose, it makes up another section of the third species – affective quality that produces an affection.

If it is neither perfective nor hurtful, it is either observed on the surface of the subject or has gone deep inside. And if it has gone deep inside, it is either easy to lose or hard to lose. If it is easy to lose, that makes it once again an affection of the third species of quality; but if it is hard to lose, that makes it an affective quality – not one that produces an affection, but one that is generated by an affection, such as in the case of someone who is ruddy from birth. For there is a manner in which someone who turns red with shame has a certain colour as an affection, and in the same manner someone who is naturally ruddy has a certain colour as a natural affection.

It should be noted that Aristotle says in the Seventh <Book> of the *Physics*[128] that qualitative change arises, not from every quality, but only from affective ones. Thus qualities that are states do not bring about qualitative change, he says, but rather a sort of road either toward destruction or toward coming into being. For a change of state is a substantial change. Continuing the inquiry the Philosopher said there are six species of change: coming into

---

[128] *Physics* 7.3.

being, destruction, growth, diminution, qualitative change, and change of place. These changes are observed in four categories: in substance, in quantity, in quality, and in the where. A change that occurs in regard to substance, he says, is called coming into being if it occurs from not being into being, whereas it is called destruction if it occurs from being into not being. A change that occurs in the category of quantity is called growth or diminution, that in the category of the where <is called> change of place. But qualitative change does not occur with every kind of quality. Thus changes in state are not called qualitative changes, but, for example, some <sort of> coming into being or destruction. For a state may be in the soul, as knowledge or virtue would be, or in the body, like health; and if one of these should change from not being to being, some <sort of> coming into being occurs, but if it is <a change> from being to not being, it is called destruction. Those, he says, should not be called qualitative changes. Therefore we say that there is a qualitative change when there is a change in affective quality, that is, one that is not substantial but rather accidental to the thing. And that is what there is to be said about these matters.

If, however, <the quality> has not permeated the whole of the substance but rather is manifested only on its surface, then if it is in inanimate objects, it is called figure, whereas if it is in living things it is called shape. This, we know, is the difference between figure and shape; alternatively, it is that figure is manifested in our own mental representation (*phantasia*), whereas shape is in physical things. So the term 'shape' will apply to every inanimate thing, I mean to stone and wood and iron and whatever other physical body partakes of figure. But if someone should ask why we don't say that colours are <a kind of> shape, since they are also manifested on the surface, we reply that colours are manifested not simply in a change on the surface; rather, the body is completely changed even in its composition. But with shape and figure, the substance <of the body> remains altogether unaffected and change occurs only on the surface. Thus if we take wax and make a triangular figure of it, and then change it again and make a sphere from the triangle, making no change of substance, we have changed only the figure. For it

5   will be none the less wax both when it has the shape of a triangle and <when it is> spherical.

9a10. States are also conditions.

Just as 'name' (*onoma*) is predicated of both noun (*onoma*) and verb, so also condition is predicated of both state and condition. A state is also a condition according to their
10   common predicate, but a condition is not also a state. For in one sense, conditions are divided into state and condition, but in another <condition is> distinguished from state.

9a14. A second kind (*genos*) of quality.

Since quality is a genus, why does Aristotle say of its species that one is primary and another secondary? We reply that in respect of being qualities it isn't that one of them is primary,
15   the other secondary. They differ only in rank, as do human being and horse. But why does he say 'genus of quality' when <quality> is the highest genus? He says 'genus' in place of 'species' to show that it is not an *infima* species but rather a subordinate genus. But it may be considered a species under quality, as when we say that animal is a genus of substance,
20   instead of a genus *under* it.

The second species of quality he gives, then, is that with respect to capacity and incapacity. He says that skilled boxers and runners are those having by nature an aptitude for one of those <activities>, that is, those who are such in capacity (*dunamei*). The first species of quality – that of state and condition – is manifested in actuality, whereas the second
25   <species is manifested> in potentiality (*dunamei*). For potential boxers or runners are said to have their aptitude with respect to natural capacity or incapacity. But if there is a boxer or runner in actuality, he is not so called with respect to natural capacity or incapacity, but rather <with respect to> state and condition.

85,1   **9a16. For <each of these things is said of someone> not because of his condition.**

We do not say they are such by being <so> in actuality, but rather by their having such a capacity.

9a21. They are said to be healthy because they have a natural capacity not to be <easily> affected <by what happens to them>.

Note that it is called capacity either in being a natural disposition to do <something>, as when we say that a boxer is capable of striking, or in being a natural disposition not to suffer, as when we say that a healthy person has the capacity not to suffer, and again we say that an ill person has the capacity to suffer. But if someone should say that an incapacity is not a quality, we refute this from its opposite. For no one is foolish enough to say that a capacity is not a quality. But it has been proved that what holds for one of <a pair of> contraries holds also for the other, for they both belong to the same genus. Accordingly incapacity, too, is said in three ways. Incapacity is said in the case of one who is not naturally prone to act, as when we say that someone who is ill has an incapacity to act. But it is also said in the case of one who is not naturally prone to suffer, as when we say that someone who is healthy has an incapacity to be affected. But again we say that someone who is ill has an incapacity not to be affected, that is, the capacity to suffer. The negation of not being affected introduces the capacity to be affected and, conversely, the negation of being affected introduces the capacity not to be affected. There is also another way of speaking. Capacity is said (i) in relation to a universal, as if we were to say that every human has the capacity to measure, or (ii) with respect to ease, so that <we say that> a certain human being has the capacity to measure instead of saying that he is capable of measuring easily. And it is similar also in the case of incapacity. For we say it, too, either with respect to something naturally prone not to measure at all, for example, a dog, or with respect to one who measures with difficulty, for example, a dullard. For example, those who are ill have a capacity to suffer something easily, so they have an incapacity to not suffer, whereas the healthy have the reverse.

86,1   9a28. [Affective qualities and affections make up] a third kind (*genos*) of quality.

Here once again he says genus (*genos*) instead of species (*eidos*). This <kind of quality> is manifested in four ways. Either (1) it is present in the entire species and it is called an affective quality, like whiteness in snow; or (2) <it is present> not in all but in some <members of the species>, although naturally and from birth, and it is likewise called an affective quality, like blackness in Ethiopians; or (3) <it is present> not by nature but is acquired and hard to lose, and it is called an affection classified under <the category of> quality, like the pallor <that results> from a long illness or from jaundice; or (4) it is acquired and easy to lose, like redness <or pallor>, as when someone turns red with shame or pale with fear, and it is called an affection classified under <the category of> being affected (for participants in these are certainly not said to be *qualified* by them). And bear in mind that those are conceived of not only with regard to the body, but also with regard to the soul.

Affective qualities <are spoken of> in two ways. Things are said to have an affective quality either from having been affected themselves, i.e. because produced[129] by an affection, or from the fact that our senses are affected in the perception of them, as with fire. For the fire itself is not affected so as to become hot, but we are affected by it and we become hot in the perception of it. It is the same with honey. Such things[130] are qualities in that <their> form and essence are in a subject, and it is because the senses are affected by them that it[131] is

[129] Reading *pepoieisthai* ('produced') with MS F and rejecting Busse's emendation *pepoiôsthai* ('qualified'). Busse's proposal has some plausibility, since being affected is not the same thing as being *produced* by an affection, and what is affected can plausibly be said to be *qualified* by an affection. But Ammonius tends to be careless about what his subject is, often shifting in mid-sentence between a quality and the thing that has it. The MS reading makes sense if it contains an ellipsis: '<a quality of theirs> is produced by an affection.' Ammonius' point seems to be that a thing with a certain quality may be said to be affected if that quality was produced by an affection.

[130] Ammonius seems to have in mind such examples as the heat in fire and the sweetness in honey.

[131] The subject of *legetai* ('said') may be either singular or (neuter) plural; here, no subject is explicitly provided. The most plausible candidate would normally be the subject of the antecedent clause, which is plural ('such things'). But in that case (as Pelletier notes) Ammonius should have written *einai* ('to be') rather than *ekhein* ('to have'): 'they are said *to be* affective qualities'. If *legetai* is singular, we must take its

said to have affective qualities. But a body that has become   20
white has an affective quality because it was itself affected. For
whiteness is accidental to it and is acquired, but is not its form
or in its essence. Now the senses are affected in these cases, too.
But since that which has itself been affected is more properly
called affective than is that which produces an affection,[132] in
the case of things that are both <affected and produce an
affection>, it is perhaps better for them to derive their name   25
from the more proper one.[133]

9b1. For honey is not said to be sweet because it has been somehow affected.

Indeed, it is not that being at first without sweetness <the honey> later received it as a result of some affection. Rather, it is, so to speak, essential.

9b11. [Now it is clear that many changes of colour] are   87,1
brought about by [an affection].

Having said that colours are affective qualities in virtue of being brought about by affections, he establishes this and shows it to be so.

---

implied subject to be *to hupokeimenon* (the subject in which the form and essence of the qualities reside) from the antecedent clause: '<the subject> is said to have affective qualities.' In either case, Ammonius' point is that hotness is (a) a quality of fire because its form and essence are in fire, and (b) an affective quality because it affects the senses of one who perceives fire.

[132] Ammonius ought to have said: '*qualities of* that which has itself been affected are more properly called affective than are *qualities of* that which produces an affection.'

[133] Aristotle conceives of affective qualities as belonging to 'external' objects; as he says, they are 'in' the objects. Such a quality is *affective* because it stands in a causal relation to an affection (i.e. to a state of the soul). He thus divides affective qualities into two classes:
  (1) Those that produce affections of the senses. His examples are the hotness of fire and the sweetness of honey, which affect the senses of those who feel the fire or taste the honey.
  (2) Those that are produced by affections. His examples are blushing from shame and turning pale with fear.
Ammonius notes that class (2) affective qualities not only are caused by affections, but also produce affections in the senses of those who perceive them. In the cryptic final sentence of the section ('But since that which has itself been affected ... .') he seems to be making (albeit none too clearly) the point that although such qualities do produce affections, this is not the proper reason for calling them *affective*. The proper reason is that they are produced by affections.

106 Commentary

9b19. Therefore, all such symptoms.

He calls colours 'accidents' (*sumptômata*) on account of their supervening (*episumbainein*) on other affections.[134]

9b27. For in the same way we are said to be qualified on account of them.

A quality is that in respect of which <things> are called qualified. So if they are not called qualified after easily removed affections, it is clear that those <affections> are not called qualities.

9b33. In much the same way [we speak of affective qualities and affections] with regard to the soul also.

Not only, he says, are affective qualities and affections manifested in connection with the body, but also with the soul.

9b35. For those that come into being at the moment of birth.

Just as blackness in an Ethiopian, which is inborn, is called an affective quality, so too is an inborn fit or a temperament called an affective quality.

10a2. It is the same with fits [that are not inborn].

Again, just as pallor resulting from a long illness is called an affective quality, so too a fit or something else <resulting> from an accident (*sumptôma*) is called an affective quality.

10a12. A fourth kind (*genos*) of quality.

He gives yet a fourth species of quality, calling it too a genus instead of a species. This is figure and shape. 'Figure' applies more broadly than 'shape', for every shape also has a figure,

---

[134] The word here translated 'accidents' is not the usual Aristotelian one (*sumbebêkota*), but an Epicurean term (*sumptômata*) for a thing's non-permanent

On Qualified and Quality

but not every figure also has a shape. The reason why Aristotle puts figure before shape is that it is more important and universal. For shape is said solely in the case of animate things, whereas figure <is said> in the case of the inanimate as well.

10a12. ... and also, in addition to these, [straightness and curvature and the like ...]

It is also with respect to these that their participants are called qualified. For example, a line is called straight after straightness and curved after curvature, and straightness and curvature are affections of a line.

10a16. Porous and dense [and rough and smooth might be thought to signify qualities].

'Might be thought to be', he says, since in truth they are not qualities. A dense thing is one whose parts are arranged so close together that it cannot admit a different kind of body; a porous one has its parts so spread out that it can admit a different kind of body. So it appears rather that the parts of these things exhibit a certain position (*thesis*). Aristotle understands *porous* to be the result of artifice; for example if someone were to fill his hand with nuts, we might call the body composed of all of them *porous* on account of its rarefaction. In fact, in the *Physics*[135] he himself defines *porous* and *dense* differently.

10a25. Now perhaps some other [type of quality might be brought to light].

Having presented four species of quality to us, he draws his conclusion and says that these are the <only> types of quality. Wanting us not to be content with what the ancients said or to remain idle, but to investigate on our own, however,

---

attributes. Cf. Epicurus, *Letter to Herodotus*, 68-73; A.A. Long and D.N. Sedley, *The Hellenistic Philosophers* (Cambridge: 1987), 33-6.
[135] *Physics* 4.9, 216b30.

108   Commentary

he says that 'perhaps some other type of quality might be brought to light'.¹³⁶

10a27. What we have mentioned above, then, are qualities.

25   Whiteness, blackness, and the like are *qualities*, he says. A thing that participates in qualities, for example a body that is white or black or sweet and so forth, is *qualified*. The qualities are participated in, and the <things> qualified participate in
89,1   and are called paronymously after them. But this is not so in all cases, as in the case of virtue. For one who participates in it is not called 'virtued'¹³⁷ paronymously after it, but rather is called 'good'. This is why he says 'or else in some other way'.

10a34. For example, a man good at running [or good at boxing ...]

5   Indeed the person good at boxing, who is so called according to a fitness that Aristotle calls a capacity, is not named after a quality. Certainly he is not named after <the quality> boxing; for boxing is a science. And besides, those who

---

¹³⁶ The division of the category of quality that Ammonius proposes may be summarized in outline form:
I. In potentiality
    A. Capacity
    B. Incapacity
II. In actuality
    A. Perfective or hurtful
        1. Affection-producing
            a. Easy to lose: affections
            b. Hard to lose: affective qualities
        2. Not affection-producing
            a. Easy to lose: conditions
            b. Hard to lose: states
                i. Of the soul
                ii. Of the body
    B. Neither perfective nor hurtful
        1. On the surface
            a. Of something inanimate: figure
            b. Of something animate: shape
        2. In the interior
            a. Easy to lose: affections
            b. Hard to lose: affective qualities (produced by an affection)
Although this division includes the four species of quality that Aristotle discusses, it is clearly more complex than what Aristotle had in mind.
¹³⁷ cf. n. 68.

On Qualified and Quality

participate in it perfectly and <are> in the <appropriate> state are paronymously called boxers after it. It is the same for the person good at running, for he is <not> named after a quality either.[138]

10b5. Sometimes also when a name has been laid down ...

But often, even if a name has been laid down for the quality, that which participates in it is not called paronymously after it, for we do not say 'virtued' but 'good'.

10b12. Justice, for example, [is contrary to injustice].

Aristotle searches for what is peculiar (*idion*) to quality. So he says that admitting contrariety is peculiar to quality. But then he rejects this, for it does not belong to all qualities. For yellow, which is a quality, has no contrary, nor does red, and similarly neither do the other qualities of this sort. But it is clear, he says, that when one of a pair of contraries is subsumed under a category, the other is also subsumed under the same one because it is not possible for us to classify it under another category.

10b26. [Qualities] admit of more [and less].

Another concomitant[139] (*parakolouthêma*) of quality is to admit of more and less. It is reasonable <to suppose> that this is not a universal concomitant. For it is said that where contrariety is manifested there is more and less, but where it is not there is not more or less. Since, then, contrariety belongs in <the category> of quality, more and less belong <there, too>; but since <contrariety> does not belong to all <qualities>, neither does more and less belong to all <of them>. For justice, they say, is hardly said to be more or less than justice, yet it is said that those things participating in justice or health participate <in them> more or less.

---

[138] Reading *oude gar* for *kai gar*, with Busse.
[139] Ammonius makes much use of this Epicurean term for a thing's permanent attributes. See n. 134 for references.

11a2. [But then it is] indisputable [that the things called after these] admit of [more and less].

And of course those things that are called paronymously after these appropriately admit of more and less. But Aristotle leaves unresolved the puzzles as to why justice is not said <to be> more or less <justice>.

Well then, we say that justice does admit of more and less. For whenever we say that one person is more just than another, it is clear that <this is so> in so far as the one participates in justice more than the other does. So justice does admit of more and less.

11a5. But triangle and square [do not seem to admit of more].

One triangle is not more or less of a triangle than another triangle, nor is a pentagon more of a circle than a square is. For if things are to be compared as circles, they must both admit the formula of a circle. But if they do not <both> admit <it>, they cannot be compared at all. For one would not say that a cow is more of a man than a horse is, since neither of the two admits the definition of a man. And so it will be the same with figures. All figures that admit the definition of a circle are equally circles and those that admit the definition of a triangle are equally triangles, and it is the same with the rest.

11a9. Whereas [none] of the things that do not admit it [is said to be more than another].

But those things that do not admit <the definition> at all are not compared. Therefore not all qualities admit of more and less.

11a15. Now none of the things so far mentioned [is peculiar to quality].

Aristotle here rejects two concomitants of quality, since they are not concomitants of quality in every way. Then he moves

On Qualified and Quality   111

on to a *proprium* in the strict sense when he says 'similar and dissimilar'.[140] Indeed this *proprium* applies to none of the other categories.

11a20. We need not be alarmed [if someone should tell us that although we proposed to discuss quality we have taken many relatives into account].

Since Aristotle was aware of having included many relatives in his treatment of quality, he says that it is not necessary to puzzle over the fact that the discussion concerns quality <rather than relatives>. In fact we subsumed many relatives under quality, for example, state and condition. For a state is said to be the state of something and a condition the condition of something. Then he solves this in two ways.

11a23. For in nearly all [such cases the genera are spoken of in relation to something].

This is the first solution to the puzzle. He says that the genera of qualities are classified under relatives but their species <are classified> under quality. For example, knowledge is said to be a relative (for it is said to be knowledge *of* something). Geometry, however, is not a relative, for it is not said to be the *geometry* of something, but perhaps the *knowledge* of something. But this solution is superficial; the later one is more precise. We are called knowledgeable, he says, not simply for participating in knowledge but rather for participating in either music or geometry or one of the other <kinds of knowledge>. Knowledge, since it is indeterminate, is a relative, but its species are not. For they are determinate, and we do not call music or geometry the music or geometry of something, but rather <we call them> qualities. Indeed we are called qualified after them. So the genus is classified under relatives, but the species under quality. So that we may understand this more precisely, let us grasp it by way of division, as follows. Some beings are subjects (*hupokeimena*), such as substance, and some are in a subject, such as

---

[140] 'Now none of the things so far mentioned is peculiar to quality. But it is qualities alone with respect to which things are said to be similar and dissimilar' (11a15-16).

accidents. And some things in a subject are in a relation (*skhesis*) and constitute (*ginetai*) <the category of> relatives, whereas some are not in a relation. Now some of those not in a relation belong indivisibly and constitute <the category of> quality, whereas some <belong> divisibly and constitute <the category of> quantity. Thus it is not paradoxical for a genus to be subsumed under relatives, but its species under quality. And this is a precise solution. But above all, there is no paradox when some things classified under another category are also classified under relatives. Rather it is altogether necessary that what is subsumed under relatives be classified under some other category as well; for it has been pointed out[141] that <the category of> relatives does not contain (*ekhei*) things that are peculiar <to it>; rather <its members> are observed in other categories.

On Doing and Being Affected

11b1. Both doing and being affected admit of contrariety.

One must be aware that the principal and primary categories are the four we have mentioned: *substance, quantity, quality,* and *relative*. The other six arise from the combination of substance with the remaining three. For from the combination of substance and quantity arise the two categories of *where* and *when*. Again, from the mingling of substance and quality arise two others: *doing* and *being affected*. From the combination of substance and relatives arise the two remaining categories: *being arranged* and *having on*.

Although he gave the definitions and concomitants of the <first> four categories, he neither stated the *propria* nor gave definitions or a division into species for the remaining six, since we are able to figure those things out from what has already been said. So we must give the definition of each as well as its division into species.

So: (1) *doing* is operating (*energein*) on something. There are two species of this. For either the agent (*poioun*) acts on

---

[141] Ammonius may be referring to his discussion of contrariety among relatives at 69,24ff.

itself, e.g. the soul knows itself, or it acts on another, e.g. heating. (2) *Being affected*, on the other hand, is being qualitatively changed by something. There are likewise two species of this. For a thing is affected either so as to be brought to destruction, e.g. being burned, or so as to be raised to perfection, as when we say that vision is affected by the visible. (3) *Being arranged (keisthai)* is a certain position (*thesis*) of the body, and this has three species: to be lying, to be sitting, and to be standing. (4) *When* is indicative of time, and also has three species: present, past, and future. (5) *Where* is indicative of place, and this has six species: up, down, right, left, in front, and behind. (6) *Having on* is an arrangement of a substance around a substance; for it signifies *having shoes on*, *having armour on*, and other such things.

On Opposites

11b16. [We must talk] about opposites, and the various ways [in which things are usually opposed].

Aristotle's aim here is to teach us about the words mentioned in the doctrine of categories that require some articulation and explanation, although from common usage they are not completely unknown to us. He speaks first about opposites. For indeed he mentioned opposites in the <discussion of> relatives, when he said that large and small are opposed not as contraries but as relatives.[142] Thus he wants to teach <us> in how many ways opposites are spoken of, and he says that they are opposed in four ways: (1) as relatives, (2) as contraries, (3) as privation and state, (4) as affirmation and negation.

So that we may have a practical understanding of how

---

[142] Ammonius apparently has in mind a passage (5b15-6a11) in the chapter on quantity, where Aristotle says that large and small are relatives and not contraries. But Aristotle does not there call them *opposites*. As Pelletier points out, the word 'opposite' (*antikeimenon*) and its cognates do not occur in the passage cited.

opposites are spoken of in four ways, let's obtain them by division. Opposites are opposed either (A) in statements, as affirmation and negation, e.g. 'Socrates walks' / 'Socrates does not walk', or (B) in things. In the latter case they either (B1) have a relation or (B2) are manifested on their own. The ones having a relation are said to be opposed as relatives, e.g. right and left; the others are opposed not with respect to a relation but on their own. These either (B2a) change into one another or (B2b) do not change. If they change, they are opposed as contraries, e.g. dark and pale; if they do not change, they are opposed with respect to privation and state, e.g. sight and blindness.

But why did he list them in this order? We reply that he began with the ones having the mildest opposition, I mean relatives. For it is scarcely in their nature to be at war with one another. In fact they bring each other in together, and if one exists the other always exists as well, and conversely if one does not exist neither will the other exist. Second he talks about contraries, for contraries are more violently opposed. Indeed, they destroy one another, and if one exists the other always perishes. Yet things <opposed> as privation and state are more violently <opposed> than these. For contraries destroy one another, as we said, but they also change into one another (for pale comes to be from dark, and conversely). But things opposed as privation and state do not change into one another. For a blind person will not recover his sight nor will a bald one grow hair. Yet more violent than this is the opposition of affirmation and negation. For this one alone is manifested in the case of everything that exists; the others are not. For the opposition between relatives is not said to apply in every case. Thus if one happens to be alone one is not said to be either on the right or on the left.

Nor do contraries apply in every case. For a substance has no contrary, and a word is not said to be white or black according to the contrariety of colours. Likewise the opposition of privation and state is not spoken of in all cases. For a stone is not said to be blind or to have sight or to be bald. But the opposition of affirmation and negation is manifested in every case. For Socrates is either said to be on the right or not to be on the right, and a substance is either said to have a contrary or not,[143] and a stone either to have sight or not to have sight. And in the same way in every case you will find the opposition of affirmation and negation in abundance. Hence it was reasonable to mention first the <opposition> of relatives, second that of contraries, third that of privation and state, and fourth affirmation and negation.

11b32. Therefore things opposed [as relatives].

Aristotle wants to show that the opposition between relatives is not the same as that of contraries, and this is how he does it. Things opposed as relatives are said to be the very things that they are *of* other things, e.g. what is to the right is <said to be> to the right of what is to the left. But things opposed as contraries are not said to be the very things they are of other things. For white is not said <to be> white of black. Therefore things opposed as relatives are different from those opposed as contraries.

11b38. Those contraries [which are such that it is necessary for one or the other of them to belong].

Having distinguished the opposition between relatives from that of contraries, Aristotle now wishes to distinguish it also from the rest. For this purpose he offers a division of contraries which he sets out as follows. Some contraries have no intermediate, such as odd and even; others have an intermediate, such as white and black and anything like that. Some of the contraries that have an intermediate are such that it is not necessary that one or the other of them be present in a subject, such as white and black. For it is not necessary that every body is either white or black; <a body>

---

[143] A subtle confusion may have crept into Ammonius' comments. The point he seems to be making here is that whether *F* is (i) a relation, (ii) a contrary, or (iii) a state (or privation), a substance, *S*, either has *F* or does not have *F*. But if so, his way of expressing (ii) is unfortunate. For his talk of a substance 'having a contrary or not' recalls his comment at 94,19 that 'a substance has no contrary'. But his point there was the altogether different one that substances themselves are not contraries (e.g. *horse* is not the contrary of anything). But a substance may nevertheless have a property which is itself a contrary (e.g. Socrates is pale, and pale is contrary to dark), and in this sense the substance may (misleadingly) be said to 'have a contrary'. Ammonius seems to be speaking this way here.

can also be grey or some other intermediate <colour>. But some are such that it is necessary that one or the other of them be present in a subject, such as heat in a fire. For cooling never takes place in it; and likewise in snow <there is> coldness and never the contrary.¹⁴⁴

20   **12a6. Also odd and even [are predicated of numbers].**

For every number is either odd or even, and no number can be found that is not like that.

12a6. Also [while] bad and good can be predicated [both of men and of many other things ...].

It is not only in the case of man that we use the <terms> *bad*
25   and *good*, but also in the case of many other things, for example, horses and dogs and the like.

12a20. In some cases [there are established] names [for the intermediates, e.g. grey and yellow between light and dark ...].

Among contraries having an intermediate, some have an intermediate that has been given a name, as white and black
96,1   have <as intermediates> pale and grey and the like, whereas others do not but <their intermediate> is signified by the

---

¹⁴⁴ Ammonius' commentary here is misleading. Let us call contraries *mediated* if they have something intermediate between them, and *bare* if they do not. Aristotle does not, in fact, divide mediated contraries in the way that Ammonius suggests. After noting (11b38, 12b27) that it is necessary for one or the other of a pair of bare contraries to belong to any subject capable of receiving them, he asserts emphatically (12b35) that it is not necessary for one or the other of a pair of mediated contraries to belong to any subject capable of receiving them. At 12b37 he notes an apparent exception: a pair of mediated contraries (heat and cold) one of which (heat) belongs necessarily to a subject (fire).

As a little reflection will show (and as Aristotle is well aware – cf. 12b41-13a3), this is not a genuine exception. Heat (and therefore heat or cold) belongs necessarily to fire. But the rule is that with mediated contraries it is not necessary for one or the other to belong to *every* suitable subject. That is, when contraries are mediated there will always be *some* suitable subject that lacks them both. A genuine exception would consist of a pair of mediated contraries one or the other of which belongs necessarily to every subject capable of receiving either. The example of heat and fire, on the other hand, is one of a particular subject to which some mediated contrary belongs necessarily. Fire is necessarily hot, but some things (e.g. lukewarm water) are neither hot nor cold. So Aristotle's rule remains intact.

negation of the extremes. For example, the mean between bad and good is not called by a name, but we make it known by denying the extremes, saying, for example, 'that which is neither bad nor good'.

> 12a26. Privation and state are spoken of [in regard to the same thing, e.g. sight and blindness in regard to the eye].

Wishing to distinguish the opposition between relatives from the opposition between privation and state, Aristotle teaches first about things opposed in respect of privation and state. He says that the thing of which the state is said is also the one in which the privation is observed.

> 12a29. We say [that a thing capable of admitting a state] is deprived [of it if the state is one that naturally belongs to that thing ...].

The Philosopher quite convincingly asserts that if we are going to say that something is deprived of something, we must consider these three points: first, whether the thing we are speaking about is capable of admitting <the state>; next, the place in which it is naturally said <to have the state>; third, the proper time at which the state should have existed. Thus, it is necessary first to consider the subject, because some things are utterly unreceptive. (For we don't say that a stone is deprived of sight, since it is totally deprived of the capacity to acquire sight; we might as well say that it is deprived of justice. Rather I think it is clear that a privation is spoken of only with respect to a pre-existing possession.) Second, it is also <necessary to consider> the part in which it is natural for it to have <the state>. (A man is capable of receiving sight, but we do not say that his foot is deprived of sight because, as we said, he does not naturally have sight in that part.) Finally in these matters <it is necessary to consider> the proper time. A young puppy naturally has sight and <has it> in the required part; yet it does not see and it is not said to be deprived of sight because the proper time has not yet arrived for it to receive sight in actuality. At first it <simply> does not see; <only> later does it become blind. So the

118 Commentary

Philosopher rightly and convincingly tells us to watch for and consider these three points. 'For it is not what<ever> lacks teeth that we call toothless' – surely not what has just now been born – 'and not simply[145] what lacks sight <that we call> blind' (12a31-32) – surely not a puppy.

97,1 **12a35. But to be deprived is not a privation and to have a state is not a state.**

With these <words> the Philosopher wishes to show that to be deprived is not the same thing as privation nor to have a state <the same thing> as a state; but they are said paronymously from the same thing. For if they were the same thing, they would both be predicated of the same thing. If a state and having a state were the same, they would both be predicated of the same thing, and similarly with regard to a privation. But in fact it is not so. For we do not call a blind <man> blindness.

12b6. But similarly[146] what an affirmation or a negation is about is not [an affirmation or a negation].

From the fact that an affirmation and a negation are statements, whereas the things signified by them are things, Aristotle shows that affirmation and negation are not the same as the things that are signified by them. But these, too, are said to be opposed as affirmation and negation, <just as> 'Socrates is sitting' <is opposed> to 'Socrates is not sitting'. By 'these' I mean the things themselves, for example, <the things signified by> 'is sitting' and 'is not sitting'.

12b16. [It is evident] that privation and state [are not opposed as relatives].

Having distinguished relatives from contraries he now distinguishes them from things opposed as privation and state. He begins with what is more obvious and agreed upon, I mean with the fact that sight is not said to be the sight of

---

[145] 'Simply' (*haplôs*) added by Ammonius.
[146] 'Similarly' added by Ammonius.

On Opposites

blindness. Later he shows, and this is doubtful, that blindness is not said to be <the blindness> of sight. For this does seem to be said.

12b18. [For sight is not said to be sight of blindness,] nor is it spoken of in any other way in relation to it.

Instead of: 'When you coin words, they are not spoken of at all in relation to things conversely related to them.'[147]

12b19. Nor, in the same way would blindness be said to be the blindness of sight.

Aristotle points out that blindness is not called <the blindness> of sight, for if it were so called, sight would also be called <the sight> of blindness. For relatives are spoken of with respect to things they are conversely related to, as with 'to the left of the right' and 'to the right of the left'.

12b26. [That the things spoken of as privation and state are not opposed as contraries is clear from the following.]

Note that it would be natural <at this point> to distinguish the opposition of relatives from that of affirmation and negation. But Aristotle omits this, since he is about to distinguish that <opposition>[148] from the other three in a single statement; instead he distinguishes the opposition of privation and state from that of contraries. He makes a division of contraries and explains them, first by means of particular cases and then in a universal statement: 'Of contraries which have nothing intermediate between them it is necessary for one or the other always to belong to the things in which they naturally occur, or of which they are predicated.'[149] We would not say that fire is odd or even or

---

[147] The point of this obscure remark may be that Aristotle often coins a word for the converse of a relative precisely so that he will have a term for what the relative is said to be related to. But its relevance to the lemma, which deals with a privation and state (blindness and sight) that both have names, is unclear.

[148] i.e. the opposition between affirmation and negation. The passage Ammonius refers to occurs at 13a37: 'It is evident that things opposed as affirmation and negation are not opposed in any of the ways we have discussed.'

[149] 12b28-9, but not verbatim.

15   that a stone is ill or healthy, since they are not at all naturally capable of receiving <these contraries>. He says 'for one or the other always to belong to the things of which they are predicated' on account of unmediated contraries; as he himself says, 'in the case of illness and health and even and odd' (12b30-31). For it is necessary for every number to be either even or odd and for every body capable of receiving these <sc. illness and health> to be ill or to be healthy.

20   **12b33. It is not necessary for everything to be white or black that is capable of receiving them.**

It is not necessary for a body to be either white or black (for it can also be grey) or for it to be cold or hot (for it can be lukewarm) unless perhaps one of them necessarily belongs to
99,1 the subject as white belongs to snow or hot to fire, i.e. to the conception itself, since just as heat is essentially combined with fire so too are cold and white with snow.

13a3. But [neither of the things just mentioned is true] of privation and [state].

5   Having set out the types of opposition between contraries, Aristotle now shows that in none of the types mentioned can the opposition between contraries be the same as that of privation and state. For in the case of contraries that have nothing intermediate, of necessity one or the other will belong to the subject, but in the case of things <opposed> as privation and state, it is not the case that of necessity one or the other is always present in the subject. Therefore the
10   opposition between contraries that have nothing intermediate is not the same as that between privation and state.[150]

---

[150] Omitting *all' oude têi ana meson* with MS F.

13a4. For it is not [necessary that one or the other of these] always [belong] to what is capable of receiving them.

Now first of all he distinguishes things <opposed> as privation and state from contraries that have nothing intermediate, arguing that one <or the other> of the latter is of necessity present in the subject. For necessarily every number is either odd or even, but not every body will of necessity be called blind or sighted. For surely a stone will not, nor in general will things that are not capable of receiving <either of them>.[151]

13a8. Nor are they among those that have something intermediate.

Next he distinguishes them from contraries that have an intermediate, arguing that it is not the case that one or the other of those is of necessity present in the subject. For it is not necessary that every body be white or black, but in the case of things <opposed> as privation and state, of necessity one <or the other> of them is present in anything capable of

---

[151] Ammonius' example of a stone is not appropriate here. For Aristotle explicitly restricts his discussion to subjects that are 'capable of receiving' (*dektika*) the contraries in question. A stone cannot be said to be blind (i.e. deprived of sight), to be sure, but that is because it is not the sort of subject that is capable of having sight. If such unsuitable subjects were allowed, Aristotle's claim that one or the other of a pair of bare contraries belongs to every subject would be in jeopardy. (Clearly not *everything* can be said to be odd or even.) In fact, Aristotle says that 'a thing for which it is not yet natural to have sight is not said either to be blind or to have sight' (13a5-6). His point is thus more subtle; it concerns only those subjects in which the state naturally occurs (cf. 12a26ff.) and depends on considering the time at which it is natural for them to have the state. (For more on Ammonius' neglect of temporal considerations, see the next note.)

Aristotle's point is better illustrated by examples of the following sort. A newborn kitten cannot see, but we would not say that it is blind on that account, for it is not natural for newborn kittens to have sight. A newborn baby lacks teeth, and so may an old man, but it is only the latter that we call toothless, for it is not natural for babies to be born with teeth. And we would never say that an earthworm is toothless or blind, for there is no time in an earthworm's life at which it would naturally have teeth or sight.

receiving them.¹⁵² He adds 'to everything'¹⁵³ since among contraries that have an intermediate there are some of which one or the other is of necessity present in a subject, as, for example, heat in fire. But nevertheless he also points out a difference these have in comparison to things <opposed> as privation and state, namely, that it is definitely one or <definitely> the other of these that is present in the subject. For in the case of hot and cold, which are contraries that have an intermediate, it is definitely heat that belongs to fire and not just one or the other of them. But with things <opposed> as privation and state it is not like that. For it is not necessary that it be definitely sight that is present in what is capable of receiving <it>, or <definitely> blindness, but whichever of the two happens to belong.

13a18. Moreover, [it is possible for there to be change] from one contrary [into another as long as there is something capable of receiving them].

Having divided contraries into those which have something intermediate and those which do not, and having compared relatives with both of them, he now distinguishes them by means of a general formula when he says that all contraries change into one another unless one of them belongs to the subject naturally and essentially. 'For change occurs', he says,

---

¹⁵² Ammonius ought to had said 'is *at some time* present in anything capable of receiving them'. In distinguishing the opposition between privation and state from the opposition between contraries of the two kinds (bare and mediated) previously marked off (11b38-12a21), Aristotle uses a subtle blend of modal, temporal, and quantificational notions. Every subject capable of receiving predicates opposed as privation and state, Aristotle says, will (i) necessarily at some time in its career but (ii) not necessarily at all times, be characterized by one or the other of them. These two features distinguish privation and state both from mediated contraries, which do not satisfy (i), and from bare contraries, which do not satisfy (ii). That is, some subject may never have either of a pair of mediated contraries (e.g. black and white) even though it is capable of receiving them (e.g. it has a colour, but its colour at any given time falls between the two extremes); in the case of bare contraries, on the other hand, every subject capable of receiving either of them necessarily at all times has one or the other. Ammonius seems not to have recognized how crucial the temporal dimension is (his commentary is devoid of temporal language with the sole exception of a single occurrence of 'always' at 99,9). As a result, he misleadingly makes Aristotle appear to have contradicted himself (compare 99,8-9 with 99,21-2).

¹⁵³ Aristotle's next sentence reads: 'For it is necessary that one or the other of these at some time belong to everything capable of receiving them' (13a8-9).

'from state into privation; from privation into state is impossible.'[154]

But what is <the meaning of> 'he restores himself to the contrary state, time permitting'?[155] That means 'if he is not too old when he starts doing philosophy'. For in that case time will not permit his progress to advance all the way to the contrary.

13a37. [It is evident that things opposed] as affirmation [and negation are not opposed in any of the ways we have discussed].

Having distinguished the three oppositions from one another he now compares the remaining one to the three and distinguishes it <from them> in a single statement by saying 'for only with these is it always necessary for one of them to be true and the other false' (13b2-3). For it is distinctive of affirmation and negation to divide in every case (*epi pantos pragmatos*) <into> the true and the false, as he teaches in *de Interpretatione*.[156] If I say 'Socrates is sitting' <and> 'Socrates is not sitting', necessarily one of them is true and the other false. And it is the same with all things <opposed> as affirmation and negation.

13b10. But nothing at all [said] without any combination [is either true or false].

Things said without any combination are clearly neither true nor false; and relatives, contraries, and things <opposed> as privation and state are said without combination. Clearly, then, these are neither true nor false. Therefore they are not the same as those said <to be opposed> as affirmation and negation.

13b12. Although it is not the case, it might certainly [seem that this is how it is with contraries said in combination].

---

[154] 13a32-4, slightly reworded.
[155] 13a30-1, slightly reworded.   [156] 17a25ff.

Aristotle raises an objection, saying that in the case of contraries not said without combination it would seem that one is true and the other false, whereas this is not the case. He resolves this by <the method of> objection and counter-objection. <He says> that, first of all, they do not always (*pantôs*) divide <into> the true and the false. For if someone should say 'Socrates is well' <and> 'Socrates is ill', then if Socrates exists (*huparkhei*), they divide, but if he does not exist, the one which says that a nonexistent person is well and the one which says that he is ill are both false. On the other hand, if they do divide <into true and false>, then they are in effect affirmation and negation; for that is what a statement (*legomenon*) signifies. For we know that of opposites in language (*en logois*), affirmation and negation are opposed in this way. Therefore <contraries said in combination> do not always divide <into the true and the false, i.e. they do not do> precisely what is distinctive of affirmation and negation.

On Contraries

13b36. A good thing's contrary is [necessarily a bad thing].

Having completed his discussion of opposites, Aristotle now wants to talk about the various ways in which contraries are said. He says that the contrary of a good thing will always be bad, but not conversely – the contrary of a bad thing is not always good. The contrary of a bad thing is sometimes good and sometimes bad – not good exclusively. For excess, a bad thing, is contrary to deficiency, which is bad, and similarly rashness is opposed to cowardice, which is bad. But such contraries are rare, since for the most part a bad thing is contrary to a good one.

14a7. Moreover, with contraries [it is not necessary that, if one exists, the other will, too].

It is clear that Aristotle is now also examining contraries as things and not as contraries. For if white exists, he says, it is not necessary for black to exist, but if it exists as a contrary, of necessity black exists. For a contrary is said to be contrary *to something*, as has already been pointed out in <the discussion of> relatives.

14a10. Moreover, if Socrates' being healthy [is contrary to Socrates' being ill and it is not possible for both to belong to him at the same time, then if one of the contraries existed it would not be possible for the other to exist as well].

He says this because contraries are destructive of one another, and when one of them exists the other would never exist in the subject in the same part at the same time. For health and illness are contraries and will never belong to the same thing simultaneously.

14a15. It is clear that [contraries naturally arise] in something which is the same [either in species or in genus].

Another concomitant of contraries is that both of them are found in a single subject. And this is reasonable. For things that are at war with and fight one another must do so by meeting in a single subject or place.

14a22. But justice and injustice are [in separate genera].

Although above he had said that contraries must be in the same genus, Aristotle now shows that they are not all in the same genus. Indeed, justice and injustice, which are contrary genera, are not found in the same genus; for justice is in the genus, virtue, whereas injustice is in the genus, vice. We reply that genera that are themselves contraries still have some common genus. Thus virtue is a state and vice is likewise a state.[157]

---

[157] At this point MS M adds: The good is thought of as the care (*sustasis*) of substance, just as evil is the abandonment (*ekptôsis*) of substance, so that the categories do not become more numerous than promised.

On Priority

14a26. One thing is said to be prior to another [in four ways].

Since Aristotle mentioned priority in his doctrine of the categories, it is reasonable for him to enumerate its meanings. He makes a division and says that there are four, but later he adds a fifth. He says, first, there is what is called priority in time, according to which we say that an elder is prior to a youth. (Notice that we say 'elder' (*presbuteron*) for the animate and 'older' (*palaioteron*) for the inanimate.) The second meaning <of 'prior'> is <that in which> the converse of an implication of existence does not hold. That is to say, that which is entailed (*suneispheromenon*) does not entail (*suneispheron*) <the other>.[158] For that is what it is for there to be no converse implication of existence. For example, if there are two things, there will necessarily be one <thing> (for one is entailed), but if there is one there will not necessarily be two (for <two> is not entailed by one). Therefore one is prior to two. Again, if there is a human being, there will necessarily be an animal (for animal is entailed by human being), but if there is an animal there will not always be a human being. For human being is not entailed by it. There are many animals that are not human beings. Therefore, animal is prior to human being. But this way of talking has to do with nature and not with time. The third is <priority> in order (*taxis*), in the way that the introduction is prior to the narrative. The fourth <is priority> in worth (*axiôma*), in the way that the commander <is prior> to the commanded. The fifth is that in which there is a converse implication of existence, but <the prior> is the cause of the other's existence.

14b7. This is perhaps the strangest [of the ways.]

This is precisely because it has been established by our choice and not by the nature of things.

---

[158] cf. n. 64.

14b11. For when there is a converse [implication of existence].

104,1

For if, Aristotle says, one of the reciprocals were the cause of the existence of the other, it would rightly be called prior.[159] For example, a father is the father of a son, but they reciprocate with each other: the son is the son of the father. If, then, the father is the cause of the existence of the son, he would rightly be called prior in nature to the son.

5

14b22. Therefore there are five ways in which one thing might be said to be prior to another.

In talking about the prior, Aristotle has also <in effect> mentioned the posterior.[160] For his account of the posterior is clear from his teaching about the prior. Indeed these <two> belong together, since they are both relatives. For the prior is said to be prior to the posterior, and posterior is said in each of the ways in which prior is said.

10

On Simultaneity

14b24. It is things that come into being [at the same time] that are said to be, simply and in the strictest sense, simultaneous.

15

Since Aristotle mentioned the simultaneous in his teaching on the categories,[161] he also discusses it <here>. Just as we said about priority, that its first meaning, strictly speaking, is with respect to time, so also here, Aristotle says. Nature is second, just as was also said about the former. This <sense> is opposed to the second and fifth senses of priority, for <with them> there is a converse implication of existence and neither is the cause of the other's existence. Examples <of naturally simultaneous things> are terrestrial, aerial, and

20

105,1

---

[159] Reading *to heteron* for *to heterou*.
[160] Reading *kai* ('also') with all MSS and rejecting Busse's *ouketi* ('not yet'), which he derives from Philoponus.
[161] 7b15ff.

aquatic animals. For one type of animal is aerial, another is terrestrial, and a third is aquatic. They are therefore said to be simultaneous, since they are <obtained> from the same genus by the same division, as Aristotle says. But if the aerial <kind> is divided, perhaps into birds and insects (*akrides*), then bird and aerial are no longer said simultaneously; rather, aerial is prior, because it is obtained from the first division of animal.

On Change (*kinêsis*)

15a<1>3. There are six kinds of change.

Aristotle once again talks about change, since he also mentioned it in what has preceded.[162] Motion is thus change (*metabolê*), and the changeable changes either substantially (*kat' ousian*) or accidentally (*kata sumbebêkos*). If <the change is> substantial, it constitutes coming into being (*genesis*) and destruction (*phthora*). (If it is from not being to being, it will be coming into being; if it is from being to not being, it constitutes destruction.) If it is accidental, the change is either in the thing <that changes>, or on it, or near (*peri*) it. And if it is in the thing itself, it is called growth and diminution; if it is on the thing it is <called> qualitative change; if it is near the thing it is called change of place. Therefore there is change in four categories – in substance: coming into being and destruction; in quantity: growth and diminution; in quality: qualitative change; in the where: change of place. Aristotle now does exactly what he did in the case of opposites: he distinguishes the forms of movement from one another.

15a25. For if it were the same, a case of qualitative change [would have at once to be a case of growth, too, or diminution ...]

---

[162] There is only one prior occurrence of the word *kinêsis* in the *Categories* (5b3). Pelletier suggests that Ammonius may have in mind Aristotle's earlier references to action and affection. Perhaps Ammonius is thinking of his own previous commentary (83,8ff) on Aristotle's discussion of change (*metabolê*) in *Physics* 7.3.

On Change (kinêsis)

Aristotle does not elaborate on any of the other <forms of movement>, since they are clear. Concerning qualitative change, he does, and says that if qualitative change were the same as growth, a thing that has grown would have to change in every way, which does not happen. Thus a square grows when a gnomon is put around it, but it is not qualitatively changed[163] in any way, for it remains still a square. The gnomon is the peripheral thing (*peripheria*) with two complements around the diagonal.

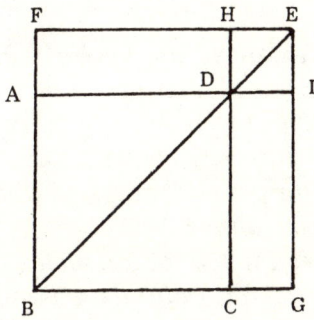

When the gnomon *AFEGC* was put around it, the square *AC* was enlarged but not qualitatively changed. For *GF* is also a square. And again when the gnomon *HFBGI* was put around it, the square *ED* was enlarged but not qualitatively changed. For *EB* is also a square. Thus the gnomon is a square with two complements around its diagonal.

So much for these matters. The rest we pass over, since it is easy.[164]

---

[163] 'Not qualitatively changed' since its shape remains the same. *Alloiôsis* (literally, 'alteration') is a change in quality, not in quantity. Hence the enlargement of a square is not a qualitative change so long as it remains a square.

[164] Ammonius offers no comments on the very brief Chapter 15, in which Aristotle discusses the various senses of 'having' (*ekhein*).

Textual Emendations

The following textual changes have been adopted in the translation:

8,5-6	*hê tês didaskalias apangelia* for *hê tês apangelias didaskalia* with Pelletier
11,2-3	*haiper eisi protaseis kai suntithetai ex onomatôn kai rhêmatôn* for *kai suntithetai ex onomatôn kai rhêmatôn haiper eisi protaseis* with Pelletier
19,10	*dikhôs* for *tetrakhôs*
28,14	*tou en hôi esti topou* for *tou mêlou en hôi esti topôi*
31,14	*proslambanei* for *prolambanei* with MSS MF
31,19	*hetera genê* for *heterogenê* with MS M
32,24	*dê akolouthôs toutô to* for *de akolouthôs touto* with Busse
34,3	*phêsomen* for *ephamen* with Busse
35,1	*deitai arnêtikou* for *deitai heterou arnêtikou* with MS F
35,4-5	*ou pantôs hê kataphasis kai hê apophasis phanerôs alêtheuei ê pseudetai* for *ou pantôs hê kataphasis alêtheuei oude pantôs hê apophasis pseudetai* with Pelletier
37,6	*en hupokeimenôi* for *kath' hupokeimenou* with Pelletier
43,1	Omitting *tout' esti ta hupallêla* with MS M
46,27	Omitting *to gar sumbebêkos en tini* with MSS MF
58,27	5a15 for 5a13
59,4	*hupomenein* for *hupokeimenô* with MS M
59,6	5a23 for 5a22
59,20	5a30 for 5a23
64,22	6a11 for 6a12
66,8	*hautê haplê* for *haplê* with Busse

Textual Emendations

66,19	*ê xulon* for *xulon* with MS M
70,15	6b19 for 6b20
72,13-14	*hê kephalê tôn pros ti· tinos gar kephalê. ean oun apodothê* for *hê kephalê ean apodothê* with MS M
76,6	*aisthêtikon* for *aisthêton*
76,22	*phêmi* for *phêsi*
80,2	*mathêsetai* for *mathêseôs* with MS F
86,14	*pepoieisthai* for *pepoiôsthai* with MS F
89,9	*oude gar* for *kai gar* with Busse
99,11	Omitting *all' oude têi ana meson* with MS F
104,2	*to heteron* for *to heterou* (sic)
104,8	*kai* for *ouketi* with all MSS

Appendix

The Commentators*

The 15,000 pages of the Ancient Greek Commentaries on Aristotle are the largest corpus of Ancient Greek philosophy that has not been translated into English or other modern European languages. The standard edition (*Commentaria in Aristotelem Graeca*, or *CAG*) was produced by Hermann Diels as general editor under the auspices of the Prussian Academy in Berlin. Arrangements have now been made to translate at least a large proportion of this corpus, along with some other Greek and Latin commentaries not included in the Berlin edition, and some closely related non-commentary works by the commentators.

The works are not just commentaries on Aristotle, although they are invaluable in that capacity too. One of the ways of doing philosophy between A.D. 200 and 600, when the most important items were produced, was by writing commentaries. The works therefore represent the thought of the Peripatetic and Neoplatonist schools, as well as expounding Aristotle. Furthermore, they embed fragments from all periods of Ancient Greek philosophical thought: this is how many of the Presocratic fragments were assembled, for example. Thus they provide a panorama of every period of Ancient Greek philosophy.

The philosophy of the period from A.D. 200 to 600 has not yet been intensively explored by philosophers in English-speaking countries, yet it is full of interest for physics, metaphysics, logic, psychology, ethics and religion. The contrast with the study of the Presocratics is striking. Initially the incomplete Presocratic fragments might well have seemed less promising, but their interest is now widely known, thanks to the philological and philosophical effort that has been concentrated upon them. The incomparably vaster corpus which preserved so many of those fragments offers at least as much interest, but is still relatively little known.

The commentaries represent a missing link in the history of philosophy: the Latin-speaking Middle Ages obtained their knowledge of Aristotle at least partly through the medium of the commentaries. Without an appreciation of this, mediaeval interpretations of Aristotle will not be understood. Again, the ancient commentaries are the unsuspected source of ideas which have been thought, wrongly, to originate in the later mediaeval

---

* Reprinted from the Editor's General Introduction to the series in Christian Wildberg, *Philoponus Against Aristotle on the Eternity of the World*, London and Ithaca N.Y., 1987.

period. It has been supposed, for example, that Bonaventure in the thirteenth century invented the ingenious arguments based on the concept of infinity which attempt to prove the Christian view that the universe had a beginning. In fact, Bonaventure is merely repeating arguments devised by the commentator Philoponus 700 years earlier and preserved in the meantime by the Arabs. Bonaventure even uses Philoponus' original examples. Again, the introduction of impetus theory into dynamics, which has been called a scientific revolution, has been held to be an independent invention of the Latin West, even if it was earlier discovered by the Arabs or their predecessors. But recent work has traced a plausible route by which it could have passed from Philoponus, via the Arabs, to the West.

The new availability of the commentaries in the sixteenth century, thanks to printing and to fresh Latin translations, helped to fuel the Renaissance break from Aristotelian science. For the commentators record not only Aristotle's theories, but also rival ones, while Philoponus as a Christian devises rival theories of his own and accordingly is mentioned in Galileo's early works more frequently than Plato.[1]

It is not only for their philosophy that the works are of interest. Historians will find information about the history of schools, their methods of teaching and writing and the practices of an oral tradition.[2] Linguists will find the indexes and translations an aid for studying the development of word meanings, almost wholly uncharted in Liddell and Scott's *Lexicon*, and for checking shifts in grammatical usage.

Given the wide range of interests to which the volumes will appeal, the aim is to produce readable translations, and to avoid so far as possible presupposing any knowledge of Greek. Footnotes will explain points of meaning, give cross-references to other works, and suggest alternative interpretations of the text where the translator does not have a clear preference. The introduction to each volume will include an explanation why the work was chosen for translation: none will be chosen simply because it is there. Two of the Greek texts are currently being re-edited –

---

[1] See Fritz Zimmermann, 'Philoponus' impetus theory in the Arabic tradition'; Charles Schmitt, 'Philoponus' commentary on Aristotle's *Physics* in the sixteenth century', and Richard Sorabji, 'John Philoponus', in Richard Sorabji (ed.), *Philoponus and the Rejection of Aristotelian Science* (London and Ithaca, N.Y. 1987).

[2] See e.g. Karl Praechter, 'Die griechischen Aristoteleskommentare', *Byzantinische Zeitschrift* 18 (1909), 516-38 (translated into English in R. Sorabji (ed.), *Aristotle Transformed: the ancient commentators and their influence* (London and Ithaca, N.Y. 1990)); M. Plezia, *de Commentariis Isagogicis* (Cracow 1947); M. Richard, 'Apo Phônês', *Byzantion* 20 (1950), 191-222; É. Evrard, *L'Ecole d'Olympiodore et la composition du commentaire à la physique de Jean Philopon*, Diss. (Liège 1957); L.G. Westerink, *Anonymous Prolegomena to Platonic Philosophy* (Amsterdam 1962) (new revised edition, translated into French, Collection Budé; part of the revised introduction, in English, is included in *Aristotle Transformed*); A.-J. Festugière, 'Modes de composition des commentaires de Proclus', *Museum Helveticum* 20 (1963), 77-100, repr. in his *Études* (1971), 551-74; P. Hadot, 'Les divisions des parties de la philosophie dans l'antiquité', *Museum Helveticum* 36 (1979), 201-23; I. Hadot, 'La division néoplatonicienne des écrits d'Aristote', in J. Wiesner (ed.), *Aristoteles Werk und Wirkung* (Paul Moraux gewidmet), vol. 2 (Berlin 1986); I. Hadot, 'Les introductions aux commentaires exégétiques chez les auteurs néoplatoniciens et les auteurs chrétiens', in M. Tardieu (ed.), *Les règles de l'interprétation* (Paris 1987), 99-119. These topics are treated, and a bibliography supplied, in *Aristotle Transformed*.

those of Simplicius *in Physica* and *in de Caelo* – and new readings will be exploited by translators as they become available. Each volume will also contain a list of proposed emendations to the standard text. Indexes will be of more uniform extent as between volumes than is the case with the Berlin edition, and there will be three of them: an English-Greek glossary, a Greek-English index, and a subject index.

The commentaries fall into three main groups. The first group is by authors in the Aristotelian tradition up to the fourth century A.D. This includes the earliest extant commentary, that by Aspasius in the first half of the second century A.D. on the *Nicomachean Ethics*. The anonymous commentary on Books 2, 3, 4 and 5 of the *Nicomachean Ethics*, in *CAG* vol. 20, is derived from Adrastus, a generation later.[3] The commentaries by Alexander of Aphrodisias (appointed to his chair between A.D. 198 and 209) represent the fullest flowering of the Aristotelian tradition. To his successors Alexander was The Commentator *par excellence*. To give but one example (not from a commentary) of his skill at defending and elaborating Aristotle's views, one might refer to his defence of Aristotle's claim that space is finite against the objection that an edge of space is conceptually problematic.[4] Themistius (*fl.* late 340s to 384 or 385) saw himself as the inventor of paraphrase, wrongly thinking that the job of commentary was completed.[5] In fact, the Neoplatonists were to introduce new dimensions into commentary. Themistius' own relation to the Neoplatonist as opposed to the Aristotelian tradition is a matter of controversy,[6] but it would be agreed that his commentaries show far less bias than the full-blown Neoplatonist ones. They are also far more informative than the designation 'paraphrase' might suggest, and it has been estimated that Philoponus' *Physics* commentary draws silently on Themistius six hundred times.[7] The pseudo-Alexandrian commentary on *Metaphysics* 6–14, of unknown authorship, has been placed by some in the same group of commentaries as being earlier than the fifth century.[8]

[3] Anthony Kenny, *The Aristotelian Ethics* (Oxford 1978), 37, n.3; Paul Moraux, *Der Aristotelismus bei den Griechen,* vol. 2 (Berlin 1984), 323-30.

[4] Alexander, *Quaestiones* 3.12, discussed in my *Matter, Space and Motion* (London and Ithaca, N.Y. 1988). For Alexander see R.W. Sharples, 'Alexander of Aphrodisias: scholasticism and innovation', in W. Haase (ed.), *Aufstieg und Niedergang der römischen Welt*, part 2 *Principat*, vol. 36.2, *Philosophie und Wissenschaften* (1987).

[5] Themistius *in An. Post.* 1,2-12. See H.J. Blumenthal, 'Photius on Themistius (Cod.74): did Themistius write commentaries on Aristotle?', *Hermes* 107 (1979), 168-82.

[6] For different views, see H.J. Blumenthal, 'Themistius, the last Peripatetic commentator on Aristotle?', in Glen W. Bowersock, Walter Burkert, Michael C.J. Putnam, *Arktouros*, Hellenic Studies Presented to Bernard M.W. Knox (Berlin and N.Y., 1979), 391-400; E.P. Mahoney, 'Themistius and the agent intellect in James of Viterbo and other thirteenth-century philosophers: (Saint Thomas Aquinas, Siger of Brabant and Henry Bate)', *Augustiniana* 23 (1973), 422-67, at 428-31; id., 'Neoplatonism, the Greek commentators and Renaissance Aristotelianism', in D.J. O'Meara (ed.), *Neoplatonism and Christian Thought* (Albany N.Y. 1982), 169-77 and 264-82, esp. n. 1, 264-6; Robert Todd, introduction to translation of Themistius *in DA 3.4-8*, in *Two Greek Aristotelian Commentators on the Intellect*, trans. Frederick M. Schroeder and Robert B. Todd (Toronto 1990).

[7] H. Vitelli, *CAG* 17, p. 992, s.v. Themistius.

[8] The similarities to Syrianus (died *c*.437) have suggested to some that it predates Syrianus (most recently Leonardo Tarán, review of Paul Moraux, *Der Aristotelismus,*

The Commentators

By far the largest group of extant commentaries is that of the Neoplatonists up to the sixth century A.D. Nearly all the major Neoplatonists, apart from Plotinus (the founder of Neoplatonism), wrote commentaries on Aristotle, although those of Iamblichus (c. 250 – c. 325) survive only in fragments, and those of three Athenians, Plutarchus (died 432), his pupil Proclus (410 – 485) and the Athenian Damascius (c. 462 – after 538), are lost.[9] As a result of these losses, most of the extant Neoplatonist commentaries come from the late fifth and the sixth centuries and a good proportion from Alexandria. There are commentaries by Plotinus' disciple and editor Porphyry (232 – 309), by Iamblichus' pupil Dexippus (c. 330), by Proclus' teacher Syrianus (died c. 437), by Proclus' pupil Ammonius (435/445 – 517/526), by Ammonius' three pupils Philoponus (c. 490 to 570s), Simplicius (wrote after 532, probably after 538) and Asclepius (sixth century), by Ammonius' next but one successor Olympiodorus (495/505 – after 565), by Elias (fl. 541?), by David (second half of the sixth century, or beginning of the seventh) and by Stephanus (took the chair in Constantinople c. 610). Further, a commentary on the *Nicomachean Ethics* has been ascribed to Heliodorus of Prusa, an unknown pre-fourteenth-century figure, and there is a commentary by Simplicius' colleague Priscian of Lydia on Aristotle's successor Theophrastus. Of these commentators some of the last were Christians (Philoponus, Elias, David and Stephanus), but they were Christians writing in the Neoplatonist tradition, as was also Boethius who produced a number of commentaries in Latin before his death in 525 or 526.

The third group comes from a much later period in Byzantium. The Berlin edition includes only three out of more than a dozen commentators described in Hunger's *Byzantinisches Handbuch*.[10] The two most important are Eustratius (1050/1060 – c. 1120), and Michael of Ephesus. It has been suggested that these two belong to a circle organised by the princess Anna Comnena in the twelfth century, and accordingly the completion of Michael's commentaries has been redated from 1040 to 1138.[11] His commentaries include areas where gaps had been left. Not all of these gap-fillers are extant, but we have commentaries on the neglected biological works, on the *Sophistici Elenchi*, and a small fragment of one on the *Politics*. The lost *Rhetoric* commentary had a few antecedents, but the *Rhetoric* too had been comparatively neglected. Another product of this

---

vol. 1, in *Gnomon* 46 (1981), 721-50 at 750), to others that it draws on him (most recently P. Thillet, in the Budé edition of Alexander *de Fato*, p. lvii). Praechter ascribed it to Michael of Ephesus (eleventh or twelfth century), in his review of *CAG* 22.2, in *Göttingische Gelehrte Anzeiger* 168 (1906), 861-907.

[9] The Iamblichus fragments are collected in Greek by Bent Dalsgaard Larsen, *Jamblique de Chalcis, Exégète et Philosophe* (Aarhus 1972), vol.2. Most are taken from Simplicius, and will accordingly be translated in due course. The evidence on Damascius' commentaries is given in L.G. Westerink, *The Greek Commentaries on Plato's Phaedo*, vol.2., Damascius (Amsterdam 1977), 11-12; on Proclus' in L.G. Westerink, *Anonymous Prolegomena to Platonic Philosophy* (Amsterdam 1962), xii, n.22; on Plutarchus' in H.M. Blumenthal, 'Neoplatonic elements in the de Anima commentaries', *Phronesis* 21 (1976), 75.

[10] Herbert Hunger, *Die hochsprachliche profane Literatur der Byzantiner*, vol.1 (= *Byzantinisches Handbuch*, part 5, vol.1) (Munich 1978), 25-41. See also B.N. Tatakis, *La Philosophie Byzantine* (Paris 1949).

[11] R. Browning, 'An unpublished funeral oration on Anna Comnena', *Proceedings of the Cambridge Philological Society* n.s. 8 (1962), 1-12, esp. 6-7.

period may have been the composite commentary on the *Nicomachean Ethics* (*CAG* 20) by various hands, including Eustratius and Michael, along with some earlier commentators, and an improvisation for Book 7. Whereas Michael follows Alexander and the conventional Aristotelian tradition, Eustratius' commentary introduces Platonist, Christian and anti-Islamic elements.[12]

The composite commentary was to be translated into Latin in the next century by Robert Grosseteste in England. But Latin translations of various logical commentaries were made from the Greek still earlier by James of Venice (*fl. c.* 1130), a contemporary of Michael of Ephesus, who may have known him in Constantinople. And later in that century other commentaries and works by commentators were being translated from Arabic versions by Gerard of Cremona (died 1187).[13] So the twelfth century resumed the transmission which had been interrupted at Boethius' death in the sixth century.

The Neoplatonist commentaries of the main group were initiated by Porphyry. His master Plotinus had discussed Aristotle, but in a very independent way, devoting three whole treatises (*Enneads* 6.1–3) to attacking Aristotle's classification of the things in the universe into categories. These categories took no account of Plato's world of Ideas, were inferior to Plato's classifications in the *Sophist* and could anyhow be collapsed, some of them into others. Porphyry replied that Aristotle's categories could apply perfectly well to the world of intelligibles and he took them as in general defensible.[14] He wrote two commentaries on the *Categories*, one lost, and an introduction to it, the *Isagôgê*, as well as commentaries, now lost, on a number of other Aristotelian works. This proved decisive in making Aristotle a necessary subject for Neoplatonist lectures and commentary. Proclus, who was an exceptionally quick student, is said to have taken two years over his Aristotle studies, which were called

[12] R. Browning, op. cit. H.D.P. Mercken, *The Greek Commentaries of the Nicomachean Ethics of Aristotle in the Latin Translation of Grosseteste, Corpus Latinum Commentariorum in Aristotelem Graecorum* VI 1 (Leiden 1973), ch.1, 'The compilation of Greek commentaries on Aristotle's Nicomachean Ethics'. Sten Ebbesen, 'Anonymi Aurelianensis I Commentarium in *Sophisticos Elenchos*', *Cahiers de l'Institut Moyen Age Grecque et Latin* 34 (1979), 'Boethius, Jacobus Veneticus, Michael Ephesius and "Alexander" ', pp. v-xiii; id., *Commentators and Commentaries on Aristotle's Sophistici Elenchi*, 3 parts, *Corpus Latinum Commentariorum in Aristotelem Graecorum*, vol. 7 (Leiden 1981); A. Preus, *Aristotle and Michael of Ephesus on the Movement and Progression of Animals* (Hildesheim 1981), introduction.

[13] For Grosseteste, see Mercken as in n. 12. For James of Venice, see Ebbesen as in n. 12, and L. Minio-Paluello, 'Jacobus Veneticus Grecus', *Traditio* 8 (1952), 265-304; id., 'Giacomo Veneto e l'Aristotelismo Latino', in Pertusi (ed.), *Venezia e l'Oriente fra tardo Medioevo e Rinascimento* (Florence 1966), 53-74, both reprinted in his *Opuscula* (1972). For Gerard of Cremona, see M. Steinschneider, *Die europäischen Übersetzungen aus dem arabischen bis Mitte des 17. Jahrhunderts* (repr. Graz 1956); E. Gilson, *History of Christian Philosophy in the Middle Ages* (London 1955), 235-6 and more generally 181-246. For the translators in general, see Bernard G. Dod, 'Aristoteles Latinus', in N. Kretzmann, A. Kenny, J. Pinborg (eds). *The Cambridge History of Latin Medieval Philosophy* (Cambridge 1982).

[14] See P. Hadot, 'L'harmonie des philosophies de Plotin et d'Aristote selon Porphyre dans le commentaire de Dexippe sur les Catégories', in *Plotino e il neoplatonismo in Oriente e in Occidente* (Rome 1974), 31-47; A.C. Lloyd, 'Neoplatonic logic and Aristotelian logic', *Phronesis* 1 (1955-6), 58-79 and 146-60.

The Commentators

the Lesser Mysteries, and which preceded the Greater Mysteries of Plato.[15] By the time of Ammonius, the commentaries reflect a teaching curriculum which begins with Porphyry's *Isagôgê* and Aristotle's *Categories*, and is explicitly said to have as its final goal a (mystical) ascent to the supreme Neoplatonist deity, the One.[16] The curriculum would have progressed from Aristotle to Plato, and would have culminated in Plato's *Timaeus* and *Parmenides*. The latter was read as being about the One, and both works were established in this place in the curriculum at least by the time of Iamblichus, if not earlier.[17]

Before Porphyry, it had been undecided how far a Platonist should accept Aristotle's scheme of categories. But now the proposition began to gain force that there was a harmony between Plato and Aristotle on most things.[18] Not for the only time in the history of philosophy, a perfectly crazy proposition proved philosophically fruitful. The views of Plato and of Aristotle had both to be transmuted into a new Neoplatonist philosophy in order to exhibit the supposed harmony. Iamblichus denied that Aristotle contradicted Plato on the theory of Ideas.[19] This was too much for Syrianus and his pupil Proclus. While accepting harmony in many areas,[20] they could see that there was disagreement on this issue and also on the issue of whether God was causally responsible for the existence of the ordered physical cosmos, which Aristotle denied. But even on these issues, Proclus' pupil Ammonius was to claim harmony, and, though the debate was not clear cut,[21] his claim was on the whole to prevail. Aristotle, he maintained, accepted Plato's Ideas,[22] at least in the form of principles (*logoi*) in the divine intellect, and these principles were in turn causally responsible for the beginningless existence of the physical universe. Ammonius wrote a whole book to show that

---

[15] Marinus, *Life of Proclus* ch.13, 157,41 (Boissonade).

[16] The introductions to the *Isagôgê* by Ammonius, Elias and David, and to the *Categories* by Ammonius, Simplicius, Philoponus, Olympiodorus and Elias are discussed by L.G. Westerink, *Anonymous Prolegomena* and I. Hadot, 'Les Introductions', see n. 2. above.

[17] Proclus *in Alcibiadem 1* p.11 (Creuzer); Westerink, *Anonymous Prolegomena*, ch. 26, 12f. For the Neoplatonist curriculum see Westerink, Festugière, P. Hadot and I. Hadot in n. 2.

[18] See e.g. P. Hadot (1974), as in n. 14 above; H.J. Blumenthal, 'Neoplatonic elements in the de Anima commentaries', *Phronesis* 21 (1976), 64-87; H.A. Davidson, 'The principle that a finite body can contain only finite power', in S. Stein and R. Loewe (eds), *Studies in Jewish Religious and Intellectual History presented to A. Altmann* (Alabama 1979), 75-92; Carlos Steel, 'Proclus et Aristote', Proceedings of the Congrès Proclus held in Paris 1985, J. Pépin and H.D. Saffrey (eds), *Proclus, lecteur et interprète des anciens* (Paris 1987), 213-25; Koenraad Verrycken, *God en Wereld in de Wijsbegeerte van Ioannes Philoponus*, Ph.D. Diss. (Louvain 1985).

[19] Iamblichus ap. Elian *in Cat.* 123,1-3.

[20] Syrianus *in Metaph.* 80,4-7; Proclus *in Tim.* 1.6,21-7,16.

[21] Asclepius sometimes accepts Syranius' interpretation (*in Metaph.* 433,9-436,6); which is, however, qualified, since Syrianus thinks Aristotle is really committed willy-nilly to much of Plato's view (*in Metaph.* 117,25-118,11; ap. Asclepium *in Metaph.* 433,16; 450,22); Philoponus repents of his early claim that Plato is not the target of Aristotle's attack, and accepts that Plato is rightly attacked for treating ideas as independent entities outside the divine Intellect (*in DA* 37,18-31; *in Phys.* 225,4-226,11; *contra Procl.* 26,24-32,13; *in An. Post.* 242,14-243,25).

[22] Asclepius *in Metaph* from the voice of (i.e. from the lectures of) Ammonius 69,17-21; 71,28; cf. Zacharias *Ammonius*, *Patrologia Graeca* vol. 85, col. 952 (Colonna).

Aristotle's God was thus an efficient cause, and though the book is lost, some of its principal arguments are preserved by Simplicius.[23] This tradition helped to make it possible for Aquinas to claim Aristotle's God as a Creator, albeit not in the sense of giving the universe a beginning, but in the sense of being causally responsible for its beginningless existence.[24] Thus what started as a desire to harmonise Aristotle with Plato finished by making Aristotle safe for Christianity. In Simplicius, who goes further than anyone,[25] it is a formally stated duty of the commentator to display the harmony of Plato and Aristotle in most things.[26] Philoponus, who with his independent mind had thought better of his earlier belief in harmony, is castigated by Simplicius for neglecting this duty.[27]

The idea of harmony was extended beyond Plato and Aristotle to Plato and the Presocratics. Plato's pupils Speusippus and Xenocrates saw Plato as being in the Pythagorean tradition.[28] From the third to first centuries B.C., pseudo-Pythagorean writings present Platonic and Aristotelian doctrines as if they were the ideas of Pythagoras and his pupils,[29] and these forgeries were later taken by the Neoplatonists as genuine. Plotinus saw the Presocratics as precursors of his own views,[30] but Iamblichus went far beyond him by writing ten volumes on Pythagorean philosophy.[31] Thereafter Proclus sought to unify the whole of Greek philosophy by presenting it as a continuous clarification of divine revelation,[32] and Simplicius argued for the same general unity in order to rebut Christian charges of contradictions in pagan philosophy.[33]

Later Neoplatonist commentaries tend to reflect their origin in a teaching curriculum:[34] from the time of Philoponus, the discussion is often divided up into lectures, which are subdivided into studies of doctrine and of text. A general account of Aristotle's philosophy is prefixed to the *Categories* commentaries and divided, according to a formula of Proclus,[35] into ten questions. It is here that commentators explain the eventual purpose of studying Aristotle (ascent to the One) and state (if they do) the requirement of displaying the harmony of Plato and Aristotle. After the ten-point introduction to Aristotle, the *Categories* is given a six-point introduction, whose antecedents go back earlier than Neoplatonism, and which requires

[23] Simplicius *in Phys.* 1361,11-1363,12. See H.A. Davidson; Carlos Steel; Koenraad Verrycken in n.18 above.

[24] See Richard Sorabji, *Matter, Space and Motion* (London and Ithaca N.Y. 1988), ch. 15.

[25] See e.g. H.J. Blumenthal in n. 18 above.

[26] Simplicius *in Cat.* 7,23-32.

[27] Simplicius *in Cael.* 84,11-14; 159,2-9. On Philoponus' *volte face* see n. 21 above.

[28] See e.g. Walter Burkert, *Weisheit und Wissenschaft* (Nürnberg 1962), translated as *Lore and Science in Ancient Pythagoreanism* (Cambridge Mass. 1972), 83-96.

[29] See Holger Thesleff, *An Introduction to the Pythagorean writings of the Hellenistic Period* (Åbo 1961); Thomas Alexander Szlezák, *Pseudo-Archytas über die Kategorien*, Peripatoi vol. 4 (Berlin and New York 1972).

[30] Plotinus e.g. 4.8.1; 5.1.8 (10-27); 5.1.9.

[31] See Dominic O'Meara, *Pythagoras Revived: Mathematics and Philosophy in late Antiquity* (Oxford 1989).

[32] See Christian Guérard, 'Parménide d'Elée selon les Néoplatoniciens', forthcoming.

[33] Simplicius *in Phys.* 28,32-29,5; 640,12-18. Such thinkers as Epicurus and the Sceptics, however, were not subject to harmonisation.

[34] See the literature in n. 2 above.   [35] ap. Elian *in Cat.* 107,24-6.

The Commentators

the commentator to find a unitary theme or scope (*skopos*) for the treatise. The arrangements for late commentaries on Plato are similar. Since the Plato commentaries form part of a single curriculum they should be studied alongside those on Aristotle. Here the situation is easier, not only because the extant corpus is very much smaller, but also because it has been comparatively well served by French and English translators.[36]

Given the theological motive of the curriculum and the pressure to harmonise Plato with Aristotle, it can be seen how these commentaries are a major source for Neoplatonist ideas. This in turn means that it is not safe to extract from them the fragments of the Presocratics, or of other authors, without making allowance for the Neoplatonist background against which the fragments were originally selected for discussion. For different reasons, analogous warnings apply to fragments preserved by the pre-Neoplatonist commentator Alexander.[37] It will be another advantage of the present translations that they will make it easier to check the distorting effect of a commentator's background.

Although the Neoplatonist commentators conflate the views of Aristotle with those of Neoplatonism, Philoponus alludes to a certain convention when he quotes Plutarchus expressing disapproval of Alexander for expounding his own philosophical doctrines in a commentary on Aristotle.[38] But this does not stop Philoponus from later inserting into his own commentaries on the *Physics* and *Meteorology* his arguments in favour of the Christian view of Creation. Of course, the commentators also wrote independent works of their own, in which their views are expressed independently of the exegesis of Aristotle. Some of these independent works will be included in the present series of translations.

The distorting Neoplatonist context does not prevent the commentaries from being incomparable guides to Aristotle. The introductions to Aristotle's philosophy insist that commentators must have a minutely detailed knowledge of the entire Aristotelian corpus, and this they certainly have. Commentators are also enjoined neither to accept nor reject what Aristotle says too readily, but to consider it in depth and without partiality. The commentaries draw one's attention to hundreds of phrases, sentences and ideas in Aristotle, which one could easily have passed over, however often one read him. The scholar who makes the right allowance for the distorting context will learn far more about Aristotle than he would be likely to on his own.

The relations of Neoplatonist commentators to the Christians were subtle. Porphyry wrote a treatise explicitly against the Christians in 15 books, but an order to burn it was issued in 448, and later Neoplatonists

---

[36] English: Calcidius *in Tim.* (parts by van Winden; den Boeft); Iamblichus fragments (Dillon); Proclus *in Tim.* (Thomas Taylor); Proclus *in Parm.* (Dillon); Proclus *in Parm.*, end of 7th book, from the Latin (Klibansky, Labowsky, Anscombe); Proclus *in Alcib. 1* (O'Neill); Olympiodorus and Damascius *in Phaedonem* (Westerink); Damascius *in Philebum* (Westerink); *Anonymous Prolegomena to Platonic Philosophy* (Westerink). See also extracts in Thomas Taylor, *The Works of Plato*, 5 vols. (1804). French: Proclus *in Tim.* and *in Rempublicam* (Festugière); *in Parm.* (Chaignet); Anon. *in Parm.* (P. Hadot); Damascius *in Parm.* (Chaignet).

[37] For Alexander's treatment of the Stoics, see Robert B. Todd, *Alexander of Aphrodisias on Stoic Physics* (Leiden 1976), 24-9.

[38] Philoponus *in DA* 21,20-3.

140 Appendix

were more circumspect. Among the last commentators in the main group, we have noted several Christians. Of these the most important were Boethius and Philoponus. It was Boethius' programme to transmit Greek learning to Latin-speakers. By the time of his premature death by execution, he had provided Latin translations of Aristotle's logical works, together with commentaries in Latin but in the Neoplatonist style on Porphyry's *Isagôgê* and on Aristotle's *Categories* and *de Interpretatione*, and interpretations of the *Prior* and *Posterior Analytics*, *Topics* and *Sophistici Elenchi*. The interruption of his work meant that knowledge of Aristotle among Latin-speakers was confined for many centuries to the logical works. Philoponus is important both for his proofs of the Creation and for his progressive replacement of Aristotelian science with rival theories, which were taken up at first by the Arabs and came fully into their own in the West only in the sixteenth century.

Recent work has rejected the idea that in Alexandria the Neoplatonists compromised with Christian monotheism by collapsing the distinction between their two highest deities, the One and the Intellect. Simplicius (who left Alexandria for Athens) and the Alexandrians Ammonius and Asclepius appear to have acknowledged their beliefs quite openly, as later did the Alexandrian Olympiodorus, despite the presence of Christian students in their classes.[39]

The teaching of Simplicius in Athens and that of the whole pagan Neoplatonist school there was stopped by the Christian Emperor Justinian in 529. This was the very year in which the Christian Philoponus in Alexandria issued his proofs of Creation against the earlier Athenian Neoplatonist Proclus. Archaeological evidence has been offered that, after their temporary stay in Ctesiphon (in present-day Iraq), the Athenian Neoplatonists did not return to their house in Athens, and further evidence has been offered that Simplicius went to Ḥarrān (Carrhae), in present-day Turkey near the Iraq border.[40] Wherever he went, his commentaries are a treasure house of information about the preceding thousand years of Greek philosophy, information which he painstakingly recorded after the closure in Athens, and which would otherwise have been lost. He had every reason to feel bitter about Christianity, and in fact he sees it and Philoponus, its representative, as irreverent. They deny the divinity of the heavens and prefer the physical relics of dead martyrs.[41] His own commentaries by

---

[39] For Simplicius, see I. Hadot, *Le Problème du Néoplatonisme Alexandrin: Hiéroclès et Simplicius* (Paris 1978); for Ammonius and Asclepius, Koenraad Verrycken, *God en Wereld in de Wijsbegeerte van Ioannes Philoponus*, Ph.D. Diss. (Louvain 1985); for Olympiodorus, L.G. Westerink, *Anonymous Prolegomena to Platonic Philosophy* (Amsterdam 1962).

[40] Alison Frantz, 'Pagan philosophers in Christian Athens', *Proceedings of the American Philosophical Society* 119 (1975), 29-38; M. Tardieu, 'Témoins orientaux du Premier Alcibiade à Ḥarrān et à Nag 'Hammādi', *Journal Asiatique* 274 (1986); id., 'Les calendriers en usage à Ḥarrān d'après les sources arabes et le commentaire de Simplicius à la *Physique* d'Aristote', in I. Hadot (ed.), *Simplicius, sa vie, son oeuvre, sa survie* (Berlin 1987), 40-57; id., *Coutumes nautiques mésopotamiennes chez Simplicius*, in preparation. The opposing view that Simplicius returned to Athens is most fully argued by Alan Cameron, 'The last days of the Academy at Athens', *Proceedings of the Cambridge Philological Society* 195, n.s. 15 (1969), 7-29.

[41] Simplicius *in Cael.* 26,4-7; 70,16-18; 90,1-18; 370,29-371,4. See on his whole attitude Philippe Hoffmann, 'Simplicius' polemics', in Richard Sorabji (ed.), *Philoponus and the Rejection of Aristotelian Science* (London and Ithaca, N.Y. 1987).

contrast culminate in devout prayers.

Two collections of articles by various hands have been published, to make the work of the commentators better known. The first is devoted to Philoponus;[42] the second is about the commentators in general, and goes into greater detail on some of the issues briefly mentioned here.[43]

---

[42] Richard Sorabji (ed.), *Philoponus and the Rejection of Aristotelian Science* (London and Ithaca, N.Y. 1987).

[43] Richard Sorabji (ed.), *Aristotle Transformed: the ancient commentators and their influence* (London and Ithaca, N.Y. 1990). The lists of texts and previous translations of the commentaries included in Wildberg, *Philoponus Against Aristotle on the Eternity of the World* (pp.12ff.) are not included here. The list of translations should be augmented by: F.L.S. Bridgman, Heliodorus (?) in *Ethica Nicomachea*, London 1807.

I am grateful for comments to Henry Blumenthal, Victor Caston, I. Hadot, Paul Mercken, Alain Segonds, Robert Sharples, Robert Todd, L.G. Westerink and Christian Wildberg.

English-Greek Glossary

accident: *sumbebêkos*
account: *logos*
action: *praxis*
activity: *energeia*
actuality: *energeia*
affected, to be: *paskhein*
affection: *pathos*
affective quality: *pathêtikê poiotês*
affirmation: *kataphasis*
agent: *poioun*
aim: *skopos*
analogy: *analogia*
animate: *empsukhos*
appear: *phainesthai*
argument: *epikheirêma*
arrange: *keisthai*

be, being: *einai*
being: *huparxis*
belong: *huparkhein*
body: *sôma*

capacity: *dunamis*
category: *katêgoria*
cause: *aition*
change (n.): *kinêsis, metabolê, tropê*
change (v.): *metaballein*
characterize: *kharakterizein*
coextensive, to be: *exisazein*
cognition: *katalêpsis*
colour: *khrôma*
combination: *sumplokê*
coming into being: *genesis*
commentator: *exêgoumenos*
common: *koinos*
commonality: *koinônia*
complete (v.): *sumplêroun*
complete (adj.): *teleios*
composite, compound: *sunthetos*
concept: *ennoia, noêma*
concomitant: *parakolouthêma*
concomitant, be a: *parakolouthein*

condition: *diathesis*
constitute: *sunistanai*
constitutive: *sustatikos*
continuous: *sunekhês*
contrariety: *enantiotês*
contrary: *enantios*
convert: *antistrephein*

define: *aphorizein, horizein*
definite: *hôrismenos*
definition: *horismos, horos*
demonstration: *apodeixis*
demonstrative: *apodeiktikos*
description: *hupographê*
destroyed, to be: *phtheiresthai*
destruction: *phthora*
determinate: *hôrismenos*
different: *heteros*
differentia: *diaphora*
discrete, to be: *diorizesthai*
discussion: *logos*
distinctive: *idios*
discriminate: *diakrinein*
divine: *theios*
division: *diairesis*

enmattered: *enulos*
entail: *suneispherein*
equal: *isos*
essence: *ousia*
essential: *ousiôdês*
examination: *diakrisis*
example: *paradeigma*
exist independently: *huphistanai*
existence, independent: *hupostasis*
explanation: *aitia*
expression: *phônê; phrasis*

false: *pseudos*
few: *oligos*
figure: *skhêma*
fitness: *epitêdeiotês*

English–Greek Glossary

form: *eidos*
formless: *aneideos*
formula: *logos*
future: *mellon*

genus: *genos*
good: *spoudaios*
grammar: *grammatikê*
growth: *auxêsis*

heterogeneous: *heterogenês*
heteronym, heteronymous: *heterônumos*
homonym, homonymous: *homônumos*
homonymy: *homônumia*
human being: *anthrôpos*

implication: *akolouthêsis*
inanimate: *apsukhos*
incapacity: *adunamia*
include: *periekhein*
indefinite, indeterminate: *aoristos*
independent existence: *hupostasis*
individual: *atomos*
inflection: *ptôsis*
instrument: *organon*
intelligible: *noêtos*
intermediate: *mesos*
intermediate, having an: *emmesos*

knowledge: *epistêmê*
known: *epistêtos*

language: *logos*
large: *megas*
limit: *peras*

magnitude: *megethos*
many: *polus*
matter: *hulê*
mean: *sêmainein*
meaning: *sêmainomenon*
middle: *mesos*
mind: *nous*

name: *onoma*
natural: *phusikos, phusiologikos*
naturally: *pephukôs*
nature: *phusis*
negation: *apophasis*
noun: *onoma*
number: *arithmos*

objection: *enstasis*

odd: *perittos*
one: *heis, hen*
opposite: *antikeimenos*
opposition: *antithesis*
order: *taxis*

paronym: *parônumos*
part: *meros, morion*
partake of, participate in: *metekhein*
particular: *merikos, tode ti*
perceptible: *aisthêtos*
perception: *aisthêsis*
perfect: *teleios*
place: *topos*
popular (writings): *exôterika*
position: *thesis*
predicate (v.): *katêgorein*
predicate (n.): *katêgoroumenon*
predication: *katêgoria*
premise: *protasis*
present: *nun*
primary: *prôtos*
principle: *arkhê*
prior: *proteros*
privation: *sterêsis*
proof: *apodeixis*
proper: *idios, oikeios*
proposition: *protasis*
proprium: *idion*

qualitative change: *alloiôsis*
quality: *poion, poiotês*
quantity: *poson*

real being: *hupostasis*
received opinions: *endoxa*
receptive: *dektikos*
reflection: *epinoia*
relation: *skhesis*
relative: *pros ti*
rule: *kanôn*

school (writings): *akroamatika*
science: *epistêmê*
scientific: *epistêmonikos*
self-subsistent: *authupostatos*
sensible: *aisthêtikos*
sentence: *logos*
shape: *morphê*
sight: *opsis*
signified: *sêmainomenon*
signify: *sêmainein*
similar: *homoios*
simple: *haplous*

144 English–Greek Glossary

simultaneous: *hama*
small: *mikros*
soul: *psukhê*
species: *eidos*
standing: *stasis*
state: *hexis*
statement: *logos*
strictly: *kuriôs*
subject, to be a: *hupokeisthai*
subject: *hupokeimenon*
subordinate: *hupallêlos*
substance: *ousia*
surface: *epiphaneia*
syllable: *sullabê*
syllogism: *sullogismos*
synonym, synonymous: *sunônumos*

teaching: *didaskalia*
theoretical: *theorêtikos*

thing: *pragma*
thought: *noêma*
time: *khronos*
transcendent: *exêirêmenos*
true: *alêthês*
truth: *alêtheia*

ultimate (genus): *genikôtaton*
understanding: *nous*
universal: *katholou*
unmediated: *amesos*

verb: *rhêma*
virtue: *aretê*

when: *pote*
where: *pou*
white: *leukos*
word: *lexis, phônê*

Greek-English Index

References are to the page and line numbers of the *CAG* edition, which appear in the margin of this translation.

abebaios, unreliable, 79,10
adiairetos, indivisible, 19,10.14
adiaphoros, indifferent, 32,8
adiarthrôtos, unresolved, 90,9
adikia, injustice, 102,19
adunamia, incapacity, 81,6.12; 82,5; 84,22.26.27; 85,9-26
agathos, good, 4,30; 6,13.14; 10,17; 13,5; 101,17
  agathotês, goodness, 6,15
agnoein
  ignore, 78,27
  be ignorant of, 81,28
  agnoia, ignorance, 70,3
  agnôstos: unintelligible, 43,21; unknown, 14,7.12; 93,11
agros, field, 19,13
aïdios, eternal, 45,18
aisthêsis
  perception, 33,25; 67,21; 74,23; 75,27-76,7; 77,1; 80,25
  sense, 82,7; 86,15-23
  aisthêtikos, sensible, capable of perceiving, 15,25; 38,21; 48,5.6; 76,6
  aisthêtos: that which is perceived, 67,21; 77,1.2; perceptible, capable of being perceived, 28,26; 41,10; 45,17; 47,2.3; 60,2; 74,23.24; 76,1.3.6.7
aitia, explanation, 7,22; 66,6
  aition, cause, 21,21ff; 67,23; 76,15; 103,20; 104,2ff; 105,1
  aitiatos, caused, 67,23; 76,15
  aitiatikê, accusative case, 68,7.11
akairos, inappropriate, 47,11
akatalêpsia, total ignorance, 2,11ff
akation, rowboat, 72,2
akhlus, fog, 15,7
akhôristos, inseparable, 28,9

akhroia, pallor, 87,18
akolouthein, follow from, 50,4; 71,13.15
  akolouthêsis, implication, 103,9-20; 104,21
  akolouthos: feature, 23,7; 23,9; natural sequence, 5,31; 24,22; consistent, in accordance with, 32,24; corollary, 78,18
akouein, understand, 57,21
akris, insect, 105,5
akroasthai, listen to, 1,9; 4,26; 6,21; 65,26
  akroamatikos, esoteric, 4,19.26.28; 6,27
  akroatês, reader, 66,11
akros, extreme, 10,13ff; 96,2ff
alêthês, true, 4,29; 5,1ff; 8,17; 10,17; 10,19; 13,5; 34,14; 64,17; 78,21.23; 92,22ff; 100,16-20; 100,23-101,7
  alêtheia, truth, 5,20; 6,28; 8,5.18; 14,18; 34,21; 50,2.20; 52,22; 53,11.13.20; 60,15; 80,8ff; 88,10
  alêtheuein, speak truly, 9,13.15; 34,15ff; 35,4; 52,19; 66,28; 67,6
  alêthinos, genuine, 21,5
alloioun, change qualitatively, 92,20; 105,24-106,3
  alloiôsis, qualitative change, 83,3-21; 105,15-23
allos, other, 21,15; 22,16; 27,27; 65,29; 91,28
allotriôs, improperly, 43,21
allotrioun, be different, 16,25
alogos, irrational, 31,25; 32,3; 42,2ff
ambluôttein, be dim-sighted, 15,7
amerês, indivisible, 6,12
  ameristos, indivisible, 91,25

145

amesos, unmediated, having
    nothing intermediate, 95,12ff;
    98,16; 99,7.10
amoibê, compensation, 78,24
amphibolos, doubtful, 97,21
amudros, faint, vague, 79,10; 82,16
anabasis, ascent, 16,27
anagein, subsume, 33,20.23ff; 69,25ff
anairein, destroy, 41,3.8; 75,22; 94,9ff
    anairesis, destruction, 96,2ff
anakamptein, to reverse, 59,17
    anakampsis, converse, 68,14
anakeisthai, to be reclining, 69,8;
    93,2
anakhôrêsis, withdrawal, 78,22
anaklinein, to be lying, 69,5.9
    anaklisis, lying, 68,21.24; 69,4
analogein, to be analogous, 26,32
    analogia: analogy, 22,5; 31,30;
        41,23; 42,8.10; 43,24; variation,
        23,23
    analogos, analogous, 26,31
anamnêsis, memory, 37,14
anapalin, conversely, 15,21; 68,16;
    76,6
anaphainein, be evident or obvious,
    1,7; 13,7
anapherein, classify, 91,11ff
anatrepein
    overturn, 50,5
    refute, 53,2
aneideos, formless, 54,5
anêkoos, untutored, 6,3
anepaisthêtos, imperceptible, 28,26ff
anepitêdeiotês, unfitness, 81,11.13
angeion, container, 29,8ff
aniatos, incurable, 82,15
anisos, unequal, 65,22; 71,13.16; 72,3
anô, up, 15,4; 64,24; 65,2; 93,4
anoêtos, unthinkable, 37,5
anomoios, dissimilar, 75,16; 91,1
anthrôpos, human being, 9,14; 15,16;
    19,19; 21,6; 27,13; 40,11; 48,6
antianeira, a woman with the
    strength of a man, 71,2
antidiastellein, to be opposed, 18,21;
    19,2ff; 20,27; 84,11
    antidiastolê, opposition, 37,6
antikeisthai, to be opposed, 16,11;
    16,14; 33,16; 63,17; 93,14-94,9;
    97,14; 101,12-21; 104,20
    antikeimenos, opposite, 16,10.16.17;
        26,18; 33,18; 34,7; 85,10; 93,7-18;
        94,13; 95,3-7; 96,8; 97,19;
        101,12.16; 105,19
antikheir, thumb, 71,4
antikrus, outright, 14,21
antilêpsis, perception, 86,15ff
antiparastasis, counter-objection,
    53.1.3.5.20; 62,4; 63,11; 101,6
antistrephein
    convert, 27,12ff; 42,18; 44,12ff;
        70,24; 71,5; 71,12-73,8; 97,24;
        98,4;101,18; 103,9ff.20
    reciprocate, 104.2.4.20
antistrophê
    conversion, 70,25; 71,1; 72,17;
        73,8-13
    correlative, 68,12
antitheos, godlike, 71,2
antithesis, opposition, 94,5-95,9;
    96,6.7; 98,7.9; 99,5.7.10; 100,14
antônumia, pronoun, 34,21
anupostatos, meaningless, 25,8
aoristos
    indefinite, 12,4; 55,11; 62,5ff
    indeterminate, 63,8; 78,31; 91,17
apagôgê, reduction, 63,27
apangelia, narrative, 1,9; 4,11; 6,25;
    8,5
apareskein, disapprove, 36,15.18
aparithmein, include, 91,4
aparithmêsis, inventory, 25,4
apatheia, freedom from emotion, 3,19
apeikos, unlikely, 79,13
apeirodunamos, of infinite potentia-
    lity, 6,12
apeiros, infinite, 12,2
aperilêptos, uncircumscribed, 6,12
aperioristos, infinite, 6,12
aperittos, not overly refined, 6,28
aphairein, take away, 73,14ff
aphanizein, make disappear, 59,4
aphorizein, define, 33,21; 46,9; 49,9;
    69,25
    aphôrismenôs, definitely, 99,25.27,
        100,1
aphuktos, exhaustive, 26,5
apodeiknunai, prove, 3,5; 50,3; 57,4;
    79,16; 85,11
    apodeiktikos, demonstrative (argu-
        ment), 2,13; 4,25; 5,8.17; 13,10.17
    apodeixis: demonstration, 6,3;
        10,22ff; exposition, 4,7; proof,
        4,25; 5,4.9; 57,13; 78,19.28
apodidonai, set out, 21,3; 43,21
    apodosis, setting out (of a defi-
        nition), 43,18

Greek–English Index

apodokimazein, reject, 65,16; 90,27ff
apographein, register, compile, 4,5.8
apokatastasis, return, 60,26; 70,26
apokathistanai, restore, 71,1; 100,10
apokrinein, to answer, 42,1.3; 70,4
apolauein, partake, 19,12
apologeisthai, defend, 80,13
  apologia, defence, 77,23
apoluein, make independent, 63,16; 76,12
aponemein, assign, 78,24
apophainein, give an opinion, 79,26
apophasis, negation, 25,18.21; 26,4.9; 34,12ff; 34,26ff; 35,1-5; 36,23ff; 85,18.19; 93,16.17.19; 94,15.19.23.29; 97,11.12.15; 98,8; 100,14.17.21; 101,2.11-13
  apophatikos, negative, 52,4ff
aporein, raise puzzles, 80,1.3ff
  aporētikos, aporetic, 6,28
  aporia, puzzle, 80,6ff
  aporos, puzzling, 80,4
aporroê, effluence, 2,24
aporroia, effluence, 28,28
apostasis, distance, 74,14.17
apoteinein, expose by slicing, 58,4
apotelesma, finished product, 35,25
apôthein, reject, 48,13
apous, footless, 31,26.28; 32,5
apsukhos, inanimate, 31,17; 81,24; 83,29; 88,4; 103,8
aptaistos, infallible, 79,11
araiôsis, rarefaction, 88,16
aretê, virtue, 23,13; 40,15ff; 70,3-6; 78,25; 81,31; 82,10; 83,18; 89,2; 102,19ff
  aretaios, virtued, 40,16; 89,2.12
argos, idle, 17,21.23; 88,21
aristeros, left, 59,19; 66,17-67,8; 67,18; 67,25ff; 69,31; 93,4; 93,22; 94,18; 95,4; 98,5
arithmos, number, 7,17; 12,4; 24,25; 25,1ff; 30,4.15.22; 49,15; 51,5; 54,13.17; 55,3ff; 57,3ff; 58,8; 59,21; 60,2ff; 62,10.25; 95,21; 98,18; 99,15
  arithmêtos, counted, 59,22ff
arkhaios, ancient, 88,21
arkhê, principle, 5,7.16.26; 6,11ff; 34,1
arkhein, to rule, 67,20; 103,19
arnêtikos, negative, 34,26; 35,1
arthron

article, 11,16ff
  joint, 8,8
artios, even, 95,12.21; 98,14ff; 99,15
asaphês, obscure, 7,7
  asapheia, obscurity, 1,10; 7,11; 25,14
asêmos, meaningless, 9,21
askêsis, ornamentation, 4,11
asômatos, incorporeal, 6,12; 54,5
astrôos, constellation, 38,13
asumplokos, without combination, 25,4
athanatos, immortal, 31,24; 32,4; 78,21ff
atmos, smoke, 29,2
atomos, individual, 13,15; 29,21; 30,4-17; 43,5-8; 45,21; 46,1.3; 49,2; 50,18
atreptos, unchanged, 83,34
authupostatos, self-subsistent, 30,8; 33,12; 35,15
autoagathotês, goodness itself, 6,12
autoprosôpos, in propria persona, 4,16.18
autos, self, the same, 51,6; 62,20ff; 63,22; 67,8ff; 76,11
auxanein, auxein, grow, increase, 28,21; 71,25-72,9; 105,24-106,3
  auxêsis, growth, 28,23.27; 83,8.14; 105,15ff
  auxêtikos dunamis, faculty of growth, 28,22
axiôma
  rank, 84,15
  worth, 103,19
  axiômatikos, axiomatic, 4,19

barus, heavy, 55,9
basanizein, examine, 8,17
basanos, testing, 80,1
bathos, deep, 43,4; 82,29.30
bebêlos, impure, 7,9
brakhulogia, brevity, 16,17

daktulos, digit, 10,2; 71,3.4
deilia, cowardice, 101,21
dein, need, 17,19; 25,19; 35,1; 40,19.26; 48,17
deixis, pointing out, 48,15.16; 49,3
dekas, ten, 12,4; 24,26
  dekaetês, ten years, 60,28
  dekapêkhus, ten cubits, 63,5
dektikos, receptive, able to take on, 51,9ff; 64,6.13; 73,14; 96,13ff; 98,15.19

dêlêtêrios, noxious, 5,19
dêmiourgos, inventor, 81,27
dermopteros, having membranous wings, 71,22
desmoun, bind, 76,12.17
deuteros
   second, 11,15; 36,3-19; 38,6-40,2; 41,19; 43,8; 51,14; 54,6.13.15; 77,7; 78,6
   secondary, 36,6.7
dexios, right, 59,18; 66,17-67,8; 67,18.25.26; 68,2.3; 69,31; 93,4.22; 94,18.24; 95,4; 98,5
diagnôsis, diagnosis, 82,17
diagônios, diagonal, 25,9
diairein, divide, 38,1.3; 98,10
   diairesis, division, 1,5; 3,21ff; 8,6; 32,20; 37,22ff; 58,1; 91,21; 93,18
   diairetos, divisibly, 19,13
diakonein, serve, 15,9
diakrinein, discriminate, 5,3; 10,21; 13,5
   diakrisis: disputation, 2,9; discrimination, 4,29.30; 10,18
   diakritikos: able to distinguish, 2,4; penetrative, 40,14
dialambanein, treat, 11,18; 22,13
dialogikos
   in the form of a dialogue, 4,15
   dialogue, 4,18ff; 7,1
diametros, diagonal, 105,26; 106,5
dianoia
   intention, 21,19
   thought, 8,14
diaphônein, disagree, 9,12
diaphora, differentia, 15,13.22; 21,15; 22,22-4,11; 23,9.28; 26,32; 31,15-32,12; 44,10.17; 45,8; 45,9-46,11; 46,22.28.29; 47,2.7.8.20; 67,25; 83,26; 99,25
diaphorein, dissipate, 28,18
diaphorêsis
   evaporation, 28,26
   effluence, 29,3
diaporein, raise difficulties, 80,2
diaporthmeuein, convey, 15,9
diarthroun, articulate, 14,13; 32,22
   diarthrôsis, articulation, 93,11
diaskedannunai, disperse, 78,22
diastasis, dimension, 54,5; 58,7
   diastatos, dimensional, 54,6.8.14
diathesis, condition, 68,17; 81,6.9; 82,10; 84,8-11.24.28; 91,7
   diathetos, conditioned, 68,18

didaskalia
   teaching, 7,7; 8,6; 67,11
   lesson, 31,14-15
diêgêsis, narrative, 103,19
diexerkhesthai, go through in detail, 60,16
diïskhurizesthai, assert confidently, 80,12
diïstanai, set apart, 64,24; 88,12
dikaiosunê, justice, 90,3; 102,17.18
diôkein, put to flight, 7,14
diorizesthai, be discrete, 31,17; 54,16ff; 56,8; 57,4.8.9.11; 58,28; 59,2; 62,9.25
dipêkhus
   two-footed, 49,15; 50,5
   two cubits, 61,1.4; 62,5; 63,5
diplasios, double, 79,4.5
dogma, doctrine, 2,14
doidux, pestle, 31,27
dokein, seem, 35,4ff
dokêsis, opinion, 52,17
dotikê, dative, 23,24; 68,6.11.17
doulos, slave, 71,6; 73,4ff.19; 74,2ff
doxazein, to judge, 52,20.21
   doxa, opinion, 52,19-53,24
dramatikos, dramatic, 4,15
dromeus, runner, 84,27
   dromikos, skilled runner, 84,22ff; 89,8
duas, dyad, 24,27
dunamis
   capacity, 51,12; 81,6.11ff; 82,5; 84,21ff; 84,25.27; 85,6-26; 89,6
   faculty, 28,22
   potentiality, 55,13; 76,23-30
   power, 55,4.8
   strength, 71,3
   dunamei, virtually, 34,20; 35,6
dusapoblêtos, hard to lose, 82,8.9.19.26.30.32; 86,6
dusôdia, stench, 28,32ff

eidikos, specific
   eidikôtaton eidos, infima species, 43,2; 84,17
eidopoios, specific, 31,15.29
eidos
   form, 1,9; 6,25; 7,3; 8,4; 21,10.13; 27,1; 27,30-28,3; 29,15; 34,3; 35,22; 36,7; 86,18.22; 105,20
   kind, 2,2; 31,25; 68,21-69,11; 83,15
   species, 13,13.14; 15,24; 26,34; 29,12-18.21.23; 30,13; 38,1-4;

Greek–English Index

39,2-12.16; 41,7.9.10.20ff;
42,2-11; 42,7-43,5; 43,6.7; 43,16-
44,2; 45,11; 45,21-46,2; 49,4;
50,18.19; 52,14; 66,7; 81,5-82,31;
83,8; 84,13.17.18.21.24; 86,2.3;
87,22.23; 88,19; 91,11-27;
92,15-20; 93,1.3.4
eikê, at random, 79,25
einai
  to be, being, 9,26.7; 10,1.12; 16,19;
    21,13; 25,5ff; 26,24; 35,16;
    36,15ff; 40,23.24; 41,17; 60,11;
    77,29
  exist, existence, 56,5; 59,12;
    103,9.11.20
eisagomenos, beginner, 36,11; 53,6;
  55,12
ekhein, have, 13,1; 33,17-20; 92,12;
  93,5
ekmisthoun, sell, 8,15
ekstasis, fit, 87,15.19
ektithesthai
  explain, 75,8
  set out, 75,6; 78,14.18
elatê, silver fir, 17,25
elatês, charioteer, 17,25
elattoun, decrease, 72,4.5.10
elenktikos, contentious, 2,3
êlithios, foolish, 78,26
ellattôn, lesser, 71,13-72,8; 74,17
elleipein, leave out, 27,11
elpis, hope, 21,28
emballein, include, 47,11
emmesos, intermediate, 95,12ff;
  99,19ff
emphainein, make apparent, 49,6.7
emphilosophos, philosophical, 79,25
empoiein, affect, 81,17; 82,7ff; 86,24
emprosthen, in front, 93,4
empsukhos, animate, 15,25; 31,17.24;
  48,5.6; 81,25; 88,4; 103,7
en, in, 26,32ff; 29,5ff
enallagê, inflection, 17,14; 18,1; 83,7
enallattein, to change, 17,21
enantios, contrary, 49,12ff; 49,15-18;
  49,20-50,12; 51,10ff; 52,13.17;
  53,8-24; 58,9; 62,3-18; 63,12-
  64,20; 63,15ff; 63,19ff; 64,25ff;
  65,3.5.6.10.16; 69,27-70,6; 74,17;
  85,12; 89,17.19; 93,13.14.16;
  94,1.9.18; 95,3; 95,10.12.27;
  97,18; 98,9; 99,5.13.19; 101,4.14;
  102,4.7.12
  enantiôsis, contrariety, 94,20

enantiotês, contrariety, 50,10ff;
  64,23; 65,14; 69,23ff; 70,18ff;
  89,16.25; 90,2
enargeia, manifest facts, 14,21
enargês, self-evident, 57,3
endeia, deficiency, 101,20
endiathetos logos, inner language,
  57,23
endidonai, grant, 53,4
endoxos, received opinion, 4,25
energeia
  action, 11,13
  activity, 3,14.15; 32,27; 69,20
  actuality, 55,11.13; 58,1; 76,27ff;
    82,3.5; 84,24-85,2; 96,24
  behaviour, 22,7
energein, operate, 92,17
enginesthai, generate, 81,16ff
engutês, proximity, 41,22
eniautos, year, 60,26
enistanai, to object, 26,15
enestôs khronos, the present time,
  93,3
enkômion, praise, 40,23
ennoein, understand, 50,15
  ennoêmatikos, notional entity, 9,9
  ennoia, concept, 9,11.23; 17,6;
    32,21; 33,9; 80,24.25.27.28
enstasis, objection, 53,1ff; 101,4.6
entos, in, within, 1,3; 2,6; 6,2
enudros, aquatic, 32,4; 105,1.2
enulos, enmattered, 37,18; 66,1.2
enuparkhein, inhere, 27,30
epagein, add, 50,13
epanapauesthai, be content, 88,21
epanô, above, 50,16
epanthein, be evident, 8,5
epeiserkhesthai, come, 49,10
ephistanai, notice, figure out, 36,14;
  92,16
epiballein, make an effort, 46,17
epibolê
  application, 78,12
  elaboration, 11,15
epigraphein, entitle, 8,3; 13,12.19;
  14,20; 66,14.18
  epigraphê, title, 7,22; 80,18; 81,2
epidiairein, divide, 54,18; 58,28
  epidiairesis, division, 59,2
epidosis, progress, 100,12
epikheirêma
  proof, 63,2.27
  argument, 41,20; 42,10; 43,24
  epikheirêsis, argument, 43,17

epiklêsis, name, 86,25
epiktêtos, acquired, 86,6.8.21
epilanthanesthai, forget, 37,19
epiluein, solve, 28,12; 46,22.25; 52,16; 91,8
  epilusis, solution, 91,10.28
epinoein, think of, 37,5; 74,2
epinoia
  conception, 99,1
  reflection, 75,1.3
  en psilêi epinoiai, in bare thought, 9,26
epipedon, superficies, 58,4.5
epiphaneia, surface, 54,17ff; 55,2-7; 58,4ff.18.20; 60,19-61,3; 82,29; 83,24-84,1
epipolaios, superficial, 4,23
epipolês, surface, 82,23.25
epiprosthen, in preference to, 8,18
episkeptesthai, examine, 33,10
epistêmê
  knowledge, 16,18; 22,4.5; 25,11; 27,14.15; 31,20; 67,22; 68,18.19; 69,18; 70,3; 73,14; 74,12.21ff; 76,18ff; 79,10; 81,30; 82,10; 83,17; 91,11.12.16ff
  science, 12,2; 23,2.10; 89,7
  epistêmôn: scientist, 60,14; knowledgeable, 91,15; knower, 67,22.23
  epistêmonikos, scientific, 5,9
  epistêtos, known, 68,19; 74,12.21ff; 75,23ff; 76,18ff
epistolê, letter, 3,24; 7,4
  epistolimaios, epistolary, 7,5
episumbainein, supervene on, 87,5
epitêdeiotês
  fitness, 51,10; 81,11.12; 82,2.3ff; 84,25; 89,5
  capacity, 96,16
  epitêdeia, aptitude, 84,22
epitêdeuein, invent, 75,2
epiteinein, increase, heighten, 51,2; 64,11
epitekhnêsis, artifice, 88,14
erastês, lover, 4,27
ereuthos, redness, blushing, 81,23; 82,21.26
  ereuthrian di' aidô, turn red with shame, 81,23; 82,21.34; 86,9
ergon, task, 60,14
erô, I will say, I am erotically affected (example of an homonymous expression), 18,19

erôtikos, erotic, 18,19
eruthros, ruddy
  ek genetês eruthros, ruddy from birth, 82,34
  ek phuseôs eruthros, naturally ruddy, 83,1
êthikos, ethical, 5,5
  êthikê, ethics, 6,1.5.18
  êthos, character, 6,1.5.23
euapoblêtos, easy to lose, 82,8.10.19.30.31; 86,8; 87,9
eukherês, easy, 106,6
euôdia, fragrance, 28,9ff
euphuês, clever, 46,17
eutaktos, well-ordered, 44,7
euthus, straight, 88,7
  eutheia, straight line, 75,16
  euthugrammos, rectilinear, 75,11
  euthutês, straightness, 88,6.8
euzôia, living well, 78,25
exêgeisthai
  exêgoumenos, commentator, 1,12; 8,11ff
  exêgêsis, interpretation, 7,16
exêirêsthai, be separated from, transcend, 37,8.10.12.17.18
exetasis, review, 43,4
exisazein, to be coextensive, 71,24
exisoun, equalize, 72,3.5
exôterikos, popular, 4,18-22

geitniazein, border on, 46,13
genesis
  birth, 15,6
  coming into being, 34,21; 45,18.20.22; 83,8.12; 105,12ff
  origin, 24,27
  genetê, birth, 82,34; 86,4; 87,15
genikê, genitive, 23,24; 68,5.11.15
genos, genus, 9,8.10; 13,13.14; 15,13.24; 21,24; 25,4; 26,32.34; 27,3; 29,12-18.20.23; 30,14ff; 31,4-12.18.22; 32,11ff; 39,2-12.16; 41,9.10.20ff; 42,14-43,5; 43,16-44,2; 44,10; 45,21; 46,1ff; 48,2-9; 49,5; 50,19; 52,14; 65,1-6; 69,6.8; 84,18; 85,13; 86,2; 87,22; 91,10-26; 102,16-20; 105,3
  genikôtatos, ultimate, highest, 13,16ff; 20,16; 44,8ff; 84,16
geômetrein, to measure, 85,21-5
  geômetrês, geometer, 58,4; 75,11; 81,8
  geômetria, geometry, 91,13.16ff

Greek–English Index   151

geômetrikos, concerning geometry, 81,8.9
ginesthai, come into being, 59,12
ginôskein, know, 2,17ff
glukutês, sweetness, 86,27
gnathos, jaw, 2,16
gnêsios, genuine, 8,2; 13,25.27; 14,1
gnômôn
  gnomon, 105,25.26; 106,4
  rule, 10,21
gnôrizein, make known, 96,4
  gnôrimos, known, 33,25; 43,20
  gnôsis, awareness, 79,10
gorgeuesthai, hurry, 22,8
grammatikê
  literary, 22,4.5
  grammar, 22,23ff; 23,1; 37,15
grammatikos, grammarian, 22,23ff; 23,1.14.24
grammê, line, 54,17; 55,2.6; 57,26ff; 58,7; 63,4; 88,7.8
graphein, draw, 21,6
gumnazein, work out, 75,27

haima, blood, 36,8; 82,25
hama, simultaneous, 3,2; 14,16; 24,18; 59,11; 64,7.12; 73,23-74,11.28; 75,3; 76,6.17.21ff; 102,10; 104,9; 104,13-105,5
haplous, simple, single, 5,11ff; 11,2.8.19; 12,1; 13,7.9; 14,22ff; 15,14; 16,20.22; 26,30; 30,8; 32,26; 33,1.3; 34,3ff; 35,18-36,1; 45,19-46,8; 66,8ff; 78,31
hêdonê, pleasure, 3,17
heis, hen, one, 21,22; 30,12; 50,5; 51,5.6
  henikos, singular, 49,6; 66,15.19
  henotês, unity, 48,18
  henoun, unite, 65,5
hektikos, consumptive, 81,35
hektos, possessor, 68,16
hêlios, sun, 19,7
hêmeis, we, 59,17; 63,7; 80,5.6
hêpar, liver, 66,25.26
heterogenês, heterogeneous, 31,15ff; 88,11.13
heterônumos, heteronym, 15,26; 16,14.24.25
  heterônumia, heteronymy, 67,17
heteros, different, 16,24.25; 31,18.25
  heterotês, difference, 23,17.24
heurêma, discovery, 14,1
heuresis, discovery, 6,28

hexis
  possession, 34,6
  state, 68,15.16; 81,6-82,10; 83,5-17; 84,8-11.24.28; 89,7; 91,6.7; 93,16ff; 94,2-29; 96,7-14; 97,4-19; 98,10; 99,7-100,24; 102,20.21
hieros, temple, 7,8
hippikê, horsemanship, 35,25.26
histanai, stand, 69,4.8; 93,2
hode, this, 48,15ff; 49,1
hoios, of what sort, 18,3; 24,27
holos, whole, 77,9ff
  holoskherês, general, 24,24
homoios, similar, 31,28; 67,17; 70,17; 74,25; 78,11; 91,1
  homoiotês, similarity, 22,2.9
homologein, acknowledge, 10,6; 73,3; 78,12; 90,7
homônumos, homonym, 13,22; 15,29; 16,8-17,6.8.16; 17,19-18,4; 18,6.7.12.20-4; 19,18; 20,1-7; 21,16-24; 22,12-24,9; 38,2-15
  homônumia, homonymy, 18,18.25; 20,10.17.23; 38,16; 67,17
homozugos, being yoked together, 19,2
hoplizein, to arm, 93,6
hopôsoun, in whatever way, 68,6
horasis, vision, 92,22
  horatos, visible, 92,22
horismos, definition, 15,23-17,7.11; 19,19-20,3; 20,14-21; 21,4-14; 22,18.19; 26,30.31; 27,9-28,11; 37,19; 38,16-19; 40,10-16; 43,18; 44,7-12; 44,29-45,3.14; 64,25; 67,12-30; 77,4-23; 78,14; 80,10-21; 90,19.21; 92,14.16
  hôrismenos, definite, determinate, 62,5; 63,6.7; 78,30; 79,18-21
  horistos, defined, 27,13; 44,12
  horizein, define, determine, 62,5; 63,6.7; 78,30; 91,18
horman, set in motion, urge on
  ho hormôn, charioteer, 17,25
horos
  boundary, 56,9.10; 57,4-58,25
  definition, 9,16; 18,24; 27,13; 78,18; 92,13
  term, 18,13
hôsanei, as if, 15,23
hosos
  hosa toiauta, things like that, 16,3; 66,23
hugiainein, to be healthy, 85,8ff

hugeia, health, 82,11ff
hugieinos, healthy, 85,27
hulê, matter, 8,4.5; 21,10-12; 27,1.30-28,1; 29,15; 34,2; 35,21; 36,7; 37,18.19; 54,5; 79,7.14
hupallêlos
    subaltern, 25,8
    subordinate, 13,15; 31,22ff; 32,11ff; 84,18
huparkhein
    belong, 27,4.6.28; 28,18; 44,20; 47,1; 50,6; 51,15.17; 52,2.3.6.8; 65,11; 67,14; 70,17; 89,16; 90,1-3; 91,25; 98,13.16.24; 99,8.27; 100,7; 102,10; 104,10
    be a characteristic of, 47,1
    be, 6,4; 21,1
    exist, 101,9
huparxis
    belonging, 26,11; 42,12
    being, 6,16; 20,28; 52,10
huperairein, overshoot, 27,10
huperballein, exceed, 27,10
    huperbolê, excess, 101,20
hupertithenai, set out above, 98,9
huphainein, compose, 4,11
huphesis, decrease, 50,12
huphistanai, exist independently, 9,27-10,1; 21,2; 25,19; 33,13; 34,1; 35,17; 41,1.4; 59,11; 63,24; 102,8
hupoballein, propose, 60,14
hupodedesthai, have shoes on, 93,5
hupoduein
    creep in, 5,1
    masquerade, 10,19
hupographê, description, 20,16
hupokeisthai
    assume, 79,17
    be a subject, 11,3; 13,14-16; 26,12; 42,12-16; 43,25-44,2
    hupokeimenon, subject, 9,6; 13,18; 16,27.29; 25,16-26,16.22; 26,25ff; 27,1-29,17.25; 29,26-30,23; 31,3.8.11; 32,15; 36,16.18.19.20; 37,3-9; 40,9.11.16; 41,1.5; 44,16.24.27-30; 45,1; 46,17.27.28; 47,7.10; 48,1.4.9.16-49,2; 51,6; 54,6; 56,3; 58,8; 65,7; 75,23; 78,10; 81,18; 82,29; 86,18; 91,22.23; 95,14.17; 96,14; 98,24; 99,8-26; 100,6; 102,8-14
hupolêpsis, conjecture, 79,10
hupomenein, last, be permanent, 56,2; 59,13

hupomnêmatika, commentaries, 4,5-12
hupopous, footed, 31,27.29; 32,5
hupostasis
    real being, 51,7.8; 63,16; 70,11
    independent existence, 53,23; 66,6.21; 67,10
hupotassein, count under, 58,9
hupothesis, hypothesis, 41,8
hupotithesthai, suppose, 64,16.17
husteros, posterior, 104,8-11
    husterogenês, later in origin, 9,9; 49,11

iatros, physician, 5,18
    iatrikê, medicine, 37,15
    iatrikos, medical, 5,18; 21,21
idea, type, 7,4
idiazein, be distinctive, 51,15
idios
    proprium: of substance, 44,11-22; 45,7; 46,6; 47,21.22; 51,5- 52,12; of quantity, 57,17.18; 65,10ff; of quality, 67,13.15; 90,28; 91,2; 92,14
    distinctive: of substance, 45,15; 50,13; of quantity, 61,9; of quality, 100,17; 101,13
    peculiar, peculiarity: of substance, 47,6; of quality, 89,15
    distinguishing mark: of substance, 49,3
    proper: definition of relatives, 78,13; parts of humans, 47,13
ikterian, to have jaundice, 67,2
    ikterikos, concerning jaundice, 86,7
isos, equal, 65,22ff; 71,2-4; 75,11.12; 78,11.12
    isotês, equality, 71,11.15
isostrophê, 'equiversion' (syn. of *antistrophê*), 71,1
isotheos, godlike, 71,2

kainotomein, innovate, 72,17
kairos
    appropriate, 47,5
    at the proper time, 96,13.21.23
kakos
    bad, 4,30; 10,18; 13,5; 101,18-21.22
    vicious, 70,6
    kakia: defect, 27,10; vice, 5,28; 70,3-7; 102,19.20
    kakizein, to fault, 27,9
    kakôtikos, hurtful, 82,6.28

kalligraphos, copyist, 35,7
kallôpizein, embellish, 7,3
kampulos, curved, 88,7
  kampulotês, curvature, 88,7.8
kanôn
  rule, 32,14; 71,15; 72,25
  standard, 10,21
kantharos, beetle, 71,23
karkinos, crab, 72,16
karpos, fruit, 17,1.3
karuon, nut, 88,15
katabasis, descent, 16,28
katadêlos, manifest, 82,16
kataginôskein, discover, recognize, 47,20; 49,3.13
kataleipein, leave, 50,15
katalêpsis
  cognition, 2,17ff
  recognition, 10,17
katalimpanein, remain, 73,12
katametrein, measure, 57,14.16
kataphasis (opp. to *apophasis*, q.v.)
  affirmation, 26,5.10; 34,12-35,4; 36,24; 93,16.19; 94,15-29; 97,11-14; 98,8; 100,17.20; 101,2-13
  kataphaskein, affirm, 36,25
  kataphatikôs, positively, 52,5
katarrathumein, lose through carelessness, 7,12
kataskeuazein
  hôs enargês, prove, 57,3
  hôs prophanôn, elaborate, 105,22
katatrekhein, to attack, 67,15
katêgorein, to predicate, 11,3; 13,14ff; 15,24; 16,20; 20,21.24; 30,6; 30,25-31,5; 31,1-12; 38,13; 41,2; 42,16; 45,11; 47,24; 48,3.7.10; 73,20; 84,7.8; 97,5.6; 98,13.16
  katêgoroumenon (opp. to *hupokeimenon*, q.v.), that which is predicated, a predicate, 31,3.6.10; 32,15; 48,4-8
katêgoria
  predication, 16,9; 26,12.16; 42,12.15; 47,26; 48,1; 66,8; 84,9
  category, 9,8; 13,4; 14,1.4-15; 16,20; 24,22; 33,4-35,17; 39,4; 46,18; 54,4.10.11; 57,20; 64,19; 65,28; 69,8-70,1; 80,17.19; 81,4; 83,10-14; 89,19.20; 91,1.29; 92,2.6; 93,10; 103,3; 104,16; 105,17
katekhein, seize, 37,14

kathêsthai, sit, 93,2; 97,14-16; 100,19
  kathedra, sitting, 68,21.25; 69,5
  kathezesthai, sit, 69,5.9
katholou, universal, 3,23-4,4; 5,10; 12,3; 13,10; 25,5-16; 26,12-28; 29,25; 30,1.9.25; 32,19; 36,4-18; 38,20; 39,3-41,17; 42,12ff; 77,8-13
  katholikos, general, universal, 75,22; 88,2; 98,11; 100,5
katopin, afterwards, 3,6
katorthoun, succeed, 2,11
keisthai
  be arranged, 13,1; 33,20; 59,4.7; 60,6; 68,24; 69,7-21; 88,11; 92,12; 93,1
  be found, 9,27
  lay down, 89,11
kenkhros, millet seed, 62,12.21ff
kephalê, head, 72,14ff; 77,13.24, 78,6
  kephalaios, main point, 4,5; 8,6.9
  kephalaiôdôs, in summary fashion, at the start, 4,8; 33,8
  kephalôtos, 'headed', 72,18.19.22
keramos, jug, 58,18
kêros, wax, 84,2.4
khalinos, bridle, 35,26
  khalinopoiêtikê, bridle-making, 35,24.25
kharaktêr
  character, 75,2
  form, 49,6
  style, 7,5
  kharaktêrizein: characterize, 21,10.13; 59,3; 70,13; derive, 78,8
khaunos, empty, 7,13
kheir, hand, 79,17ff
khersaios, terrestrial, 38,14
khliaros, lukewarm, 98,23
khreia, what is needed, 46,28
khrêsthai, use, 25,14; 35,26
khrêsimos, useful, 1,7; 6,10; 7,20; 13,3ff
khrôma, colour, 26,6ff; 82,26; 83,30; 87,2
  khrônnunai, be coloured, 5,2
khronos
  time, 21,25-22,1; 26,33; 28,17; 29,5.6; 54,11.18ff; 58,13; 59,11; 60,22-7; 62,10; 64,2-12; 66,11; 69,12.13; 74,13-75,6; 81,22; 93,2; 100,10-12; 102,9; 103,6-18; 104,18
  tense, 11,16.17

khumos, humour, 82,26
kinein, to change, 2,21ff; 53,12
  kinêsis, change, 3,7; 14,16; 55,10-13; 60,24.25; 105,7-20
klimax, staircase, 16,29
klinê, bed, 31,28
koinos, common, 6,11; 17,10; 18,5ff.22; 19,10.19; 20,3.28; 31,21; 36,7; 42,7; 44,18-21; 55,6; 56,9.10; 57,4-58,25; 72,26; 75,2; 84,9; 102,20
  koinônia, commonality, 15,8; 20,9; 22,22-24,10; 38,16.17; 49,7
  koinônikos, sociable, 11,9
  koinônein, have in common, share with, 23,26-24,3; 46,29
koleopteros, sheath-winged, 71,23
kosmein, to discipline, 6,1
kouphos, light, 55,9
kratunein, to support, 8,16; 9,2
krinein
  to judge, 67,21
  bring to trial, 78,28
  krisis, examination, 80,1
ktêsis, possession, 96,18
kuklos, circle, 70,27; 90,15.16.20
kuôn, dog, 2,3ff; 38,13.14
kuriôs
  primarily, 56,6
  principally, 92,6
  properly, 21,14; 55,4; 86,23.25
  strictly, in the strict sense, 30,8; 31,29; 47,9; 50,2; 60,18; 61,8; 62,6; 63,3; 65,18ff; 90,28; 104,18
  kurioteron, more important, 88,2

legein, say, call, 26,24; 36,15ff; 40,4.19; 41,17; 67,28
  legesthai kata, be said of, 31,2.6; 32,15; 41,13; 43,3
lêmmation, small assumption, 31,14
leptomerês, subtle parts, 28,33
lêthê, forgetfulness, 37,14
leukos, white, 6,13; 51,2; 60,16; 80,26ff
  leukotês, whiteness, 6,14; 40,12.13; 44,30; 45,2; 51,2; 86,4; 88,25
lexis
  speech, 7,2.3
  text, 9,3; 17,6; 33,14
  word, 14,6-16; 57,22
logikê, logic, 6,4.6; 10,9.11; 13,3.4
  logikos, rational, 31,24; 32,3; 42,2
logopoiein, compose, 5,27

logopoiia, composition, 5,27
logos
  account, 14,7; 15,10-17,8; 19,20-20,26; 24,22; 65,21; 67,28; 78,10; 104,9
  argument, 2,17; 15,1; 75,27
  definition, 27,20.32; 80,23
  discourse, 5,28; 7,3; 26,20
  discussion, 8,9.10; 22,12; 34,5; 47,2.5; 54,3; 55,12; 62,3; 91,6; 101,16
  explanation, 36,11
  formula, 90,16; 100,5.15
  language, 57,23; 101,12
  lecture, 1,9
  proposition, 13,9
  reason, 28,25.29
  reasoning, 2,6; 79,22
  relation, 43,11
  sentence, 7,13
  statement, 5,11.23; 11,2; 52,17-53,24; 54,17; 55,3ff; 57,11-19; 60,10; 93,19; 97,12; 98,8.11
  study, 9,21; 11,5
  thought, 37,12; 66,1.3
  word, 4,11
  writing, 6,2
lumainein, do damage to, 53,4.5
lusis, solution, 91,14

makhaira, knife, 20,24
makhesthai
  fight, 63,20
  oppose, 64,14
  makhomenon, contradictory, 50,13
malakos, mild, 94,5
mallon, more, 36,14; 41,20ff; 42,20; 50,10-51,1; 61,5; 65,13.14.15; 70,16.19-21; 89,23-90,25
manos, porous, 88,9.12-16
mathêma, teaching, 5,18
  mathêmatikos, mathematical, 5,5; 6,7.19; 66,2
megas, large, 49,17; 62,2ff.16; 63,2-12.22-8; 64,18; 71,3; 75,13; 93,13
  megethos, magnitude, 55,7.8; 79,4
meiôsis, diminution, 83,8.14; 105,15.19
  meiousthai, shrink, 28,17
melania, blackness, 86,5; 87,14; 88,25
mellein
  mellôn khronos, to mellon, the future, 17,3; 58,13; 59,15.16; 74,16; 93,3

Greek–English Index   155

mêlon, apple, 28,9ff
melos, limb, 8,7
mên, month, 60,25
meros
   part, 4,7; 9,13; 26,33-28,3; 29,10-22;
      38,2.7; 45,13.14; 46,22-47,17;
      49,7.9; 51,10; 77,6-78,7; 79,23;
      96,19-22
   particular, 98,11
   merikos, particular, individual,
      3,22-4,3; 25,6-17; 26,12-29; 29,24-
      30,2; 32,19.20; 36,4-16; 37,2.13;
      40,20-41,23; 44,24ff; 77,9-12
   meristos, divisible, 91,26
mesos
   centre, 65,2.3
   intermediate, 95,27
   mean, 9,25
   middle, 80,6
metaballein, to change, 51,6.8;
      53,8.11ff; 83,18; 93,23-94,14;
      100,6.7; 105,10ff
   metabolê, change, 2,24; 83,7-21;
      83,32-84,3; 100,9; 105,10-19
metapherein, derive, 69,4.7
   metaphora, metaphor, 7,2; 22,9
metaskhêmatizein, to change, 7,3
metekhein
   partake of, 19,10-14; 40,17;
      46,15.16; 80,22; 81,1; 83,30
   participate in, 6,15; 20,10; 67,22;
      86,10; 88,6.26-90,11; 91,15.16
   methektos, being partaken of,
      19,10.13.14
   methexis, participation, 22,3
methodos, method, 5,7-29
metrein, measure, 59,22; 60,1.25
mikros, small, 49,17; 62,3.16-64,11;
      93,14
mixis, mixture, mingling, 65,16; 92,10
mnêmê, memory, 21,26
monas, monad, 24,24
   monadikos, unique, 19,7
monimos, permanent, 32,3
monos, only, 19,2-7; 50,5; 73,8
   monoeidês, uniform, 4,13
morion, part, particle, 34,26; 35,1;
      55,1.2; 56,2.8.9; 57,5.26-58,26;
      59,1-7; 60,3-11; 66,24; 88,11-13
morphê, form, shape, 22,9; 81,7.24.25;
      83,25-34; 87,23-88,3
mousikos, musical, 23,10
   mousikê, music, 91,16ff
muriakis, ten thousand times, 34,16

nôdos, toothless, 96,26
noein, conceive, 76,18-20
   noêma: concept, 9,1-10,13; 12,1;
      thought, 4,9; 6,27; 8,4; 11,10; 15,9
   noêtos, intelligible, 41,9; 45,17;
      47,3-12; 60,5
nosein, be ill, 85,8ff
   nosêma, illness, 86,7
nosôdês, ill, unhealthy, 85,26
nosos, illness, 82,15ff; 86,7
nôthês, dullard, 85,25
nothos, spurious, 8,2; 13,27
nous
   mind, 58,1
   understanding, 27,14
nukhthêmeron, day (24 hours), 60,26
nukteris, bat, 71,22
nun, now
   ho nun khronos, to nun, the present,
      58,14; 59,11.15.16; 74,14-17

oikeios, proper, 15,12.24; 25,15; 27,27;
      29,20; 41,26; 42,1; 43,20; 62,2;
      71,18ff; 72,17-73,12; 78,12.26
oikhesthai, be gone, 63,22
oikonomikos, economical, 5,6
oikothen, on one's own, 15,5
ôkhrian, pale, 86,9
ôkhriasis, pallor, 86,8
ôkhros
   pale, 81,22; 96,1
   yellow, 89,17
oligos, few, 60,17-61,2; 62,7-10; 62,25-
      63,23; 72,5.8
onkos, volume, 7,1; 55,4
onoma
   name, 1,5; 2,10; 5,2.11; 15,10-17,20;
      18,22; 19,19-20,26; 21,27; 22,17-
      24,10; 25,14.15; 26,16; 38,17.19;
      40,10-15; 44,29-45,3; 72,12-26;
      89,11; 96,3
   noun, 5,13-26; 11,3.6.16.18; 13,8;
      14,16.21.24; 24,18.19; 57,19; 84,7
   term, 83,28
   word, 18,11; 81,26-9
   onomatopoiein, make up a name,
      coin words; 72,20.25; 97.24
   onomatothetein, invent a name,
      6,29; 72,12.16
opisthen, behind, 93,4
opsis, sight, 94,3; 96,15; 97,20; 98,3
organikos, instrumental, 4,29; 5,6ff
organon, instrument, 5,3; 10,20;
      35,25

orgê, temperament, 87,15
ornis, bird, 71,17; 105,4.5
orthê, nominative, 23,24
ouranios, heavenly, 45,18
ousia
  being, 21,1
  essence, 27,25.27; 31,7; 77,29;
    86,18.22; 100,7
  substance, 6,16; 11,13; 12,5; 15,25;
    17,11; 19,12.20; 20,26; 21,1; 23,1;
    24,26; 25,6-32,19; 26,2; 27,29;
    28,4.18.19; 30,2.25; 31,16;
    33,11.13; 34,5-35,21; 36,3ff;
    37,22-38,21; 39,15; 40,20.25;
    41,20ff; 43,4.9-44,3;
    44,6ff.10.16ff; 45,7-46,16; 46,22-
    47,16; 47,19-48,6.14.15;
    49,1.2.8.11.13ff; 50,6.10-20; 51,5-
    52,1.11; 53,8-25; 54,3ff; 58,9-11;
    61,9; 62,3; 64,6; 65,12-66,19;
    69,19-30; 77,7.8; 78,6.10; 80,11;
    83,7-84,3.19; 91,22; 92,7-93,5;
    94,19.24; 105,11.17
  thing, 26,24
  ousiôdês, essential, 32,11; 45,20;
    83,22; 86,28
  ousiôdôs, essentially, 31,1; 45,11
oute, nor, not, 50,21.22.25.26; 53,11;
  94,18.19
oxus, sharp, 20,24

palaios, ancient, 58,5; 67,12.15; 70,2;
  103,7.8
parabolê, comparision, 43,6
paradeigma
  diagram, 25,12
  example, 29,25; 39,14
  exemplar, 30,25
  original, 22,9
parakoloutêma, concomitant, 27,26;
  47,19; 48,13; 49,13; 50,9.15; 51,5;
  69,23ff; 70,16.24; 73,23; 75,22;
  77,4; 78,14; 89,23; 90,27; 92,13;
  102,12
  parakolouthein, be a concomitant,
    49,4; 51,15; 57,18; 89,24; 90,28
parakousma, mistaken notion, 81,9
parakrouesthai, mislead, 5,21
paralambanein, recognize, 35,22.23;
  36,10
parapetasma, curtain, 7,8
paraphuas, offshoot, 69,24
paraplêrôma, complement, 105,27;
  106,5

pareispherein, introduce, 30,3;
  77,5
parelêluthôs, past, 58,13; 74,14; 93,3
parelkein, be redundant, 35,7
paremballein, insert, 32,7
parepesthai, go along, 27,25.26
parienai, pass over, 106,7
paristan
  inform, 34,12
  present, 8,13
parônumos, paronym, 21,20; 22,21-
  24,12; 69,3.17; 72,21; 88,27-89,11;
  90,7; 97,4
parrêsiastikos, speaking frankly, 2,3
pas, all, 25,2; 70,17
paskhein, be affected, 13,1; 33,16.17;
  67,24; 85,7-27; 86,10.13-23;
  92,3.10.19.20
patêr, father, 104,5
pathêtikos, affective, 3,18
  pathêtikê poiotês, affective quality,
    81,6-82,32; 83,5-21; 86,3.5.13-20;
    87,2-20
pathos, affection, 81,6-83,2; 86,2.6-
  87,12; 88,8
pêdalion, rudder, 71,29ff
pêdaliôtos, 'ruddered', 72,6.7.8
pêkhuaios, one cubit, 61,3
pentagônon, pentagon, 90,15
pephukôs, naturally, by nature,
  85,14-24; 96,22
perainein, be definite, 63,4.5
peras, limit, 25,2; 58,16
periairein, strip off, 73,11
periekhein, include, 38,4; 39,15;
  58,16ff; 67,18.19
periergia, overelaboration, 7,2
perikleiein, to limit, 12,4
periorizein, include, 27,12
periphereia, peripheral thing, 105,26
periskelês, harsh, 7,6
perithesis, arrangement, 93,5
peritithenai, put around, 105,25;
  106,1.3
perittos
  odd, uneven, 95,12.21; 98,14-18;
    99,15
  excessive, 9,10
perix, surrounding, 65,2.3
pezos, terrestrial, 32,5; 105,1.2
phaidrunein, brighten, make beam,
  4,11
phainesthai
  appear, 57,17; 88,13

Greek–English Index

be evident, 6,26; 7,4
be obvious, 1,10
phainomenos, observable, 49,2
phaios, grey, 96,1; 98,23
phalakros, bald, 94,14
phantasia, representation, 83,27
phaulos, bad, 95,24; 96,2ff
philanthrôpos, kind, 33,8
philosophos, philosopher, 38,13
phônê
  expression, 13,17; 18,8.9.22; 25,21; 32,26.27; 33,2; 38,2-15; 52,10
  sound, 15,14
  speech, 11,10
  tone, 20,24
  voice, 15,9; 57,14
  word, 8,22-10,11; 11,8.15.19; 13,8; 14,22.24; 17,17; 18,4; 25,13; 26,23; 93,9; 94,19
  meta phônês, spoken, 57,14
phrasis, expression, 6,28; 7,6; 8,5
phronêsis, prudence, 22,3
phthainein, anticipate, 46,21
phthartikos, destructive, 102,7
phtheiresthai
  be destroyed, 28,4.5; 94,10
  pass away, 59,12
  perish, 53,24
phthongos, voice, 20,24
phthora, destruction, 45,18.21; 83,6.8.13.17.20; 92,21; 105,12-17
phuein, grow, 94,15
phulattein, preserve, 51,6
phusiologia, inquiry into natural causes and phenomena, 36,1
  phusiologikos, natural, 5,5
phusis, nature, 2,10; 3,25; 11,9; 15,8.12; 21,2; 28,22.25; 36,6.8; 40,4; 42,4; 45,20; 52,4; 57,8; 63,5; 65,5; 66,22.24; 73,21.23-74,11; 74,13-75,8; 82,14-25; 83,1; 84,22; 86,6; 100,7; 103,17; 104,5.19
  phusikos, natural, 6,7.19; 59,15.16; 81,12; 83,2.28.30; 84,26.27; 86,4
piptein, fall, 37,13.19; 57,20
pithanos, plausible, 4,25
platanistos, plane, 23,5
platanos, plane, 23,5
platos, horizontal, 43,6
plêroun
  complete, 9,7
  satisfy, 15,12
ploion, boat, 72,2ff
pneuma, breathing, breath, 17,9-18,5; 82,25
poiein, do, 13,1; 33,16; 34,25; 35,2; 67,24; 85,6-15; 92,3.11-17
  poiêtikos, efficient, 21,21.22
  poioun, agent, 67,24; 70,13; 92,18
poikilos, diverse, 4,14
  poikilia, intricacy, 8,4
poios
  sort, 49,8.10
  what sort of, 1,11.12; 7,15; 20,14; 33,23; 37,22; 46,18; 61,7.8; 66,7; 81,35
  to poion: quality, 12,5; 39,5; 54,10; 65,7; 66,8; 68,9; 82,2ff; 83,10; 89,15.17.23; 90,1.25-8; 91,5-27; 92,7.10; 105,18; qualified, 80,14-81,2; 86,10; 87,8; 88,6-27
poiotês
  quality, 6,14; 23,3; 46,16; 54,7; 69,19; 70,2; 80,14-18; 80,21-81,3; 81,5-82,32; 83,4-15.22.23; 84,13-24; 85,10.11; 86,2.7.13.18ff; 87,8.9.11.22; 88,10.19-23; 88,25-89,11; 89,15-18; 91,11-25
  being of a sort, 49,7
polemein, be at war, 94,6
politikos, political, 5,6
poluônumos, polyonym, 16,5-13
polus, many, 41,5ff; 60,17-61,2.4; 62,7-10.25; 63,6.8.13.23; 71,13-72,9; 87,23; 101,22
poluskhedês, complex, 66,9
porisma, corollary, 40,8; 78,19
posos
  how many, how much, 1,11; 7,15; 60,27; 61,1
  to poson, quantity, 12,5; 31,16.17; 49,14; 50,14; 53,25ff; 54,1.4.16ff; 55,4; 57,3; 57,11-18; 58,7.10.28; 60,16-18; 61,7-9; 62,5.6; 62,16-63,12; 64,16-20.23; 65,10.12.21-7; 66,3.10.13.20; 68,9; 69,11.27; 83,10.13; 91,26; 92,7ff; 105,17
  posotês, quantity, 28,25
potamos, river, 2,25
pote, when, at some time, 13,1; 69,12ff; 92,29-93,3
pou, where, somewhere, 13,1; 59,4; 60,6; 64,20; 69,12ff; 83,10.14; 92,9; 93,3; 105,18
pous, foot, 22,6.10
pragma, thing, 9,1-10,12; 11,19; 15,7.17; 17,17; 18,16; 20,15.17; 21,9; 22,2-24,6; 40,25; 66,15-67,7;

69,25; 75,25-77,2; 78,12; 92,1;
    93,20
pragmateia, treatise, 6,1
pragmatikos: really, 31,9; practical,
    93,17
praxis, action, 60,18-27; 78,25
    praktikos, practical, 4,28.30; 5,2.5;
    10,16.17
presbuteros, elder, 103,7.8
pro tôn katêgoriôn, pre-categories,
    14,3-11
proairesis, choice, 103,23
proapodidonai, give previously,
    77,15.21
probainein, advance, promote, 57,13;
    100,12
prodêlos, clear beforehand, 8,1
proêgeisthai
    introduce, 10,11
    precede, 13,8
proepinoein, think, 76,30
prokalumma
    curtain, 82,24
    veil, 7,10
prokatarkhein, to found, 1,16
prolambanein
    anticipate, 7,15
    be a prerequisite, precede, 1,11;
    105,9.10
pronoia, providence, 78,24ff; 80,4
prooimion, introduction, 65,28;
    103,18
prophanês, clear, 105,22
propherein, utter, 53,24
prophorikos, spoken, 52,17; 57,23.24
    prophorikos logos, spoken language,
    57,23
pros ti, relative, 13,1; 49,18; 54,10;
    62,16-63,20; 64,18.19; 65,3; 66,4-
    11.14-21; 66,22-67,11.15.16;
    68,15; 68,22-69,20; 69,23-70,8;
    70,10.11.16.20; 71,5-15; 72,23;
    73,11-15.23; 74,11; 75,21;
    76,11-25; 77,7-78,16; 78,30-79,22;
    80,10-12.16.20; 91,4-92,1.7.11;
    93,13-95,9; 96,6; 97,18; 98,4.7;
    100,5.24; 102,5; 104,10
prosekhês
    connected, 32,22
    immediate, 36,12; 42,3
proskhrêsthai, be used for, 54,14
prosôpon
    character, person, 4,16.22
    personality, 7,3

prosplekein, attach to, 69,26
prosupakouein, supply, 35,6; 50,16
protasis
    premise, 53,4
    proposition, 5,13.14; 11,3; 18,14
proteros, prior, 14,16; 36,6-9;
    59,15.16; 74,12-21; 75,6-76,20;
    81,22; 103,1-105,5
prôtos, primary, first, 11,8ff; 13,7;
    14,22; 35,21; 36,3-37,1; 38,6ff;
    43,8-44,22; 47,23; 54,12ff; 59,18;
    73,20; 84,13.14; 92,6
proüparkhein, pre-exist, 96,18
pseudein, be false, speak falsely,
    34,15-35,5; 52,19; 67,4.6
    pseudês, false, 4,22.30; 10,17; 13,5;
    34,14
    pseudos, falsehood, falsity, 34,22;
    52,22; 53,11-14; 100,16-20;
    100,23-101,7
psilos, bare, 9,26.27
psimmuthion, carbonate of lead,
    80,27
psukhê
    soul, 2,23-3,6.19; 6,23; 15,4; 37,2-18;
    59,21-60,4; 75,23; 78,21-28; 80,8;
    81,30-82,10; 83,17; 86,12; 87,12;
    92,18
    mind, 7,12
psukhrotês, coldness, 81,14.20; 95,19
psuxis, coldness, 81,16; 95,18
ptaisma, blunder, 82,22
ptênos, aerial, 32,4; 71,19ff; 105,1.2.4
pteron, wing, 71,17ff
pterôtos, winged creature, 71,25ff
ptôsis
    grammatical form, 23,20.22.24
    inflection, 17,14-18,5
puknos, dense, 6,27; 88,10-17
puktês, boxer, 84,27; 89,9
    puktikê, boxing, 89,6
    puktikos, boxer, 84,22ff; 89,5
pur, fire, 46,15; 81,16; 86,16; 98,15
    puretos, fever, 81,35
    purettein, have fever, 82,13
    purion, firestick, 80,7
    purros, red, 89,18

rhêma, verb, 5,13-26; 11,2ff.17.18;
    13,8; 14,22.24; 17,10; 18,18-25;
    24,19.20; 34,21; 57,19; 84,7
rhêtos, remark, 32,22
rhoê, flux, 2,24
rhopê, weight, 55,5.9

Greek–English Index 159

rhusis, flow, 2,24
rhutidoun, shrivel, 28,17.20

saphêneia
  clear knowledge, 6,29
  clearness, 53,6
saphês, clear, 7,5
seira, chain, 14,25
sêmainein
  apply, 52,8
  indicate, 11,10; 42,3
  mean, 9,17.22; 17,22-18,19;
    39,11.12; 44,21; 51,13; 57,22;
    71,2; 78,1; 80,3; 81,28
  refer to, 36,25
  signify, 5,12; 10,3.5.8; 11,19; 21,12;
    26,1; 34,14.30; 36,2; 42,2; 44,21;
    48,15; 49,5.6; 52,9; 57,15; 78,12;
    93,5; 96,2; 101,11
  sêmainomenon: meaning, 20,28;
    32,26-33,2; 103,4.8; 104,18; signi-
    fied, 11,14; 14,17; 20,19.20;
    97,12.13
  sêmantikos: meaning, 9,20.22; sem-
    antical, 18,22; signifying, 11,13;
    48,16
  sêmeion: point, 33,23-34,1; 58,1;
    sign, 82,17
skazein, be defective, 75,21
skeuos, utensil, 31,26ff
skhêma, figure, 29,16; 81,7.24; 83,25-
  84,5; 87,23-88,4; 90,19-20
skhesis, relation, 37,7.13; 41,21;
  54,11; 56,6; 64,19; 66,24; 73,19;
  76,12.17; 78,2.13; 91,23
  kata skhesin, relatively, 31,12
  skhetikos, relational, 36,2
skhizopteros, creature with feathered
  wings, 71,20.22
skia, shadow, 27,26
skopein, consider, 96,12.14
skopos, aim, 4,21; 7,17.21; 8,21ff;
  9,11ff; 11,17; 13,1; 93,9
skulakion, puppy, 96,22
sôma, body, 3,3.9; 6,14.15; 15,4.6;
  28,2; 29,11; 30,19; 31,22; 37,18;
  40,12-15; 44,30ff; 54,18; 55,6;
  58,7.19.21-59,7; 62,8.12; 65,24-
  66,2.24; 67,9; 68,23; 76,2-5; 78,22;
  79,18; 81,29-82,11; 83,18-34;
  86,11.20; 87,11; 88,12-15.26; 93,1;
  95,15; 98,18.22; 99,16.20
  sôma mathêmatikon, geometrical
    solid, 66,2

sômatikos, corporeal, 58,10
sophistês, sophist, 5,20; 66,27
  sophistikos, sophistical, 5,21
sperma, seed, sperm, 17,1.3; 36,8
sphaira, sphere, 84,3
  sphairikos, 84,5
sphalma, error, 35,7
sphodros, violent, 94,9ff
splên, spleen, 66,25.26
spoudaios, good, 23,13; 40,17; 70,5.7;
  78,23; 89,3.12; 95,24; 96,2
stasis, standing, 68,21.23; 69,4.5
sterein, be deprived, lack, 96,11-23;
  97,4
  sterêsis, privation, lack, 19,6; 33,23-
    34,9; 93,16-94,28; 96,6-97,19;
    98,10; 99,7-100,24
stoa poikilê, Painted Stoa, 1,18
stoikheion
  element, 36,7
  letter, 5,25.26
strephein, revolve, 70,27
  strophê, a return to one's starting
    point, 70,25
sukophantein, defame, 70,12
sulan, derive, 54,12
sullabê, syllable, 5,25.26; 11,4ff;
  22,25-23,23; 57,15
sullogê, aggregation, collection, 5,11;
  11,2
sullogismos, syllogism, 5,9-21; 6,3;
  11,1ff; 13,9.10.17
sumbainein, follow, 63,28; 64,12
  sumbebêkos, accidental, accident;
    3,8; 17,12; 20,23-8; 21,17; 23,2;
    25,6-32,19; 37,9; 39,6; 40,23ff;
    41,1; 43,17-44,2; 45,9.12;
    46,13-16; 46,23-47,15; 49,8.10;
    58,8; 60,19-61,8; 65,24; 73,18-20;
    77,8; 86,21; 91,23; 105,11.13
  sumbebêkuios, accidental, 32,12;
    83,23
sumballein
  be useful, 1,4; 13,5; 14,5
  join, 63,20
  include, 5,23
sumperasma, conclusion, 88,19
sumperilambanein
  include, 26,7; 34,20.21; 52,13
  comprehend, 28,11
sumplekein, combine, 32,26; 69,30;
  70,1
  sumplekomenos, compound, com-
    bined, 25,3; 34,24

sumplokê, combination, 9,4; 24,14-19; 32,23-33,4; 57,19.21; 92,8.11; 100,23-101,5
sumplêroun, complete, constitute, make up, 27,25.27; 28,5; 45,11; 47,1; 77,4
sumplêrôtikos, constitutive, completing, 28,3; 46,16
sumpseudein, to be false together, 101,9
sumptôma, accident, 87,5.19
sunagein
  draw together, 39,10
  deduce, 40,8; 78,18
  interconnect, 50,15
  imply, 9,19
  sunagôgê, uniting, 49,7.9
sunairein, destroy, 35,14.15
sunanaginôskein, connect, 24,20
sunanairein, destroy, 74,6.19
sunanaphainein, become evident, 7,21; 78,19.29
sunaptein, meet, join, be connected, 56,9.10; 57,5.9ff; 58,10
sunathroisis, gathering, 49,9
suneidenai, be conscious of, 82,22
suneisagein, bring in together, 63,18; 94,6
suneispherein, entail, 35,13.14; 74,20; 103,10
sunekhês, continuous, 31,17; 54,16.17; 56,9; 58,2-59,2; 62,7.8.12
  sunekheia, continuity, 56,3
sunengus, close, close together, 75,14; 88,11
sunêtheia, usage, 14,13.15; 72,17-26; 93,11
sungramma, writing, 3,21ff
sunistanai
  consist of, 45,14
  constitute, 46,28; 75,11
  exist, 25,9; 40,20
sunkeisthai, be a compound, 5,13
sunkerannunai, combine, 45,20
sunkhôrein, concede, 62,4; 63,12
  sunkhôrêsis, 50,3; 53,20; 62,15
sunkrinein, compare, 90,16.17.24
  sunkrisis, comparison, 41,19
sunônumos, synonym, 13,22; 15,23-16,23; 19,18-20,10; 22,12-24,11; 48,1-14; 52,9
sunousioun, combine essentially, 99,2
suntagmatikos, systematic, 4,4-15

suntaxis, organization, 14,2
sunteinein, stretch, 7,12
suntelein, contribute, 5,8
sunthesis, combination, 7,6
sunthetos
  (of substances), composite, 34,3-5; 35,18-36,2; 45,20-46,8; 54,7
  (of expressions), compound, 5,11; 33,2.3; 57,15; 66,9
suntiktein, produce, 63,20
suntomos, concise, 7,5
sunuphistanai, co-exist, 56,2
sustasis, existence, 49,11
  sustatikos, constitutive, 15,13; 21,15; 44,10
sustrephein, make terse, 6,27
suzugia, pair, 25,7ff; 77,9

tattein, fix on, 41,16
t'auton, the same, 51,6-12; 52,12; 55,5; 58,9; 97,3-11
taxis
  location, 47,6; 66,5.7; 80,17.19
  order, 7,22; 13,6.10.24; 14,21; 15,1; 17,13; 35,11; 37,17; 54,4.10; 56,2; 59,5.15-17; 94,4; 103,18
  ordering, 4,10.12; 38,22
tekhnê, method, 68,14
telein, assign, 69,17
  teleios, complete, perfect, 9,13.16; 25,2
  teleiotês, perfection, 92,21
  teleiôtikos, perfective, 82,5.6.28
  telikos, final cause, 21,23
  telos, end, 7,19
têrein, observe, 71,11
tetras, tetrad, 24,25.27
  tetragônon, square, 75,11.12; 90,15; 105,24ff
  tetragônismos, squaring (of the circle), 75,18
tetradikos, fourfold, 24,23
theôrein, contemplate, think of, 66,1.3; 77,2
  theôreisthai: be manifest, 70,19; 83,25.27.32.33; 84,24; 86,2; 87,11; 89,25; 93,21; 94,16.23; be observed, 66,25; 81,3; 82,29; 83,9; 92,1
  theôrêma: observation, 47,6.11; investigation, 79,26
  theôrêtikos, theoretical, 4,28.29; 5,1.4ff; 10,16
theos, god, 37,2

Greek–English Index

theios, divine, 26,2; 35,20.21; 36,25; 37,8.15
theologia, theology, 6,20; 35,28
theologikos, theological, 5,4; 6,7.8
thermasia, heat, 81,16.21; 82,14
thermotês, heat, 46,15; 81,15.20; 95,17
thesis
    application, 11,8.19; 13,7
    coinage, 18,12
    position, 14,22.23; 55,1-3; 56,6; 59,1.3.13; 60,3-12; 62,9; 66,22; 68,22ff; 69,15; 88.13; 93,1
thnêtos, mortal, 31,24; 32,4
thrasutês, rashness, 101,21
threptikos, concerning nourishment, 28,21
thronos, chair, 31,27
thuiskê, censer, 31,27
thumiama, incense, 29,2
tiktein, give birth, 96,27
tis, particular, 48,16
tode ti (literally, 'a this'), a particular, 48,15-49,5; 52,9
toios ê toios, such and such, 21,7
tonos, accent, 17,14-18,5

topos, place, 1,17; 3,1-15; 26,33; 27,18-28; 28,14.31; 29,9; 32,4.7; 54,11.18ff; 56,6; 58,16-59,7; 67,25; 69,11-13; 83,9.15; 93,3; 96,13; 102,14; 105,16.19
tragelaphos, goat-stag, 9,26
trigônon, triangle, 84,2ff; 90,14.22
trikhêi diastaton, three-dimensional, 54,6-8
tripêkhus, three cubits, 62,6
tropê, change, 81,18
tukhê, chance, 21,17.27; 79,13
tunkhanein, happen to
    ei tukhoi, for example, 3,29
    hôs etukhen, by chance, 79,25
tuphlos, blind, 96,27; 97,8
    tuphlotês, blindness, 94,3; 97,8.20ff; 98,3
    tuphlôttein, become blind, 96,25

xestês, pint, 59,22ff
xulon, wood, 11,12ff

zêtêsis, research, 79,26
zôê, life, 2,2; 32,3
zôion, animal, 19,11; 21,9ff; 31,11.12; 32,2ff; 38,21ff; 103,17; 105,1

Subject Index

References are to the page and line numbers of the *CAG* edition, which appear in the margin of this translation.

accidents, *sumbebêkota*
  are in substances not as parts, 47,15
  are not third substances, 43,15-22
  belong among the realities, 21,1
  do not constitute substance of the subject, 28,5
  have their being in particular substances, 40,24-41,5
  need to be in a subject in order to exist, 25,18
  only accidents inhere, 27,29
  particular accident, *merikon sumbebêkos*, 26,25-29,23
  universal accident, *katholou sumbebêkos*, 29,25
account, *logos*
  each thing is made known both by a name and by an account, 15,10
  includes both definition and description, 20,14-22
  of being (*logos tês ousias*), 17,10-21,3
affection, *pathos*
  a sub-species of quality, 81,6-83,2; 86,2.6-87,12
  being affected, *paskhein*: a secondary category combining substance and quality, 92,10; species of, 92,19ff
  affective quality, *pathêtikê poiotês*: and affection constitute a species of quality, 81,13ff; either produces or is generated by an affection, 81,15ff; affective quality vs. affection in relation to things vs. sensations, 86,13ff
affirmation (see also negation), *kataphasis*
  is generated from a substance and an action, 34,25
  not in all cases obviously true or false, 35,4ff
Archimedes, 75,14
arrangement, *keisthai*
  category arising from the combination of substance and relatives, 92,12
  definition and division into species, 93,1ff

be, being, *einai*
  in bare thought vs. independent existence, 9,26-10,12; 70,11
  predicated homonymously of the ten categories, 16,19ff
  is *form*, 21,13
  'is' vs. 'is said of', 26,24; 36,15ff; 40,23ff; 41,17; 60,11
  of other categories requires category of *substance*, 35,16
  of *relatives*, 77,29
beings, *ta onta*: division of, 10.12; 25,5-25,12
belong, *huparkhein*
  belonging in a subject divisibly vs. indivisibly, 91,25ff
  contraries belonging to a subject, 98,13-24; 99,27; 100,7; 102,10
  differentiae belong to a subject as intelligible parts, 47,1-17
  features belonging to: substance, 51,13-52,14; quantity, 65,11ff; relatives, 67,14ff; 70,16ff; quality, 89,15ff; 90,1ff
  not belonging as a part is differentia in definition of particular accidents, 27,4ff
  opposites belonging to a subject,

Subject Index

99,8.27
proprium of *x* belongs to *x* alone, 51,15ff
relatives belong together, 104,10
vs. *inherence*, 27,27ff

capacity, *dunamis*
species of quality, 81,10ff; 84,21ff
fitness for natural things, 81,11ff
natural disposition either in relation to a universal or with respect to ease, 85,5-27

category, *katêgoria*
signifies nothing true or false, 34,12ff
neither an affirmation nor a negation, 34,18-27
said without any combination, 32,20ff
four principal and primary categories: substance, quantity, quality, relative; the other six arise from the combination of substance with the remaining three, 92,5ff
origin of, 24,21-25,4

cause, *aition*
paronyms called after efficient or final cause, 21,21ff
cause and effect as relatives, 67,23; 76,15
priority of, 76,15; 103,20; 104,2ff; 105,1

change, *kinêsis*
is either substantial or accidental change, 105,9ff
is found in four categories: substance (coming into being and destruction), quantity (growth and diminution), quality (qualitative change), where (change of place), 105,17ff
vs. actuality (*energeia*), 55,10ff

change, *metabolê*
species of: generation, destruction, growth, diminution, qualitative change, change of place, 83,9
found in four categories: substance, quantity, quality, where, 83,10

colour, *khrôma*
division by means of affirmation and negation, 26,6ff
in respect to affecting quality and affection, 82,21ff; 87,1-3
distinguished from figure and shape, 83,30ff

coming into being, *genesis*
as a species of change, 83,8.12
of a proposition from a substance and an action, 34,19ff
of substances, 45,18ff
substantial change constitutes *genesis*, 105,12ff

common, *koinon*
boundary, 56,9ff; 57,1-9; 57,25-58,25
said in two ways: what is partaken of indivisibly vs. divisibly, 19,10-14
with respect to: *homonyms*, 15.17-16,6.20ff; 17,10; 18,5f.20ff; 19,17ff; *synonyms*, 15,17-16,6.20ff; 19,17ff; *proprium*, 44,18-21

concepts, *noêmata*
Aristotle's aim concerns only, 8,20-9,16
words and things mediated through, 9,17-10,14

condition, *diathesis*
perfective actuality not producing an affection and easy to lose, 82,9ff
state and condition constitue a species of quality, 81,7ff
two senses of, 84,6-11

continuity, 54,16-55,3; 57,25-58,26
line, surface, body, time, and place are continuous quantities, 54,17-18
the parts of a continuous quantity meet at a common boundary, 56,9-10
exhaustive division of the continuous is possible only in thought, 58,1

contraries, *enantia*, 101,14-102,21
and substance, 49,12-50,12; 52,13.17; 53,16-24; 58,9; 64,6; 69,27; 94,19
definite quantities do not have contraries, 62,3-18; 64,15-65,18; 69,27
division of, 95,10-96,4
do not always divide into the true and the false, 100,22-101,13
examined as things and not as contraries, 102,1ff
found in a single subject, 102,11ff

have independent reality,
63,15-25
need not be in the same genus,
102,16ff
never coexist in a single subject,
63,27-64,9; 102,6ff
quality admits, 70,2
species of opposites, 93,13ff; 94,1ff;
95,1-27; 98,10ff; 99,10ff
subsumed under the same category,
89,19ff
vs. relatives, 63,15-25; 69,23-70,8
conversion, *antistrophê*
of relatives, 73,1-13; 97,24; 98,4
is really 'equiversion', 70,25-71,8
convert, antistrephein: definition
and thing defined must convert,
27,12ff; proprium and that of
which it is the proprium must
convert, 44,12ff; priority preclude
converse implication of existence,
103,9ff; relatives ought to be convertible, 71,9-73,1
counter-objection (see also objection),
antiparastasis, 53,1ff; 62,4; 63,11;
101,6
Cratylus, 3,1
Cynics, the, 2,2.7
Cyrenaics, the 1,17

definition (see also synonyms, homonyms, heteronyms, polyonyms),
horismos
a kind of *logos*, 20,14-21
some things cannot be defined, e.g.
supreme genera, 20,15; 26,30ff;
44,7-12
should be made of genus and constitutive differentiae, 21,14
of what is in a subject and of what is
said of a subject, 40,7-16; 44,29-
45,3
vs. description, 20,14-22
Democritus, 1,15
demonstration, *apodeixis*
instrument to distinguish true and
false, 10,15-22
is a syllogism, 11,1
description, *hupographê*
there is homonymy among things
signified by, 20,17
a kind of *logos*, 20,21
differentiae, *diaphorai*
are different when genera are
different, 31,18ff
are intelligible parts of substance,
41,3-13
are simple substances, 45,17-46,10
can divide genera in many ways,
32,1ff
constitute the subject, 46,28
differ from accidents, 46,20-47,2
essential (but not accidental)
differentiae of subordinate
genera are always the same,
32,9ff
of heterogenous things are always
different, 31,15
of substances cannot be accidents,
but must be substances, 45,5ff
divine, *theion*
the divine is completely unrelated
and transcendent, 37,5ff
division, *diairesis* exhaustive by
means of negation and affirmation, 26,4ff
four-fold and ten-fold division of
things, 32,19ff
in thought vs. actual, 58,1
of the *Categories* into three parts,
14,3ff
doing, *poiein*
category arising from the combination of substance and quality,
92,10
definition and division into species,
92,17ff

Epicurus, 1,15

figure, *skhêma*
and shape constitute a species of
quality, 81,24ff
is applied to inanimate objects,
81,24ff
is manifested only on surface, substance remains unchanged,
83,24-84,5
is manifested in our own representation, 83,28
every shape also has a, 87,21
form, *eidos*
being of a thing, 21,13
and quality, 86,18.22
is prior by nature, 36,7
proper definitions are derived from
it, 21,14
not an accident, 27,30ff

Subject Index

genus, *genos*
  'different genera' said in many ways, 31,19ff
  each has specific differentiae, 31,15ff; 32,11ff
  intelligible vs. perceptible, 41,9ff
  not all are secondary substances, 39,1-12
  notional entities, 9,8ff
  of contraries, 65,1-6; 102,16-20
  of quality, 84,13ff; 86,2; 84,22; 91,10-26
  of substance, 15,13; 41,20ff; 50,19; 52,14
  secondary substances, 43,15-44,4
  predicated accidentally and relatively of a subject, 31,12
  predicated of species, 13,14; 29,20ff; 41,20ff; 42,14-43,5; 48,2-9
  signifies a plurality and a certain quality, 49,6ff
  ultimate genera, *genikôtata*: are only predicated, 13,17; entitled 'categories', 13,19
Gorgias, 22,8
grammatical form, *ptosis*
  variation of the last syllable, 23,23

having, *ekhein*
  category arising from the combination of substance and relatives, 92,12
  definition and division into species, 93,5ff
  there is a category of having, but not of being had, 33,15-22
Hedonists, the, 3,16
Heraclitus, 2,25
heteronyms, *heterônyma*
  things differing in both name and definition, 15,27
  are not entirely different, but are the same in their subject, 16,24-17,3
homonyms, *homônuma*
  things having in common their name, but differing in definition, 15,29-16,4
  always have the same accent, inflection, and breathing, 17,5-18,14
  are not synonyms, 19,15-20,12
  division of, 21,16-22,10
homonymy, *homônumia*
  among verbs, 18,18-25
  among accidents, 20,23-21,2

in something, *en tini*
  genus in the definition of particular accident, 26,32ff
  is said in eleven ways, 29,5-23
incapacity, *adunamia*
  capacity and incapacity constitute a species of quality, 81,10ff
  is unfitness for natural things, 81,11ff
  is a quality said in three ways, 85,9-27
individuals, *atoma*
  are subjects only, 13,15
  not predicated of anything, but are in subjects, 30,4-23
  beings that are one in number, 30,18
inhere, *enuparkhein*, only accidents inhere, 27,29
intelligible, *noêton*
  differentiae are intelligible parts, 41,3ff

knowledge, *epistêmê*
  contrary to ignorance, 70,3
  differentia in definition of man, 27,14; 73,14
  homonymous, 22,5
  infallible awareness, 79,10
  is a relative, 67,22; 68,18; 70,3; 74,9-75,25; 76,17-77,2; 79,10; 91,11
  opposites known by the same knowledge, 16,18
  quality in the soul, 81,30
  species of knowledge are qualities, 91,10-21
  state of the soul, 82,10; 83,17
  what is known is prior to knowledge, 74,9-75,25

Lyceans, the, 2,1

man, *anthrôpos*
  individual man is an example of primary substance, universal man is called a secondary substance, 39,14-40,2
mathematical body, 66,2

negation, *apophasis*
  not in all cases obviously true or false, 35,4ff

Subject Index

appropriate means of defining substance, 36,22ff
and affirmation: as *opposites*, 93,16ff; 94,15ff; 98,8; 100,14ff; 101,1-13; generated by combining items from different categories, 34,26ff; not the same as what they signify, 97,11ff; provide an exhaustive division, 26,4ff
and truth, 34,12ff; 100,14ff; 101,1-13
number, *arithmos*
as a quantity, 54,13; 57,1-9; has no contrary, 49,15; is discrete, 54,17; 57,1-9
contrariety and, 95,21; 98,18; 99,15
in the soul vs. in perceptible things; the latter is composed of parts having position, the former is not, 59,20-60,9
one in number, 30,4.15.22; 51,5; 58,8
opposed to relatives, 62,25

objection, *enstasis*
and counter-objection, 53,1ff
one (see also number, substance), *heis, hen*, 21,22; 30,12; 50,5; 51,5.6
opposites, *antikeimena*, 93,7-101,13
four kinds of opposition, 93,15-17; affirmation and denial, 94,15ff; 100,13-101,13; contraries, 94,9ff; 95,1ff; 98,6-100,12; privation and state, 94,10ff; 97,18-100,129; relatives, 94,5ff
order, *taxis*, of the study of logic, 13,6

paronyms, *parônuma*
commonality and difference with respect to both the name and the thing, 22,22-23,19
not exactly in the middle between homonyms and synonyms, 23,25-24,12
neither in a subject nor said of a subject, 30,2
particular, *to merikon*
not said of any subject, 25,17
particular accident, *merikon sumbebêkos*, 26,25-29,23
particular substance (see also primary substance), *merikê ousia*, 25,5ff; 26,18; 36,4; 40,19ff.
perception, *aisthêsis*

Categories is concerned with things known by perception, 33,25
is a relative, 67,21
is the basis of our conception of quality, 80,25
what is perceived is prior to perception, 74,23ff; 75,26-76,8; 77,1
Peripatetics, the, 3,14
philosophical schools, 1,14-3,20
Plato, 2,7; 3,5.9; 6,24; 18,10
his refutation of Protagoras, 67,2-8
his refutation of the undecided (*ephektikoi*) philosophers, 2,13
invented the word 'quality', 81,25
on relatives, 70,10-14
said that reference to the divine is by negation, 36,26
polyonyms, *poluônuma*
things differing in name, but having definition in common, 16,5
Porphyry, 9,9; 25,7; 41,7
position, *thesis*
a species of relatives giving rise to category of being arranged (*keisthai*), 69,6-21
predication, *katêgoria*
and substance, 41,2; 45,11; 47,24
in language, 11,3; 20,21.24; 38,13
of genera, species and individuals, 13,14ff; 15,24; 30,6; 42,16; 45,11; 48,3ff
simple vs. compound, 66,8ff
transitivity of, 30,24-31,12; 48,3ff
priority, *proteron*, 103,1-104,12
five meanings of, 103,3-21
the prior and the posterior are relatives, 104,8ff
privation, *sterêsis*
not a being, but a privation of being, 34,9
not the same as to be deprived, 97,1-8
spoken of only with respect to a pre-existing possession, 96,5-28
proprium, *idion*
belongs to all and only that of which it is the proprium, 44,13
of quality, 67,13.15; 90,28; 91,2; 92,14
of quantity, 65,10ff
of substance, 44,11-22; 45,7; 46,6; 47,21.22; 51,5-52,12
Protagoras, 66,26-67,2

Subject Index

puzzle, *aporia*
  raising a puzzle is the route to the resolution of the puzzlement, 79,24-80,13
Pythagoras, 1,15

qualified, *poios*
  is what partakes of quality, 80,25-81,3
  on qualified and quality, 80,14-92,2
  things qualified participate in quality but are not always called paronymously after them, 88,25-89,13
qualitative change, *alloiôsis*
  change (*metabolê*) in affective quality, 83,22
  accidental change (*kinêsis*) in the category of quality, 105,14-19
  distinguished from growth, 105,24ff
quality, *poiotês*
  alteration arises not from every quality but only from affective ones, 83,4ff
  features of: contrariety and more or less are not features of all qualities, 89,15-91,1
  further division of: fitness/actuality; perfective/hurtful; producing/not producing an affection; hard/easy to lose, 82,2-83,2
  genera of qualities are classified under relatives but their species under quality, 91,10-92,2
  is defined in terms of the qualified, 80,21-81,3
  is that in respect of which things are called qualified, 87,8ff
  many relatives are subsumed under quality, 91,3-92,2
  on qualified and quality, 80,14-92,2
  location of the category, 80,20
  species of quality: (1) state and condition, manifested in actuality, 84,20-85,3; (2) capacity and incapacity, manifested in potentiality, 84,24-85,26; (3) affective quality and affection, 86,1-87,20; (4) figure and shape, 87,21-88,4
quantity, *poson*, 54,1-66,3
  composed of parts having position vs. not so composed, 55,1ff; 56,1-6; 58,27-60,12
  continuous (line, surface, body, time, place) vs. discrete (number, statement), 54,16ff; 56,7-58,26
  definite and indefinite, 62,5-13
  determinate, 63,1-9
  distinctive characteristics of, 61,9-66,4
  division of, 54,16-55,3
  has no contrary, 62,1-66,4
  in the strict sense and per accidens, 60,14-61,8
  opposites such as large and small are not quantities but relatives, 62,15-64,21
  position among the categories: quantity rightly occupies the second position, 54,3-15
  propria of quantity
  not having a contrary, 65,15ff
  being called both equal and unequal, 65,20-66,3

relatives, *ta pros ti*, 66,5-80,13
  being and essence of a relative is nothing other than its relation to another, 77,27-78,16
  contrariety: some relatives, but not all, admit it, 69,22-70,8
  convertible if properly specified, 73,1-23
  division of 67,16-25
  independent things in themselves or bound in relation: can be thought of either way, 76,8-17
  knowledge of: as one knows one relative, so also will one know the other, 78,29-79,8
  more and less: some relatives, but not all, admit it, 70,15-27
  one species of relatives, position, gives rise to one of the categories, 69,6-21
  position among the categories, 66,5-13
  reality of, 66,21-67,10, 70,10-14
  simultaneous by nature, 73,22-74,8
  species of, 68,13-69,21
  title: why is it 'On relatives' and not 'On relative'?, 66,13-21
  universal parts are not relatives, 79,15-23
  what is subsumed under relatives is necessarily classified under some other category as well, 91,29-92,2

shape, *morphê*

applies to animate objects,
81,24ff
figure and shape constitute a
species of quality, 81,24ff
manifested only on surface, substance remains unchanged,
83,24-84,5
simple, *haplous*, see under words, substance, predication
simultaneity (see also under relatives, contraries), *to hama*, 104,13-105,6
its first meaning is with respect to time, its second with respect to nature, 104,15ff
soul, *psukhê*
definition of substance applies to the individual soul, but not to the transcendent one, 37,10-20
number in the soul vs. in the perceptible thing, 59,21-60,4
is the subject that the sciences are in, 75,23
category of quality as applied to, 81,30-82,10; 83,17; 86,12; 87,12
species (see also under quality, relatives, change), *eidos*
is more a substance than a genus is, 41,19-42,20; 50,18ff
not all are secondary substances, 39,1-16
signifies a plurality and a certain quality, 49,6ff
species in genus vs. genus in species, 29,12-23
species of substance are called secondary substances, 43,15-44,4
subject for its genus, 13,14; 15,24
state (see also condition, privation), *hexis*
change of state is substantial, 86,5ff
of the soul and of the body, 81,34
one species is a perfective actuality that is hard to lose and does not produce an affection, 82,9ff
state and condition: constitute a species of *quality*, 81,7ff; 84,8-11.24; as *relatives*, 91,6ff
vs. privation, 93,16-94,29; 96,7-14; 97,4-19; 98,10; 99,7-100,24
statement, *logos*
does not receive contraries in virtue of receiving anything itself, 52,15-53,25

has no reality at all, 53,22ff
is a discrete quantity, 57,10-24
made up of things not having position, 60,10ff
Stoics, the, 1,18
subject, *hupokeimenon*
and contraries, 102,8-14
and opposites, 95,14ff; 96,14; 98,24; 99,8-26; 100,6
constitution of, 46,28
destruction of, 28,3ff
differentiae of, 46,28; 47,7ff
in a subject vs. said of a subject, 9,6; 25,16-26,22; 29,25-30,22; 30,25ff; 36,16ff; 37,3ff; 40,8-17; 44,16-30; 47,7ff; 48,15ff; 91,22ff
subject and accidents, 25,19ff; 27,23ff; 28,5ff; 41,1ff; 46,17ff; 91,22ff
substance vs. subject, 25,21-26,16; 28,9ff; 36,16ff; 41,1ff; 46,17ff; 47,7ff; 48,15ff; 58,8; 91,22ff
with respect to existence, 26,11ff
with respect to name and definition, 16,27ff; 40,8-17; 44,27ff
with respect to predication, 13,13ff; 26,11ff; 30,25ff; 32,15; 40,8-17; 48,4ff
substance, *ousia*, 35,10-53,25
ancients' definition leads to absurd consequence that some substances are relatives, 77,3-25
Aristotle uses 'is' when talking about, 26,24
composed of genus and constitutive differentiae, 15,11-16
composite (see simple vs. composite)
definition of 'substance':
cannot be given, since substance is an ultimate genus, 44,9
applies neither to God nor to the transcendent soul, 37,1-20
division, manner of, 37,22-38,22
concomitant features (*parakolouthêmata*) of: being said synonymously of everything, 47,18-48,14; not admitting of more or less, 50,8-51,3; not being in a subject, 44,5-46,10; not having a contrary, 49,12-50,7; being one in number and receptive of contraries, 51,4-52,14; signifying a particular this, 48,12-49,11
general sense: the reality of each

Subject Index

thing, 21,27
not every substance is a subject, 25,22-26,16
not in a subject, 25,20
other categories presuppose category of, 35,10ff
primary vs. secondary: have their name and definition in common, 38,17; particular substance is called primary, universal secondary, 36,3-21; primary is included (in divisions) under secondary, 38,6ff; 39,15; primary substances serve as subjects both for the existence of accidents and for the predication of universals, 42,12ff; secondary substances are not in a subject, 44,27-45,4; species and genera are secondary substances, 39,2ff; without primary substances neither universals nor accidents would exist, 41,13-17
proprium of: being one in number and receptive of contraries, 51,4-52,14
self-subsistent, 33,13
simple vs. composite, 35,18-36,2; *Categories* is concerned with composite substances, 34,4; prime matter and form are simple substances that are inferior to the composite, 35,21ff; substance of the gods is simple substance that is superior to the composite, 35,20ff
ultimate genus that cannot be given a definition, 44,5ff
vs. subject (see under subject)
surface, *epiphaneia*
and quality: in respect to affection, 82,24ff; in respect to figure and shape, 83,24-84,1
species of continuous quantity, 54,17-55,7; 58,18.20; 60,19-61,3
vs. superficies, 58,4ff
syllogism, *sullogismos*
collection of propositions composed of nouns and verbs, 11,1ff
demonstration is a kind of syllogism, 11,1
synonyms, *sunônuma*
things having in common both name and definition, 15,17-24

things, *pragmata*
are characterized either by their matter or by their form or by both, 21,10
time, *khronos*
is the measure of change, 60,25
natural order of, 59,10-19
truth, *alêtheia*
affirmation and negation divide in every case into true and false, 100,16ff
and falsehood do not derive from statements or opinions, but come into being by things being altered, 53,7-17
in assertions, 34,14ff; 52,22; 53,11ff
requires combination of subject and predicate, 34,14ff; 100,23ff

universal accident, *katholou sumbebêkos*
both said of a subject and in a subject, 29,25
universal substance, *katholou ousia*
said of a subject but not in a subject, 25,16ff
universals, *ta katholou*
do not need primary substances in order to exist, but in order to be said of something, 40,18ff
not prior to the many but in the many, 41,6-11
said of a subject, 25,16
utility of Aristotle's philosophy, 6,9-15; 13,4-11

virtue, *arêtê*
is a quality, 70,2-6; 81,31; 82,10; 83,18; 89,2; 102,19ff
as a contrary, 102,19ff
shares neither its name nor its definition with its subject, 40,15

when, *pote*
category derived from species of quantity, 69,11ff
category arising from the combination of substance and quantity, 92,9
definition and division into species, 93,2ff
where, *pou*
category derived from species of quantity, 69,11ff

category arising from the combination of substance and quantity, 92,9
definition and division into species, 93,3ff
words, *phônai*
Aristotle uses 'is said' when reasoning about, 26,23
simple: first application prior to nouns and verbs, 11,8; 13,7.9; 14,22; signify simple things by means of simple concepts, 12,1; 15,14
writings, Aristotelian, *sungrammata*
division of, 3,21-5,31
form of the narrative in, 6,25-7,6
way of teaching in, 7,6-14
interpretation of, 7,15-8,10
systematic (*suntagmatika*) vs. notebooks (*hupomnêmatika*) 4,4ff
popular (*exôterika*) vs. axiomatic (*axiômatika*) [= school works (*akroamatika*)], 4,18ff
theoretical vs. practical vs. instrumental (division of school works), 4,28ff
commentator on, 8,10-19

Xenocrates, 3,11-13